COLLECTIVE BARGAINING:

How It Works and Why

A Manual of Theory and Practice

Thomas R. Colosi
and
Arthur Eliot Berkeley

2nd Edition, 1992

 A PUBLICATION OF THE
American Arbitration Association

Library of Congress Catalog Card Number:
85–72636
ISBN Number: 0–943001–03–X

COLLECTIVE BARGAINING: HOW IT WORKS AND WHY (2nd Edition). Copyright © 1992 by the American Arbitration Association. Printed in the United States of America. All rights reserved. No part of this book may be used or reproduced in any manner whatsoever without written permission, except in the case of brief quotations embodied in critical articles and reviews.

First Edition, 1986
Second Edition, 1992

ORDER FROM:

American Arbitration Association
140 West 51st Street
New York, NY 10020–1203
212–484–4011

Charts 1—15 and 17 designed and developed by Thomas R. Colosi.

Chart 16 designed and developed by Arthur Eliot Berkeley.

Dedication:

*The first edition was dedicated to the memory of our fathers,
Angelo F. Colosi and Louis S. Berkeley, who were men of peace.
This second edition we would like to rededicate to them and also
to our children whom we hope may live in a world at peace:*

Jennifer, Thomas, Christopher and Samantha Colosi
and
Hillary and Lewis Berkeley

A Koan*

How do you negotiate?

Three students of Zen sat by the bank of the river with their master. He handed them each a stone and asked, "How do you hold a rock?"

The first student commented that, "The way to hold a rock is to be certain that you understand the nature of the rock and its history."

The second student replied, "The way to hold a rock is to be certain you harm no one with your rock."

The third student said, "The way to hold a rock is to be certain you are in harmony with nature and the cosmos."

An untutored fisherman overheard this conversation and spoke up. "There is no one way to hold a rock. Each rock is different and each person is different. The way you hold a rock is the way you hold a rock."

The Zen master smiled.

---

*In Zen theory, a Koan is a question that can only be answered in its own terms.

Contents

Foreword
to the Second Edition

Over the past five years since the first edition of this book was published, some revisions have been made—not through dissatisfaction on our part with the book as a whole, but as a result of the predicted changes in the labor–management culture and a growing body of information about these changes.

As a result of these changes, the collective bargaining process is more important—and sometimes more difficult—than ever in establishing and maintaining a healthy relationship between the parties. A healthy relationship, however, will create opportunities for more effective collective bargaining with change management and problem solving as critical work products.

Rather than deal with what appears to be a "chicken or the egg" question, the authors contend that a positive collective bargaining is the result of a positive relationship and a positive relationship is the result of hard work.

Why work hard for a positive relationship? The actual act of collective bargaining involves contact hours between the parties. What should the parties actually be doing during these contact hours at the table?

DISCOVERY

Each party should be discovering information it does not know. Each party knows what it knows but the purpose of the hours of contact with the other party is to find out what the other party knows. A poor relationship will yield little information whereas a good relationship will create a freer flow of information—in a process where information and knowledge are power, a positive relationship is critical.

EDUCATION

Since contact hours should be used to share well-researched information that is designed to have the other party see things differently if they are in disagreement, it is critical that the other party is listening to the new information. Effective listening does not occur within a negative environment. A positive relationship enhances the opportunity for the new information to have maximum impact.

CREATING DOUBTS AND UNCERTAINTIES

When the other party is in disagreement, it is important that the effective negotiator create doubts and uncertainties in their minds as to the viability of their position. In a negative relationship, a party will not allow doubts to be created. In fact, the other party will not become vulnerable enough even to allow uncertainties to creep into their mind-set. A change of behavior is usually preceded by a change in mind-set and a change in mind-set is preceded by a creation of doubts.

CREATING ADVOCACY

In collective bargaining, it is rare that the ratifiers engage directly in negotiations during the contact hours. Top management has negotiators (staff or outside consultants) who report to top management and recommend settlement (or not) under certain conditions. Union officials (local and national) look to the union membership to ratify the contract they chose to recommend. Each negotiating team should be attempting to gain advocacy for its position and to take care of its interests with the other negotiating team. It is easier to enlist the other teams as your advocates if a positive relationship has been established. As John Galsworthy once said, "If you do not think about the future, you cannot have one."

ENHANCING ENFORCEMENT

A positive relationship will usually yield a high-quality future dispute resolution clause, such as grievance mediation and/or grievance arbitration. A positive relationship not only allows the parties an opportunity to focus on their immediate problems but also should cause them to think about potential future problems, anticipate changes and consider what kind of systems should be jointly developed to absorb the future. Hard work expended during the bargaining process to enhance a positive relationship is a wise investment.

ENHANCING IMPLEMENTATION

If the collective bargaining process involves the exchange of promises and commitments, the keeping of those promises and commitments should be vital. A positive relationship, maintained through the "close" of the bargaining, will help to insure the keeping of those promises. A negative relationship will usually result in promises being misunderstood, commitments being half-kept, misapplication and misinterpretation with an increasing number of grievances and arbitration cases. All of the above obviously works against the maintenance of a positive relationship, making it even more difficult for the parties to engage in change management and problem solving.

FACT VERSUS ASSUMPTION

A positive relationship will create an environment in which information advanced by a party based on sheer assumption will be accepted as "fact" by that party. In a negative relationship, parties continually use their valuable time to find evidence as proof on facts that they are using to try to convince the other side. In a positive relationship, for the most part, assumption based on information is accepted as fact by each side.

PREDICTABILITY

As teachers of a more positive approach to collective bargaining, we have been asked many times whether negative behavior, shouts, yelling, insults, intimidations, threats, etc., are at all useful in a collective bargaining relationship. Our answer is that if you engage in those kinds of negative behavior and you can predict with deadly accuracy the behavioral reaction of the other side as a result of your behavior and the other side's behavior serves your interests, then by all means proceed. The wise negotiator is one who is able to predict the behavior of others. All behavior then should be designed to enhance the ability to predict.

Preface

What is this book and who needs it?

These are two good questions that deserve answers. First, this is a manual of the theory and practice of collective bargaining, how it works and why. It is not a textbook (there are already a number of fine textbooks available, suitable for either undergraduate or graduate study). It is not a "how to do it" book (such works tend to be too long on anecdotes and too short on presenting any unifying theory from which the reader can find applicable approaches to a current situation). This, then, is a book that looks at *how* collective bargaining *actually works*. The theories presented are edited by the experiences of not only the two authors, but of the many practitioners who have been able to examine in a new light their experiences with the concepts discussed here.

If this is what this manual is, who really needs it? After all, there is a long history of collective bargaining in this country, and haven't the parties gotten along very well so far without a manual like this?

Not really, we submit. The challenges of the 1990s are different from those faced earlier, and new approaches to labor–management relations must be undertaken. The concepts and notions presented will enable a negotiator to better understand not only those across the table but, perhaps even more important, those on one's own side.

Put simply, we must better understand how collective bargaining works if collective bargaining is to work. This manual is an important step, but only the first step.

In many ways, examining the authors' backgrounds is instructive in learning the nature of the book. Both authors are graduates of Cornell's School of Industrial and Labor Relations, both worked as advocates for employees and employers, and both have worked—and continue to do so—as neutrals. They thus bring the perspectives of three sides of the table to their work.

Tom Colosi is an officer of the American Arbitration Association and a third-party neutral and spends much of his time training advocates and neutrals about the workings of dispute resolution. His coauthor, Dr. Arthur Berkeley, is a full time associate professor at the Memphis State University's School of Business, where he teaches this subject in an academic setting. Colosi has taught as an adjunct for the University of

Maryland Law School and at Cornell's School of Industrial and Labor Relations. Berkeley is involved in training programs as well as serving as an arbitrator. The cross pollination of the academic and practical is blended not only in the two authors, but in the book itself.

Federal Circuit Judge Harry T. Edwards once coined the phrase ''pracademic'' to denote a welding of pragmatic and theoretical approaches. This book, like its authors, is pracademic in its approach, and it is as much at home in the classroom as a companion to any of the collective bargaining texts as it is in training or continuing education programs.

The Beginning

*"No issue can be negotiated unless you first
have the clout to compel negotiation."*

—SAUL ALINSKY
Playboy, March 1972

IN THIS SECTION we introduce our subject and a working definition of negotiation:

A process that affords the parties and/or the disputants an opportunity
to exchange promises and commitments in an effort to resolve their
differences and reach an agreement.

Why Negotiate?

There are many ways to resolve disputes. The traditional way has
always been to simply overwhelm your adversary and in so doing achieve
the settlement you desire. History is replete with tales of invasions, mur-
ders, torture and other forms of annihilation. Employee relations is not
without its own litany of violence: the Homestead Strike, the Haymarket
Riot, the Ludlow Massacre and the Republic Steel–Memorial Day 1931
carnage are but a few of the most egregious illustrations of violence and
turmoil.

It is often said that no one wins a lockout or strike—even a peaceful
one. The employees lose wages, benefits, economic security and sometimes even their jobs; the employer loses production, services are not performed as customers or clients expect, the continuity of the enterprise
is disrupted and ultimately, at least in some cases, the enterprise is dealt
such a mortal blow that it never recovers fully.

But there are additional casualties to be counted, and they are often
not parties to the initial dispute. Customers who are not served may turn
elsewhere and never return; they sometimes may not even enjoy the luxury of that choice and may be irreparably harmed no matter what the

ultimate outcome of the initial dispute. If the air traffic controllers go on strike (regardless of the merits or lack thereof of their demands, and regardless of the legality or illegality of their actions), some of the consequences to the public are immediately apparent. Flights are delayed or canceled, travelers' plans are disrupted and tempers may run short at airports. But the ripple effect felt in society is enormous: airlines may lay-off thousands of employees when there are fewer flights and passengers, and the airlines' contractors may also have to lay off employees, thus contributing to a broader societal economic downturn that will be exacerbated when enterprises serving travelers—such as taxi, bus and limousine companies, hotels, motels and restaurants, and car-rental operations—all face a reduction in demand.

In sum, then, a strike or lockout in our society not only creates a high inventory of loss to the disputants but may also cause a high inventory of loss for nondisputants as well.

These drastic "self-help techniques" are called "street-and-field processes" because that is where they occur—away from the negotiating table. There is no quarrel with those who argue that sometimes the strike or lockout is "necessary," and no judgments are made about what is "good" or "bad" labor relations. The point to be emphasized is a basic one: the table processes allow the disputants to resolve their dispute with the lowest inventory of loss, not only to themselves but to society, in the vast majority of cases. The table processes defined and discussed in this manual are those dispute settlement techniques that occur at a negotiating table and include negotiation, mediation, fact-finding (sometimes called advisory arbitration or special masters), interest arbitration, med–arb and grievance arbitration.

The Difficulty with Elections

While democratic elections as a dispute settlement process are absolutely necessary in many situations, the difficulties with using the electoral process are manifold. Initially, it is not always an appropriate way to resolve a dispute, especially a labor–management dispute in which there may be many complex issues. Further, the electoral process is a yes/no, win/lose proposition. After the parties negotiate the issue to be voted, one either votes aye or nay, Republican or Democrat, or for or against the new tax proposal, but there is no compromising or fashioning of a solution that may better fit the dispute.

The real value then of using settlement negotiations, rather than turning to an election, is that it allows the disputants flexibility in designing by mutual agreement their settlement, and, as discussed later, the very process of negotiating in itself conveys many benefits to the parties. There are numerous situations where the electoral form of decision-making is appropriate. Many of the rules of the election process, however, are subject to negotiation.

Animus Negotiandi

Animus negotiandi is a term we have created to describe the desire to negotiate. This desire is a prerequisite for successful negotiations; indeed, without it, the parties will probably not reach agreement. Notice that both sides must have this desire in order for negotiations to reach a successful conclusion.

The law can create only a duty to bargain, not the desire to bargain. Thus, often one party may be physically at the table but absent in spirit. Not surprisingly, one party may take action designed to create in the other party the spirit to negotiate.

As an illustration of this, consider that, before the 1974 amendments to the Taft–Hartley Act, private not-for-profit hospitals were not covered by national labor laws. If there were no applicable state laws, the parties were left to their own devices. Absent the statutory duty to negotiate, there were some not-for-profit hospitals that did not wish to negotiate with unions. The union often resorted to strike activity to compel the reluctant management to recognize the union and negotiate a contract. Note that, even though management was not legally required to negotiate with the union, when faced with the interruption of services, the desire to negotiate was created and contracts were reached.

It is easy—but incorrect—to interpret the *animus negotiandi* to mean anything more than the desire to reach a settlement by means of negotiation. It does not mean either party necessarily possesses any positive feeling for the other side. Put another way, management and labor do not need to love each other to have the *animus negotiandi*; all that is required is the desire to negotiate, which, hopefully, will lead to a resolution of the dispute.

Negotiations Defined and Examined

Negotiations may be functionally defined as the process which affords the disputants an opportunity to exchange promises and make binding commitments in an effort to resolve their differences. It is the exchange of promises and commitments that is the essence of the process; indeed, collective bargaining can be divided into two phases: promise making (contract negotiations) and promise checking (contract administration).

Negotiation merely provides the opportunity. If the parties have the *animus negotiandi*, they will use the opportunity to resolve their dispute.

If not, they may merely go through the motions and rely on self-help techniques or street-and-field processes such as the strike, lockout, wild-cat or sabotage in an effort to energize the negotiation process.

Consider commercial or business negotiations that occur everyday, such as between a soft drink producer and a retail grocery chain. If Pepsi-Cola cannot exchange promises with Safeway, it can sell to A&P, and Safeway may contact Coca-Cola or 7-Up. The parties *may*, but do not *have to*, negotiate with one another. In collective bargaining, because of the structure provided by law, the parties *must* deal with each other—a critical point of difference, which will be discussed in greater detail later.

In any negotiation, however, the parties have similar and different interests; the process of negotiation allows them the opportunity to recon-cile these differences. In the soda example above, Pepsi-Cola and Safeway both have a similar interest—the sale of soda. Yet their interests differ because Pepsi-Cola is concerned with the sale of its product at the most commercially advantageous price, and Safeway is concerned with both customer satisfaction and the profitability of its stores. Thus, Pepsi-Cola may seek a higher price than Safeway wishes to pay. In the process of negotiation they may well be able to resolve their differences, perhaps settling on a price that affords each side a comfortable profit. Of course, sometimes the parties are not capable of resolving their differences, and negotiations must be terminated without reaching an agreement.

Often, through constant dealing with one another, the parties are able to more easily recognize the other's interests and quickly resolve dif-ferences. Other times, the parties do not constantly interact, or perhaps their relationship is based on one single transaction, such as the sale by the owner of a coal mine to a steel company. In such singular transac-tions as corporate mergers and acquisitions, often it is this lack of knowledge of the other party that hampers the exchange of promises and may well lead to errors and miscalculations that cause the proposed tran-saction to fail to come to fruition.

Points to Ponder

In this manual, our focus is on collective bargaining between labor and management, but many of the lessons are applicable in other set-tings. As you read this book, you might want to consider whether or not the notions set out here have universal application directly or would need modification.

The Parties

---

*"Which side are you on, boy,
which side are you on?"*

—TRADITIONAL UNION SONG
first heard in the
West Virginia coalfields

IN THIS SECTION we introduce the two parties to labor–management negotiations and examine the diversity on each side of the table.

"Who's Who?"

There are two sides at the table—employer/management and employee/union—yet it is often far more complex than simply one on one.

The Union Side

Unions or employee associations are multipurpose organizations. They fulfill individual employee needs in the social, political, pragmatic, philosophical and economic spheres.

Social: the need to belong to and be part of a group. The need to have shared experiences is a basic human need, and a union can afford the individual employee the opportunity to be a vital part of a functioning group. For example, unions and employee associations will often have their own social programs and rituals—the union membership meeting, the annual dinner, picnic, etc.

Economic: many employees join and support unions because they believe it is the most effective means of obtaining job security, wage increases and more extensive fringe benefits. Often they will view a union as a service organization and will closely judge its performance in order to decide whether the union and its leadership are worth continued support. For instance, if members believe they could do better with another group representing them, or with no representation, they may well do something about it: support another group or stop paying dues to the union.

Political: a union is a political institution in that its leadership is selected by the ballot box. While some employee organizations choose to separate the functions into elected leadership and appointed staff, even the "nonpolitical" staff is appointed by those principally involved in the political process. It is a basic human trait that those in power want to retain power. If a union's leadership is going to be judged upon its ability to produce for the members, then those who wish to retain power will assiduously seek to satisfy their member voters.

Philosophical: there is a long history of ideological commitment to social change in the labor movement. Many labor leaders and union members are concerned not only with delivering more for their own members but also with influencing a broader range of societal concerns, such as distribution of wealth, equal opportunity for those previously denied fair treatment, and better health care and education for all. For example, leaders like Leonard Woodcock and the late Walter Reuther of the United Auto Workers were in the vanguard of those advocating national health insurance.

Pragmatic: unions are a vehicle for an individual to have an effect on changes in his/her immediate work environment. Not all employee concerns are financial. Such issues as the nature of supervision and discipline, health and safety, shift rotation and scheduling are often more vital to an employee than a wage increase, and they will judge their union's effectiveness by how these factors are improved. Medical employees, such as nurses and physicians, are normally vitally concerned about the quality of patient care and will demand changes in the medical care environment through the collective bargaining process.

The above briefly illustrates the number of pressures and concerns a union may bring to the bargaining table. Without including such subjective factors as individual ambition or personality conflicts, it becomes readily apparent that the employee representation side of the table may well have a lack of unity that can manifest itself in interparty conflict. Thus, one faction of the union bargaining team may seek a goal diametrically opposed by another faction of the same team. Consider the conflict between skilled and unskilled employees in the auto industry. Their union negotiators must produce an additional wage increase for the skilled-trades workers, yet that wage increment addition should not be so large as to inflame the unskilled employees who are numerically in the majority.

The experience of many skilled union negotiators is that their bargaining is not only with management but rather that some of their most difficult negotiating is done within their own team and the membership at large. This diversity of concerns and priorities on the union side is often forgotten by management negotiators who tend to speak of their opposite numbers in the monolithic "they." Also worth remembering is that a management bargaining team may have an equally diverse makeup.

The Employer Side

The term "management" may apply in such diverse settings as a small business owned by an individual or family, a large business owned by many stockholders, or a nonprofit institution such as a hospital, school or government agency. Although the concerns of management will vary with the setting, there are nonetheless certain basic factors that are constant.

Management's concern is just that: to manage successfully the enterprise or institution in the way it thinks best. If a system for employee representation does not exist, the style of management decision-making is unilateral, or one-sided. To be sure, there are many laws and regulations governing employment in the private and public sectors that affect management decision-making. For example, there are minimum-wage laws, occupational health and safety laws, agency staffing manuals and the like. Yet basic decisions are made on a unilateral mode in such areas as hiring, promotion, scheduling and employee transfer.

With the presence of the union, there is a process of bilateral, or two-sided, decision-making. This is often a rude shock to management and may require some adjustment. It is worth noting that some managements will never accept the presence of a union and will allocate substantial resources to undermine the union and the bargaining process. While this may be of doubtful legality, depending upon the actions taken, it is one possible response to a union's presence. The authors' view is that such efforts are generally counterproductive and serve to generate enormous ill will as well as hefty legal costs.

A union negotiator, fully aware of the schisms and contrasting pressures and priorities on his or her own side, will often speak of management as if it had no schisms or contrasting pressures or priorities. Consider, however, that sales and marketing people are concerned that there be no interruption in production, while those in accounting and finance are more concerned that labor costs not exceed a certain level. The production-line supervisors may want greater control over employees in disciplinary matters, while engineering and methods staff usually want greater latitude over employees in their areas of concern. Indeed, the term "office politics" probably did not originate in a unionized company.

One should not overlook different philosophies present on the management side. It is simplistic to say that everyone in management is totally opposed to the union. Note that many first- and second-level supervisors may have had experience as rank-and-file workers. Most school super-intendents were once classroom teachers, and many supervisors in in-dustry and government financed at least part of their education by work-ing in lower-level positions. Thus, often there is some sympathy for the goals of the union on the part of various members of management. Work-ing as part of the bargaining unit in the past, or simply supervising employees on a daily basis, may create a bond of sympathy or empathy. Then again, the relationship may be such that the supervisor must get along with his or her employees in order to get the work done. A school principal who is the target of a barrage of teacher grievances and com-plaints may not be seen as an effective supervisor; the production manager whose employees never make quota is not building an enviable record.

Additionally, it is the policy of most managements that, whatever the negotiated settlement may be, all members of supervision receive a bit more in compensation in order to maintain the wage differential as well as demonstrate management's concern for their welfare and acknowl-edge their unique contributions to the success of the enterprise. Therefore, because their salary and benefit increases are directly related to the union negotiated settlement, some supervisors may wish the union well.

For example, if we consider negotiations between a not-for-profit hospital and its registered nurses, we may appreciate the situation of the director of nursing, a management employee with understandable em-pathy toward the nursing staff, who may also nurture some hope of in-creased personal gain should the nurses achieve a generous settlement.

Without belaboring the point, it should be clear that each side is far from a monolithic like-minded army. There is a way to classify the team components that many have found useful, and it is discussed in "Three Dimensions to Every Team . . . " in Section 6.

Clarity of Parties

Lawyers use the phrase "real party in interest" to designate that per-son or group having a financial or commercial interest in the outcome of litigation to which they are not a party of record. A simple illustration might occur in an automobile negligence case wherein Ms. Smith is su-ing the person who caused the accident, Mr. Jones. In fact, Ms. Smith has already recovered her damages from her automobile insurance com-pany, and that company is suing Mr. Jones to recover the money it paid out. Thus, the real party in interest, the true plaintiff, is the automobile insurance company, although that company is not a party of record.

In collective bargaining, we often find that there may be a similar lack of clarity of parties, which can serve to create barriers to true dispute resolution. Take as an example negotiations for a new agreement between the teachers' representative and the school board. A potential difficulty to reaching agreement is that the board is not self-funding, and thus any commitment it makes to the teachers lacks finality, both legally and premaritally. As a result, the teachers' representative may wish to negotiate with a representative of the county council, the funding body, and may charge that they are not negotiating with the real party in interest.

A similar claim may be made by the board when it notes that whatever agreement it reaches at the table must in turn be ratified by the teachers, and is nonbinding until then. And, as the board might argue further, it is not unheard of for the membership to turn down a proposed agreement by a negative ratification vote.

It should be clear that the true nature of the parties is of great importance. The lack of clarity of the parties frequently can radically alter what occurs at the bargaining table.

It appears that this is currently more of a problem in the public sector than in the private sector, where labor and management have had the benefit of more than 50 years of history, legislation and administrative and judicial action to help guide them. In many public sector relationships, the parties are still in the early phases of their relationship; when the government is the employer, unique problems are presented. For example, unlike a private company, the government provides services to the general public, which are often free, and enjoys what frequently amounts to a monopoly. There is usually just one police, fire and sanitation department in any one locale and their services are paid for by tax dollars. In addition, there is the political process whereby decisions are made that directly affect the collective bargaining relationship. If a mayoral candidate is elected because of the support, financial and otherwise, of public employee unions, greater sympathy is often expected when contracts are being negotiated.

This leads to the concept of the "end run," a maneuver in which one party seeks to obtain through the executive and/or legislative and political process that which they were unable to achieve at the bargaining table. For example, the union might "cut a deal" with the county council for an eight-percent pay raise after the school board agreed only to a six-percent increase; or the school board might approach the county council and seek a lower salary increase than that agreed upon with the union. In either event, the end-run maneuver can be utilized due to a lack of clarity of parties, their power, authority and composition.

Points to Ponder

As human beings, we tend to consider groups as homogeneous. We constantly use this shorthand for simplicity. We hear people say things like, "The federal government makes us do this," or, "The liberals support this but conservatives oppose it."

So pervasive is this tendency to generalize that the authors, for the same reason, will do this in the next section, but not before making this apology. We engage in generalizations about groups of individuals to construct a realistic theory of the way collective bargaining works. We freely acknowledge that there are some exceptions to every general rule. Nevertheless, the exceptions are few and do not undermine our theoretical construct.

The Conflict

"What's in it, man—
What's in it for me?"

THE STORY OF BO DIDDLEY

IN THIS SECTION we introduce the essential nature of labor–management conflict clearly encapsulated in Theory "U" and Theory "M."

Preconditions for Unionization

For collective bargaining to occur, a union or employee association must be chosen to represent eligible employees, usually through the electoral process. What are the preconditions for employee organization?

First, the employees must feel distinct, as a group, from management. If the employees identify with management, share its values and goals and believe all interests, then worker and manager are the same and there will be no impetus to organize into a separate hierarchy. Additionally, even if management is perceived as being different from the workers, many employees may aspire to management and for that reason will reject unionization.

Second, the employees must feel some dissatisfaction with management policies, practices or personalities. If employees perceive inequity, such as favoritism for promotion, insufficient pay increases or inconvenient work scheduling, to name but a few potential trouble spots, then they will begin to sense the need for some means to rectify the situation. Unionization is one possible route they may select if they do not believe management will resolve these problems satisfactorily.

Third, given a sense of difference between employees and managers plus unsatisfied employee concerns, the next key element is a sense of employee commitment to the job and employer. Though at first this may seem contradictory, it is in reality complementary; if there is dissatisfaction at the workplace, the most common action is to leave, and in fact this is often what occurs. Consider the numerous fast-food outlets, only

11

a small minority of which are unionized. Many employees express the dissatisfaction and alienation described above, but most employees have only a temporary commitment to the job. Their real interests lie elsewhere, in school, family or another job. Lacking this commitment, these employees are more likely to change jobs than seek to adjust conditions through unionization.

Fourth, there must be a supportive legal environment for unionization. Until the passage of the Wagner Act (National Labor Relations Act of 1935), most private sector employees had no legal protection for union activities, and consequently most employees had some real fears concerning their futures should they join and support a union. Similarly, it was not until the 1960s and 1970s that many public employees, given newly enacted state and local laws protecting their rights to unionize, began to join and support unions in large numbers.

A final element is the interest of unions in organizing and representing employees, and the employees' perception of unions as institutions and symbols.

Historically, the American labor movement was divided into two categories: craft and industrial unions. Craft unions represented employees with a specific skill, such as carpenters or electricians, and were initially successful because of the irreplaceability of its members in the event of a dispute. Put simply, if all the skilled shoemakers who worked for the April Shoe Company refused to work until and unless the company granted a desired increase in wage rates, the company had little choice if it wished to continue production. Either the company conceded to the union's position or sought to outlast their shoemakers. Thus, the union's protection was not found in the courts or administrative bodies but rather in the unique skills of its members.

Conversely, industrial unions were not nearly as powerful because they represented unskilled and semiskilled employees who were more easily replaceable in the event of a dispute. Industrial unions organized employees vertically, meaning, for example, every production and maintenance employee in a steel mill—whether he or she worked in the hearth, tin mill, did janitorial services or kept track of inventory—was represented by a steelworker's union.

Given the difficulties of representing unskilled and semiskilled employees, it was not surprising that most craft unions, which organized workers horizontally, by skill, were reluctant to represent any employee but a skilled one. This posture changed rapidly, however, in the tumultuous 1930s, when the Committee for Industrial Organization, which later became the Congress of Industrial Organizations (CIO), became successful through aggressive organizing campaigns and the new legal protections afforded to private sector employees by the Wagner Act.

Despite great increases in union membership, some employees expressed reluctance at becoming part of a union because of what they perceived as the blue-collar and low-status image of unions. White-collar professional employees, such as registered nurses and school teachers, often preferred to be represented by organizations that originated as professional associations, and rejected union representation.

In the 1950s and 1960s, many private sector unions unfamiliar with the unique rules concerning government employment, such as the narrower scope of bargaining, were reluctant to organize and represent public employees. This has changed dramatically in recent years, and now many private sector unions eagerly seek to represent white-collar, service, professional and female employees, perhaps realizing that these workers represent growth areas of employment. At the same time, many observers have noted that such professional organizations as the National Education Association and the American Nurses Association have become increasingly oriented toward collective bargaining.

Why Employers Oppose Unionization

No doubt the vast majority of employers who must deal with unions would prefer not to. The reason is not what is commonly supposed: that unions tend to negotiate wage levels higher than employers might otherwise pay. Although numerous studies have demonstrated that unionized workers do in fact receive more money for comparable work done by nonunionized employees, this is not employers' principal objection to unionization.

The main reason for opposition to unions is more basic; it concerns the issue of control of the work environment. In a nonunionized enterprise, the employer has great latitude in the running of the operation and direction of its employees. As long as the employer is in compliance with applicable statutes, the style of decision-making may be unilateral. In deciding who to hire and at what compensation level, who to lay off or terminate, promote or transfer, the nonunionized employer has great latitude. So long as these decisions are not made on the basis of sex, race, age, ethnic background, religion or the like, which could violate laws such as the Equal Employment Opportunity statutes, the employer may treat employees as choice dictates.

Consider Abbott Distributing Corporation, a small nonunionized firm run by the Abbott family. When Sally Abbott, the firm's comptroller, wishes to reorganize the office, she makes the following decisions: Carl Rollins, who has been with the firm for eight years, will be let go. Barry Rollins, who has been with the firm for two years, will be promoted to head of accounts receivable. Debra Myers, who has been with the firm for seven months, will be promoted to head of accounts payable. Joan Watkins, a six-year employee, Larry Wilkens, a 10-year employee, and Myra Stephens, an employee of three months, will all be terminated and replaced by a new electronic data-processing system. Marsha North, the receptionist, will now work from 8 A.M. to 4 P.M. instead of from 9 to 5.

Assuming Ms. Abbott made these decisions with no discriminatory intent, the decisions are final and the employees adversely affected have little recourse except litigation. To many people, especially employers, this is as it should be, with the employer possessing discretion in the direction of the enterprise. If Ms. Abbott is to be held accountable for the performance of her department, and if that department is vital to the success of the total enterprise, then many would argue that the manager must be able to make important personnel and operational decisions free of concerns other than optimal efficiency of the enterprise.

To many others, unilateral decision-making is inherently unfair to the employees, who should have a voice in decisions affecting their working lives and economic security. Under most union–management contracts, Ms. Abbott would not be able to make the changes described without, at least, consulting the union. Under many contracts, she would have to negotiate the changes and the impact.

To begin with, Ms. Abbott chose to terminate employees in apparent disregard for their seniority. Under most union–management contracts, layoffs and terminations must be affected by inverse order of seniority, with the most recently hired being the first fired. In a similar vein, promotions within the bargaining unit are also often controlled by seniority, with the employee having the greatest length of service being entitled to first opportunity for promotion.

Under many union–management contracts, the employer is not free to introduce technology that displaces employees without first making provisions for the economic security of the affected employees, such as providing a retraining program or a new position elsewhere in the organization, or making a financial settlement (e.g., severance pay or early retirement pension for displaced employees).

Marsha North, the receptionist who had her work schedule altered, has no choice in a nonunionized enterprise but to work the new schedule or find a job elsewhere. Under most union–management contracts, an employee's work schedule may not be unilaterally altered by management. Contractual provisions usually mandate extra compensation for work schedule changes, and, sometimes, they are prohibited unless the union and the employee consent.

If a worker is fired for alleged misconduct, such as insubordination or excessive absenteeism, a nonunionized private sector employee typically has no recourse except to find another position. A union representing an employee will be concerned about whether an employee was fired for just cause. If the union does not agree that the employee deserved to be terminated, it will represent him or her in a grievance procedure that could culminate in binding arbitration.

Many employers oppose unionization because it transforms the work environment, causing an increased formalization of behavior, with rules for many activities previously handled in an informal, personal manner. For example, before unionization, when James Abbott, the traffic manager, needed someone to work overtime, he would ask Tom Wagner first because he was a young man with a growing family and he wanted all the overtime work possible. James never asked Dave Hoffman to do overtime because James knew that Hoffman had grown children, was nearing retirement, and preferred to go home and spend time with his grandchildren.

When James scheduled vacations, he knew Hoffman liked two weeks during the deer-hunting season, while Wagner wanted time off during Christmas and Easter school holidays when his children were at home. And when the position of driver–coordinator promotion opened up, Abbott knew Wagner wanted it because the money was better and that Hoffman was not interested because he was nearing retirement. James did not post the opening; he offered the promotion to Wagner.

Were there a collective agreement in effect, Abbott's style of management would, of necessity, be subject to transformation. Usually, overtime distribution, vacation scheduling, promotional opportunities, etc., are governed by seniority, and there are procedural steps to be followed by the employer for these matters.

Many employers consider these union strictures as barriers to efficient operation of the enterprise, as well as impediments to dealing with employees on a personalized, individual basis.

To union organizers and their supporters, as with management, procedural guidelines are necessary to protect employees from the vagaries of favoritism and the perils of subjective judgment. Some union organizers will argue that if the employer did not engage in abuse of discretion, the union would not have been voted in by the employees, and that objectively made decisions and clear procedural guidelines make for better management and ultimately greater organizational efficiency.

Be that as it may—and controversy on these points has raged fiercely over past decades—there can be no question that the introduction of a union mandates a different mode of decision-making and management. By law, the union is the sole and exclusive collective bargaining unit representative of employees, and as such has certain rights and obligations. The employer may no longer deal with the unionized work force unilaterally. For better or for worse, fundamental relations between employer and employee are affected by unions.

Turning our attention to the public sector, what is the applicability of the above to government employees, who for many years have enjoyed the protections of the various provisions of civil service laws that provide job security and due-process protection?

The answer is complex, reflecting as it must the disparate pressures on government as an employer and as a protector of the public interest. Over many years, a system of civil service laws, rules and regulations evolved that gave government employees job security rights and established an administrative procedure through which those rights could be protected. The focus until the mid 1970s was rarely on layoffs, cutbacks or RIFs (reductions in force), but rather on protection from disciplinary termination without just cause, alterations of medical insurance and retirement benefits and other matters.

In return for what generally came to be accepted as lifetime job security, state and local government employees earned lower wages than their private sector counterparts. In the 1960s and 1970s, unions began aggressively seeking to represent public employees. Numerous statutes, ordinances and executive orders were issued that gave a large number of government employees the right to join and support unions and employee associations, and (except in the federal sector) engage in collective bargaining for wages and other economic matters. Many government agencies remaind neutral, neither supporting nor opposing unionization.

The result of this new climate was a dramatic increase in wages and benefits for government employees. Police, fire, sanitation, road maintenance, janitorial, custodial, clerical and professional employees, such as teachers, librarians and social workers, swelled union membership rosters to unprecedented numbers. The traditional union goals of adherence to seniority in making personnel decisions such as promotion, transfer, layoffs and grievance arbitration were in many instances grafted onto already existing civil service protections, with the net result that employees often had to select remedies among a myriad of possibilities.

Many government managers, concerned that civil service protections made it difficult to operate in what they felt were the most efficient ways, decried the additional procedural safeguards of union–management agreements and sought to limit the scope of areas in which they must bargain.

To sum up the discussion at this point, employers generally oppose unionization of their employees because of the necessity to engage in bilateral decision-making and the concomitant reduction in flexibility of operations and restriction in the scope of management decision-making, as well as the style of employee relations. The scope of negotiations is thus the battlefield on which the fight for power takes place. This will be examined in Section Four. First, however, it is necessary to explore the differing beliefs and perceptions of labor and management.

Ideological Clashes

Although trade unions in this country have for the most part eschewed the ideological conflicts with management favored by western European socialist and communist unions, they too seem fundamentally opposed to employers. Sometimes this conflict appears to be one that questions which party has superior judgment about the mission, operation and function of the organization.

For example, if one analyzes the stream of arguments presented during collective negotiations between a school board and its teachers, many issues, such as class size, number of planning periods and amount of tuition reimbursement, can be viewed as questions of conflicting judgments. The school board may argue that class size, number of planning periods and tuition reimbursement, while not ideal, are appropriate for budgetary circumstances. The teachers' representative may well question the board's judgment by arguing that a decrease in class size, an increase in planning periods and tuition reimbursement will result in better-quality education. The school board may counter with the position that they think money could be better spent elsewhere, and that proposed changes are not worth the financial commitment, which, says the board, it cannot afford. The teachers' representative may respond that the board can and should be willing to expend money to improve the quality of education.

However, the problem is that the mission of the board is not simply to provide better education but to live within its budget. It must avoid a local tax increase that could have unpleasant political ramifications for the board, comply with federal guidelines on facilities—access for handicapped students, pay increased fuel bills to heat or cool the schools, pay for buses to transport students, and so on and so on. All of these demands must be met in some way if the board is to continue to function. And so the parties at the bargaining table appear to be arguing about money—and they are—but they are also bargaining over questions of judgment founded on the bedrock issue of who knows best, the board or the teachers, regarding prioritizing demands and running a school system.

From this simple illustration it can be observed that each party, in addition to whatever internal schisms it faces, must also deal across the table with an adversary who has a different philosophical and ideological base, one which can make reaching agreement more difficult. Certainly, the first step in solving this dilemma is to begin by analyzing the philosophic position from which the other side views the issues to be negotiated.

Theory "U" and Theory "M"

Douglas Murray McGregor is best known for his characterization of two approaches to the human side of enterprise. He labeled them Theory "X" and Theory "Y" and argued that these are distinct approaches, two distinct belief-systems about people in organizations. Here, we will use Theory "U" to designate the union belief-system, and Theory "M" as the employer belief-system guiding management negotiations.

In employee relations, employers and unions in both public and private sectors are opposed to one another not only on wage or salary issues but, more fundamentally, they have opposing belief-systems. As McGregor noted, these beliefs may not be explicit but are nevertheless persuasive and deep-seated. While it is true that any description of a belief system attributable to a large and amorphous group harbors within it generalizations that are broad and obviously not shared by all members of the group, these beliefs predominate and often are manifested in actions not comprehensible to those unfamiliar with underlying assumptions. The situation can be further clouded by the unwillingness and/or inability of many group members to articulate their philosophical underpinning. For instance, a management negotiator may propose a merit pay system and a union negotiator might respond reflexively with opposition to any merit pay system. Neither side may articulate the underlying philosophical rationale behind its position, but each is "coming from a different place" and may not fully understand or appreciate the other side's ideological mind-set.

Certainly, some labor–management strife may be attributed to a lack of trust. A constant refrain heard at the table by union negotiators is the employer's exasperated statement: "Why must this particular clause be included in the agreement when we've been doing it for 12 years and have no intention of stopping now? You can't put everything in a contract!" To which the union negotiator may respond "First, because you've been doing it, why not put it in writing? Second, we want as complete and detailed an agreement as possible because we don't trust you."

Perhaps at least some of this distrust could be due to an unfamiliarity with the other side's beliefs. It should be remembered that most adversaries have never been on the other side of the table and have rather limited social and professional interactions with their opposite numbers.

The two belief-systems will be presented as they prevail during negotiations, with the rationale given for each position.

What is the goal of each side?

Theory M: Unions constantly seek more money for less work, and this is bad.

Theory U: Employers constantly seek to pay less money for more work, and this is bad.

Samuel Gompers, the father of the American Federation of Labor, is alleged to have stated the basic tenet of business unionism: *More, Now!* Union negotiators are convinced that, if the employer is not constantly pressured and scrutinized, it will get more work out of employees for less money. Management negotiators believe that unions do not understand the economic importance of increased productivity, and higher pay is merited only if the worker is more productive. Union negotiators believe their members are underpaid and need to catch up (with other employers' rates, inflation, etc.); management negotiators believe employees are already fairly paid, or paid higher than is justified.

What is the current pace of work?

Theory M: Unions block all forms of technological change out of a reactionary, self protective, shortsighted impulse; all workers can become more productive by working faster and smarter.

Theory U: Management will introduce machines that speed up the pace and increase the amount of work an employee must do; employees are already working hard enough.

Management believes every job or process must be as efficient as possible in order to compete effectively, and that to force management to adhere to old techniques will lead to the demise of the employer and, thus, the termination of employees. Unions believe employees are already putting forth all the effort they can, and any new technology is a ruse to get more work out of an already overworked person. If more work is desired, let the employer pay more for it.

Is the amount of work to be done finite or infinite?

Theory M: The amount of work to be done is infinite and will expand only if employers are free to experiment, to be innovative, and to remain competitive.

Theory U: The amount of work to be done at any one time is finite and therefore must be protected constantly against any erosion.

Union representatives believe it is irrelevant and a waste of time to attempt to discredit any variant of the "Lump of Labor Theory." Their concern, for example, is an elevator operator who is being replaced by an automatic elevator. Can he feed his family with the concept of "maximum revenue product"? Additionally, they raise questions about the safety and reliability of any new, unproven technology. Management representatives claim that, if they were always to maintain the status quo in technology and never displace workers, we would still have a buggy-whip industry while other nations drove automobiles. Managers see union insistence upon lifetime job security plans and retraining as unduly financially burdensome and not in the best long-run interests of the enterprise, society or the employees themselves. Technological progress and innovation are seen as the only means to real job security; to oppose this is to oppose not merely progress, but reality itself.

Upon what basis shall personnel decisions be made?

Theory M: Management must be free to make personnel decisions (hiring, promoting, reassigning, laying off, etc.) solely on the basis of an employee's ability to do the job.

Theory U: Management will make subjective personnel decisions that reward management favorites and punish union supporters; the union must ensure objective decision-making in all personnel mailers.

Unions argue for seniority as the key variable—or the sole variable—in personnel decisions, because it is objective and clear to everyone. Older employees deserve more benefits as a reward for their good and loyal service. Unions view any plan labeled as a "merit" plan merely a device to institutionalize favoritism. Managers believe they can determine who the most capable employees are and they must, to remain efficient, be able to reward quality work. Age and length of service, employers believe, do not determine who the best workers are; indeed, often the best workers are the younger ones, and they must be rewarded to encourage their continued efforts.

Does the employee obtain "ownership rights" in a job?

Theory M: Unions should cooperate with management's need for flexibility in operations; sometimes a reduction in wages or benefits is appropriate.

Theory U: Management can introduce any change it desires so long as it does not adversely affect the position of an employee; no reduction in wages or benefits is ever justified.

Many managers believe that the true cost of employee unionization is not in higher wages but in reduced management flexibility. Many contracts contain work rules that managers claim are unrealistic, anachronistic and wasteful. They believe union negotiators should realize the importance of realistic work rules to the continued existence of the enterprise and allow management the opportunity to be technologically innovative and efficient. Union representatives will usually answer that, as long as provision is made to protect employees from financial loss, management can be as innovative as it wishes, but the union will countenance no reduction in wages or benefits, no "roll-backs," no "give backs." The union will often seek to negotiate "buy backs" that provide for the payment by management to employees who surrender job rights or benefits. However, the concept of "give back" is an anathema to a union negotiator.

Union officials believe that the employees' efforts make an enterprise successful, and it is only equitable that, as a reward for good and loyal service, an employee should obtain a sort of ownership right in the job, and such rights should not be subject to casual termination at an employer's whim. Indeed, just as shareholders develop rights in an enterprise and reap benefits, so also should employees. After all, shareholders speak of their "equity rights"; why then shouldn't employees also enjoy some equity? After all, the union argues, what else does an employee have if not his or her job?

Management negotiators consider this argument a variant of Marxist rubbish. An employee indeed shares in the success of an enterprise by receiving substantial wages and fringe benefits in return for expending labor. According to management negotiators, an employer owes no additional obligation to employees, and any attempt to create or enforce such an obligation will lead only to enormous misallocation of resources and a rigidity of operations that will paralyze management and result in a loss of employment. This, paradoxically, is the very result the union alleges it seeks to avoid.

Upon what basis shall the employee's compensation rate be established?

Theory M: Compensation rates should be based on the level of employee performance for maximum productivity.

Theory U: Compensation rates should be based upon the nature of the job for maximum equity.

Unions argue that you pay for the job, not the worker, which serves to minimize the role of subjective employer performance appraisals. Since virtually all employees, given proper training and equipment, can meet reasonable performance standards, it is only divisive to pay workers doing the same job at different rates, which serves to turn union members against fellow members. While a slight exception may be made for some length-of-service bonus that rewards loyalty, basically everyone should be paid the same amount for doing the same work. And that amount should be what the highest paid worker receives, when wage rates are being equalized. Not surprisingly, when there are "step" scales, with longer-service employees receiving higher compensation, unions argue that the scale should be as flat as possible, with all employees "maxing out" (reaching the top step) in as brief a period as possible.

Wrong, argues management. The way to motivate employees and achieve greater productivity is by monetarily rewarding individual effort. Because not all individuals work equally hard, it is wrong to reward all for the efforts of a few. Doing so will discourage individual initiative and lead to "soldiering" on the job, a phenomenon in which employees all do the same minimal amount of work. "Soldiering" and other counter-productive phenomena are encouraged by flat salary scales that take no account of these individual differences. And, finally, if there is to be uniformity of wages, it should not, must not, and will not be set at the highest level of the rate scale, but, rather, to be fair, should be set at the middle of the scale to renew average performance.

If the employer does pay a premium for length of service, the unions argue that the employer will seek to replace the more experienced, older loyal worker with a younger, less experienced and, more important, less expensive worker. Employers counter that, given restrictive rules foisted upon them by unions, they have no choice but to keep "dead wood." Whenever they can, they will place the most willing and capable worker on the job, and that person is often a younger, more ambitious individual, one who is not complacent but eager to perform to the extent of his or her abilities.

On the question of interemployer uniformity of wages, unions maintain that what is fairest and least divisive is to pay industry standard wages, or similar wages for similar work throughout the particular industry. This reduces friction within the union and increases feelings of solidarity. If there is to be an increase in wages and benefits, all members should receive the same amount because their work is the same.

Typically, each employer maintains that its own particular circumstances are somewhat unique and therefore require a settlement different from—and perhaps justifiably lower than—other employers. Each employer can prove the many ways in which their production or organizational structure and operation differ from competitors, how their financial and market posture is different, and how their ability to pay what the union terms the industry standard is thus impaired. And, finally, the employer in question can always show how another employer is paying less than the union is seeking. Therefore, the employer argues that its competitive position would be unjustifiably eroded by the union's standards.

Not surprisingly, unions can—and do—point out that there are employers who pay wages and benefits in excess of the industry rate. Also, unions are extremely reluctant to permit any employer to pay less than what is deemed the industry standard, for, if they permit one employer an exception, inevitably a competitor will demand the same, or a more extreme, concession, all of which can lead to an unraveling of the union's goal of uniform provisions for its members.

What is the appropriate level of executive compensation?

Theory M: Managers more than earn their salaries.

Theory U: Managers are paid too much.

Unions say that managers are overpaid and enjoy too many expensive perquisites, such as stock options and country club memberships. The money could be better spent on raising employee wages and/or newer plant equipment. *Nobody* is worth half a million dollars a year, it is argued, because so many managerial decisions, such as corporate acquisitions or divestitures, are incorrect and foolish; top managers should not earn 10 or 20 times what an average union employee makes. Is the high-living chairman of the board worth the money that 40 employees sweat to earn on the assembly line? Definitely not, avers the union.

Not true, argue business leaders. In fact, the direction of an enterprise is an enormously demanding pursuit, one which does not stop precisely at 5 P.M. Friday. Managerial responsibility is so broad, time consuming and challenging that it goes on all the time, even at the golf course or over dinner. Furthermore, good executive talent is difficult to find, and if the individual is not paid well, the manager will take his or her talents where the compensation package is more attractive.

In the public sector, where top positions are generally filled by political appointment, this dispute concerns the skills, abilities and competence of agency and bureau chiefs. Unions allege that these appointees lack an appreciation of the true mission of the agency and are too concerned with political decision-making and maintaining appearances to do a really effective job of leadership.

In contrast, it is contended that political appointees are in office to implement the will of the electorate, which is rightly seen as paramount in a democracy. Additionally, political appointees should not become concerned with the day-to-day operational details of an agency, but rather should provide overall direction and policy, consistent with the goals and philosophies the voters have selected. And, finally, they argue, "political" decisions are valid both premaritally and philosophically, and to be blind to their validity is to misunderstand the true nature of government.

What determines the outcome of representation elections?

Theory M: Most employees would not vote for or support a union if the union did not engage in campaign conduct that is either deceptive, coercive or both.

Theory U: Most employees would vote for and support a union if not for deceptive employer antiunion campaigns and coercive activities, which violate either the letter or the spirit of the law or both.

The statutory and administrative foundation of labor relations provides for the exercise of employee free choice and the freedom of communication by the employer, if it is not to be coercive. Unions contend that the reason they lose so many representation elections is because employers take actions that threaten employees and/or deceive them into not registering their true feelings of support for the labor movement. After losing an election, unions frequently file unfair labor practice charges against an employer, alleging that the employees did not really have the opportunity to make a free choice.

Employers note that many unions lose representation elections, and some unions that have won election victories are decertified later by disappointed or angry workers. This clearly demonstrates, they contend, that unions do not enjoy the support of workers as labor movement leaders allege. When a union wins a representation election, it is because the employees were deceived by union campaign propaganda or threatened with loss of economic security or even bodily harm unless they supported the union cause.

Thus, while many employers staunchly maintain that they keep a stance of complete neutrality in these matters and that employees are free to make their own untrammeled free choice, unions argue that this is far removed from the reality they experience during organizing campaigns.

What causes strikes?

Theory M: Unreasonable and unrealistic union demands cause strikes.

Theory U: Intransigent management positions cause strikes.

Management negotiators argue that to meet unreasonable union demands promulgated by a minority of employees would effectively prevent the enterprise from meeting its production or service goals, and therefore they are forced to resist these demands even if that means enduring a strike. Union representatives argue that they strike only reluctantly, when members authorize the action because their goals are not being met. Unions believe management overstates the cost and effect of union demands, which are only opening ploys. If the employer would approach negotiations without an antiunion attitude, a mutually satisfactory contract could be reached without a strike.

Who knows best what employees really want?

Theory M: The union leaders are out of touch with the true feelings of the members and their desires.

Theory U: Management does not truly understand the employees and is not concerned with meeting their needs.

Quite often during negotiations, management's representative will state that the offer the union is characterizing as totally unacceptable would, in fact, be perfectly acceptable to a majority of the membership. Further, on issues relating to union security, management will argue that such points as compulsory union membership, dues check-off or released time with pay for union stewards to process grievances or pursue union affairs are concerns of only a vocal minority of employees and should not stand as a barrier to reaching agreement. Union representatives will typically counter with the statement that it is management, isolated in its administrative offices, who is out of touch with employees' true feelings, desires and needs. Only rarely will management's offer be put to a ratification vote without the endorsement or support of union leadership to test management's allegation that the offer is acceptable; the usual result is a negative vote. Management will counter that the offer would have been acceptable but for the incitement by union leaders to reject the offer.

On issues of union security, union negotiators will most often argue that the more stable and secure the union is as an institution, the more responsible it can be as a bargaining representative and, thus, it is better—not worse—for management to have a strong, well-entrenched union. The more insecure a union is, they argue, the more likely it is to be militant and possibly irresponsible in an effort to prove itself.

Management dismisses this argument as self serving. It is not the role of management to strengthen the union, and, indeed, if management were to do that it could possibly be seen as an unfair labor practice. Furthermore, if the union were well-run and truly met employee needs, all would join willingly and none would require the coercion of a union shop arrangement.

Should an employee be compelled to support the union?

Theory M: No employee should be forced to support a union.

Theory U: An employee should be expected to support the union that represents him or her.

Because under law a union must represent the interests of all those in the bargaining unit, unions argue that all employees should bear the cost of contract negotiation and administration. If a person works in an employment setting where he or she benefits from a union negotiated and administered agreement, it is unfair to take without giving a fair share. Indeed, many union advocates argue that, if an individual does not want to actually join the union, he or she should proffer a payment for union services rendered. After all, this argument runs, a union performs a service that costs money, and all should share in meeting that cost because all reap the benefits. The analogy to government taxation is sometimes made with the union maintaining that, while citizens may not necessarily agree with government policy, taxes are paid by all citizens to support the running of the government.

Management in turn contends that philosophically it is wrong to force any individual to join any organization, most especially a union, because so many employees oppose the basic tenets of unionism. Additionally, if a union must represent all employees fairly, regardless of union membership, this ensures equitable treatment for all, something all Americans support, and unions would not view this as a burden if they truly sought to advance the interests of all employees instead of a favored minority. Finally, compulsory membership diminishes the employer's control of the workplace because, first, some unions are controlled by restrictive admission procedures, and, second, some very good potential employees will not accept employment if they must join a union, all of which means that the employer is not free to hire the best person for the position.

This argument is especially heated in the public sector, where unions seek agency shop provisions in their negotiated agreements that provide that an employee does not have to join the union if unwilling, but must, if not a dues-paying union member, tender a fee-for-service payment to the union. The fee-for-service sum, not surprisingly, is usually closely equivalent to union dues. Given the choice of paying dues or a fee for service of the same amount, the majority of employees join the union. The debate is also affected by the unique nature of public employment. If, as many argue, public employment is the right of every citizen, the requirement of union dues payment as a condition of retention of one's job is directly in conflict with this right. Unions argue that, just as a public employer may require payment of a compulsory pension contribution, so it may also compel payment of union dues without abridging any constitutional right or freedom. After all, unions argue, it is through their efforts that salary, benefits and working conditions of all public employees have improved. If unions are to continue their work and advance and protect the interests of all, everyone must contribute.

Reconciling Philosophical Differences

This section sought to introduce and explore the two differing belief-systems in industrial relations. In contract negotiations, these underlying differences are never resolved. More immediate things such as wages, hours and the terms and conditions of employment are, in fact, settled. Thus, each side gets a settlement they can "live with," one which meets immediate needs but cannot completely meet the philosophical and ideological goals of the two belief-systems. Perhaps this is the reason that, although contract negotiations may occur only once every year or two, collective bargaining in the form of contract administration goes on continuously. And even though grievance arbitration may put the specific controversy to rest, it does not at all put to rest the philosophic controversy; rather, it should be seen as a temporary truce in a war that does not end but only changes its form, not its essence. Indeed, this essence appears to be composed of deeply contrary philosophical positions.

The implication of this philosophical opposition is perhaps especially meaningful in times of economic uncertainty. When management seeks a "give back" or a "roll back" of existing benefits, it must be ready to contend with the union belief that management executives are grossly overpaid and that management must open its books for close financial inspection and also endure meaningful economic sacrifice. Anything less will result in an overwhelming refusal to consider any reduction in current benefits. Further, management must, if at all possible, provide for something in return to the union in addition to a promise that concessions sought will result in maintenance of employment levels. This is necessary because the concession is thus not a "give back" but rather a "buy back," something different and far more palatable to the union. As an illustration of this point, consider that, when Chrysler obtained significant wage and benefit concessions from its unionized employees, in return it gave the union a seat on its board of directors as well as participation in a profit-sharing program, which could be financially significant to the employees.

In contrast to the Chrysler approach, General Motors found itself in serious trouble when, shortly after achieving significant concessions from its unionized employees, it announced a new and enriched bonus formula for 6,000 top executives who had not enjoyed large bonuses for the past two years. The union forcefully and convincingly argued that this new executive bonus plan violated the spirit of its concessionary contract, which called for "equality of sacrifice" by management. Under mounting union criticism and the threat of serious job actions, management hastily withdrew the bonus plan. Although the union president was quoted in the April 3, 1982, *Wall Street Journal* as saying, "I hope in some period of time that this whole regrettable, unfortunate incident will be behind us," it is highly doubtful whether it will ever be forgotten. Its consequences for the parties' future relationship may be significant.

Thus, the ramifications of the theoretical underpinning of each side is not merely a subject for abstract discussion, but rather one of great pragmatic day-to-day significance that is worthy of further study. If, as many thoughtful observers believe, industrial relations in the United States in the 1980s and beyond must be harmonious and cooperative, the first step must be a greater appreciation of the belief-system of the other side. This section, it is hoped, is a precursor to that necessary first step.

Points to Ponder

In many areas of negotiation, are there not the same kinds of theories, or assumptions, based upon subjective perceptions at work?

For example, consider race relations. Might there not be a similar set of assumptions between those negotiating on behalf of blacks and those representing a corporation, a majority of whose leaders are white? If the specific issue were the nature of a proposed affirmative action program, might we not expect each team to come to the table with preconceived expectations and beliefs?

Do you think it might assist each team to have some understanding of the other side's belief-system and values?

The Battlefield

*"I've got to know
what is and isn't mine."*

—TONY ORLANDO AND DAWN
Tie a Yellow Ribbon

IN THIS SECTION we discuss some subjects that cause disputes.

Scope of Bargaining

When the union and employer sit down to negotiate an agreement, there are certain limitations on what they may and may not negotiate about. To take some extreme examples, the parties are not free to negotiate higher benefits for only those members of the bargaining unit who are dues-paying members of the union, nor may the parties agree to violate applicable laws, such as minimum wage provisions of the Fair Labor Standards Act.

Whether the negotiations take place under the National Labor Relations Act in the private sector or under various federal, state or local laws or ordinances, there are usually three broad categories into which negotiations may be classified, although particulars will vary with applicable governing laws.

The first category contains *mandatory* items of bargaining, which the parties must negotiate. The failure to do so constitutes an unfair labor practice. In the private sector, wages, hours and conditions of work are considered mandatory subjects. It must be noted that, while something may be mandatory, the law is explicit about concessions *not* being required. Put simply, as long as the employer is willing to discuss wages with the union at reasonable times and places, the employer is not required to make any compromise. Admittedly, the courts have often had great difficulty in distinguishing hard bargaining, which is legal, from a refusal to bargain in good faith, which is illegal.

In the public sector, the mandatory scope of negotiations is often far narrower than in the private sector. State or local legislatures may decide that certain subjects may not be appropriate for bargaining, which leads into the second category, prohibited subjects. In the private sector, the closed shop (a union security arrangement requiring union membership as a condition for obtaining a job as well as a condition for retaining that job) is illegal, and the parties may not even negotiate over such a provision, much less agree to one. In the federal sector, wages, a mandatory item in the private sector, is a prohibited subject.

There is a third category of items, called permissive, which consists of subjects that the parties may discuss and negotiate, if both desire. For example, internal union affairs are neither mandatory nor prohibited, and so they fall into this category. If the employer wanted to discuss the union's plan for conducting a contract ratification vote, an internal union matter, the union would not have to discuss it with the employer, but could if it wished. Similarly, internal management affairs, broadly called management rights, are usually not subjects of collective negotiations. Such matters as the nature and conduct of the employer's advertising campaign or financing arrangements are matters the employer may, if it desires, discuss with the union.

In sum, then, the three categories of subjects—mandatory, prohibited, and permissive—are found in both public and private sectors. However, the content of each category can vary markedly, depending on applicable law and judicial interpretation. Finally, it should be noted that the content of each category changes over time in a field as dynamic as collective bargaining.

Subjects of Bargaining

At this point, it is probably appropriate to identify the actual subjects of bargaining. As noted in the preceding section on "Scope of Bargaining," each sector (by statute and administrative and judicial decision) has its own particular range of topics.

In all but the federal sector, wages and all forms of employee compensation are topics of mandatory bargaining. This covers, to name only a few, such items as sales commissions, bonuses, overtime, hazard or "dirty work" pay, shift differential, on-call or call-in pay, probationary, learner, apprentice or new employee wages, special equipment operating rate, and advanced preparation or certification rates.

Usually, provision is next made for payment for time *not* worked. This covers vacations, holidays, paid sick leave, personal leave, religious holidays and sabbaticals. Eligibility for all the above is generally clearly detailed. Items such as bereavement or funeral leave have in many contracts become paid time off over recent years, but some agreements cover this under unpaid leave, or leave without pay, which encompasses items such as education leave, leave for union business, military service or paternity leave. Maternity leave, which initially was without pay, has tended to come under the category of paid leave because of changes in the law and societal trends.

Employee fringe benefits, such as health and life insurance, pension plan and profit sharing, are detailed, as are product or service discounts, optical, dental or legal services, free samples, tuition or training reimbursement, uniform or equipment allowance and free parking.

Union security provisions, including mandatory membership, agency shop and/or dues check-off, union use of bulletin boards, access to employees, paid time off to handle grievances and other union business, special seniority status for union officials, and distribution of union literature, are covered in most contracts.

Management rights are an important part of virtually every contract and provide for the employer to maintain unilateral decision-making power over such matters as the right to manage and direct the enterprise, the sole right to determine the number, location, function, operation and mission of each facility, the product or service, the method of manufacture for providing the service, schedules, financing, advertising, promotion and pricing. Further, the employer seeks a statement that it may hire, lay off, transfer, promote and otherwise assign employees to work, that it may reprimand, suspend, discharge or otherwise discipline employees for just cause, and that it may generally manage the enterprise and maintain order and efficiency in its facilities and institute, promulgate or change rules, regulations, policies and practices "not otherwise inconsistent" with the terms of the contract. It is this last phrase, coupled with the "just cause" for discipline provision, that limits employer discretion and provides a role for the union in the day-to-day affairs of the enterprise.

In the section of the contract dealing with discipline, the grievance procedure is laid out and usually the selection of the grievance arbitrator, the sharing of the costs and the arbitrator's authority are specified. Thus, while management is given great latitude in the management rights section, that latitude is tempered by the union's right to challenge any decision, especially concerning personnel, that violates contractual guidelines.

Most contracts typically contain extensive provisions, often quite detailed, that govern personnel decisions, such as seniority, promotion, layoff and recall. The parties negotiate over definitions and extent of seniority in making personnel decisions, which are vital to both the employees and the operation of the enterprise.

Typically, other contractual clauses may deal with health, safety, non-discrimination, affirmative action and career-ladder or upward-mobility programs. To be sure, each contract addresses issues specific to the industry. Problems of academic freedom, licensure, contracting out, plant closing, RIFs, malpractice insurance, medical examinations, grooming, financial responsibility, bonding and the like make each contract unique.

Finally, the agreement typically provides in some way for the stability of relations between the parties. The union will agree not to strike or sanction job actions during the term of the contract. In return, the employer may promise not to lock out employees. The date the agreement terminates gives the parties the right to strike or lock out and, in so doing, utilize bargaining power (discussed in the next chapter). Most agreements contain a "zipper clause," noting that each side had a full and unlimited opportunity to engage in negotiation, that the agreement reached is final and binding, and that each side surrenders its right to bargain collectively for the term of the contract. Just as a zipper closes a garment, so a "zipper clause" closes the agreement, stating that there are no other agreements or understandings except those contained in the contract.

As stated in the beginning of this section, each agreement is unique because of its legal background and the nature of the enterprise. Nonetheless, most contracts cover similar items and address similar problems. Certainly, mention must be made of the federal sector, in which employees and managers are not permitted to bargain over wages and are otherwise restricted in subjects of negotiation. Even in this sector, however, many of the other issues, such as aspects of union representation and employee discipline, are bargained over.

Points to Ponder

It should be noted that it may be a lengthy and tortuous process that occurs in each sector to determine which subject falls into each of the three categories described previously.

For example, the status of many items under the 1978 Civil Service Reform Act is a matter constantly filling the dockets of the Federal Labor Relations Authority as both labor and management seek to explore the limits of the law.

But this is a never-ending process, as those familiar with the evolving nature of the Wagner (1935) and Taft–Hartley (1947) Acts and the decisions of the National Labor Relations Board would most certainly agree. This process of testing the limits of the law is not removed from partisan politics, with NLRB decisions often bearing the mark of the majority political party.

Thus, we see a complex interplay between politics, administrative agencies, judicial determinations, and legislative actions—all of which shape the subjects and scope of bargaining in each sector.

The Battle

"If you're too delicate to exert the necessary pressures on the power structure, then you might as well get out of the ballpark."

—SAUL ALINSKY
Playboy, March 1972

" 'Yes, that's sad,' sighed Vlassitch. 'We foresaw that, Petrushka, but what could we have done? Because one's actions hurt other people, it doesn't prove that they are wrong. What's to be done! Every important step one takes is bound to distress somebody. . . . What's to be done!' "

—ANTON CHEKHOV
Neighbors

IN THIS SECTION we discuss the weapons of conflict in industrial relations and their uses and abuses.

Weapons of Conflict

When most people consider the topic of weapons of conflict in industrial relations, they think first of the strike. To be sure, the strike (and the threat of a strike) is very powerful, but the union has two other principal weapons: the boycott and the picket line. After a discussion of these, we will consider the weapons an employer has at its disposal.

The Union's Weapons

A strike may be defined as an organized withdrawal of employee services. Union leaders have traditionally contended that the right to withhold one's labor is the basic, fundamental and inalienable right of every working person; employers have not been in agreement, arguing that this right, if it is indeed a "right," is far from absolute and must be subject to restraints.

In the pre-Wagner Act (1935) days, unions faced almost insurmountable legal obstacles to organizing and conducting successful strikes. Since the advent of the Wagner Act, the National Labor Relations Board and the federal courts have generally upheld the right of private sector employees to strike upon expiration of a collective bargaining contract and have enjoined or penalized any accompanying violence.

In the public sector, the legality of the strike weapon has not yet been established, and, indeed, most strikes by government employees are illegal and, as such, subject to injunction and other penalties. While many public sector labor leaders argue forcefully for the right to strike, they often emphasize that their members would not abuse that right and harm the public interest. Rather, they wish to have a right everyone else enjoys because having it would greatly enhance their bargaining power.

Others argue that public service is unique, and that employees, by accepting a public employment position, surrender their right to strike. Certainly, they argue, police, firefighters and sanitation, health care and public transportation workers are simply too critical to society to be allowed to withhold their services. Some would no doubt broaden this list to include everyone in education and all other branches of government.

In any event, many legislators appear unwilling to enact public sector collective bargaining laws for fear that these laws will encourage strikes. Supporters of this legislation argue that having these laws in place will serve to provide for the orderly resolution of disputes and thus make strikes less likely. This argument continues to rage whenever public sector collective bargaining laws are being considered. It demonstrates graphically the enormous concern employers and employees share on this issue.

Indeed, it is the fear of strikes that gives the weapon such potent force. As any statistical analysis will quickly demonstrate to even the most casual observer, the vast majority of contracts are reached without a strike. Nonetheless, the possibility of a strike weighs heavily on both sides of the table. To the manager, there can be no frustration greater than having the enterprise brought to a halt by a labor dispute. Everything is in working order, but no workers are at their jobs. Similarly, the employee is earning no income, with no certainty as to when he or she will work again. As for the union, it is faced with an immediate loss of dues-income because striking workers cannot be expected to pay dues. Further, the union must cope with enormous administrative and logistic costs as well as expending money in the form of strike benefits.

There is a perverse economic paradox at work concerning payment of strike benefits: although the sum each striker receives may be small, especially by today's inflationary standards, the aggregate total of benefits paid per week (plus administrative costs) may be enormous to the union. Consider 1,000 strikers, each receiving $50 per week in strike benefits, and assume the strike lasts six weeks. When administrative costs, publicity expenses and other assistance, such as financial counseling, are added together, the total cost to the union could be in excess of $400,000—a sum that might bankrupt the local union's coffers and burden the entire union's treasury. However—and this must be emphasized—no union worth its salt will back off from a strike simply because of the costs involved. To do so would undermine the purpose of the union, which is the effective and vigorous representation of its members.

Mention must be made of various refinements of the strike weapon. In the late 1930s, CIO unions, such as the Auto Workers, used the sit-down strike, wherein employees sat down at their workplaces, refusing to work or leave the premises until progress was made in meeting their demands.

In certain public and private sector jobs, extremely detailed operational rules and procedures exist but typically are circumvented for greater efficiency and higher productivity. Sometimes, employees will strictly adhere to rules and procedures as a costly protest gesture to demonstrate their discontent to management. The cost, however, is not borne only by those employees who withhold their services and thus do not receive regular pay. The cost is also borne by the employer, customers and even the public.

For example, employees of Gotham Mass Transit are public employees not legally allowed to strike. Dissatisfied by the tenor and pace of negotiations, they begin a "work-to-rule" slowdown by following all safety rules to the letter—rules that are customarily not followed during rush-hour traffic. Bus drivers refuse to drive their buses if they are too crowded, which, of course, they always are at peak time. The problem with this technique is that the employer may quickly suspend operational rules and then discipline any bus driver who does not conform with the new procedures. Additionally—and importantly—such a "work-to-rule" slowdown greatly inconveniences the public in a situation in which public support is very critical.

A wildcat strike is a work stoppage unauthorized by the union leadership. If it occurs during the term of a contract, it may well be a violation of the contract. Most contracts contain no-strike clauses wherein the union agrees not to strike during the term of the agreement. Often the language expressly states that, should any work stoppage occur, the union will not only formally disavow the action, but union leaders will take immediate steps to stop the strike.

In the public sector, employees not permitted to strike legally have sometimes utilized the device of a great number of employees calling in and reporting illness. Police call this device "blue flu," while school teachers call it a "sickout." Whatever it is called, administrative and judicial interpretations have generally held such concerted actions to be a *de facto* work stoppage and upheld penalties assessed against individuals and unions.

Other public employees, such as nurses, who have an organizational as well as a personal conviction against use of the strike weapon, have on occasion utilized the device of mass resignation; they all submit a letter of resignation, signed and dated a month ahead. If no significant progress is made toward improving conditions, the resignations will ensue. If satisfactory progress is made, the resignations will be withdrawn. This can be a very effective device, but, as will be noted in the next section, when dealing with bargaining power, the resignations must be seriously intended to be a truly powerful weapon. Only if the nurses are *actually* ready to surrender their jobs will this get results. Obviously, to be an effective weapon, costs must be borne and imposed on the other side. In certain situations, employees will not use the strike in any of its permutations; they may choose instead to use the picket weapon.

Many people equate a picket line with a strike, and, although most strikers do maintain a picket line, it is possible to have a strike with no picket line, and, conversely, to have a picket line with no strike. A picket line is a group of employees who station themselves outside the employer's premises and carry signs to demonstrate dissatisfaction. They may chant, hand out leaflets, harangue passersby, repel replacement workers (called scabs) or urge potential patrons or other employees not to cross the picket line and enter the employer's establishment.

The dilemma society faces in regulating picketing comes from the dual nature of the activity. As a communication device, it is protected as free speech, a constitutional right; but as a form of economic behavior, it is subject to regulation and restriction. Thus, it has become necessary to classify picketing and regulate some types but not others. For example, in the private sector, if the union is engaging in picketing aimed at unionizing employees, it is usually conducted by nonemployees. This is seen as *purposeful economic activity* and thus is often regulated. If, however, the picketing is conducted by employees and is orderly and nonviolent, with the aim of conveying the information that the employer does not pay wages meeting union standards, this is seen as *communication* and generally not subject to regulation—it is deemed free speech.

Nowhere is this dichotomy between striking and picketing, between purposeful economic activity and communication, more clear than in the public sector, where strikes are generally unlawful. Many public sector unions have sought to utilize the picket line to influence public opinion, especially concerning political figures. Thus, before or after the school day, public school teachers will, for example, picket the school superintendent's office or the men's haberdashery store owned by the chairman of the school board. Such picketing is usually upheld as an exercise of free speech and is legal unless it runs afoul of laws governing boycotts.

A boycott is an organized refusal to deal with—and in so doing punish or coerce—an enterprise or its owners. Unions have often been found to have conducted an illegal secondary boycott, which means refusing to deal with Company A, with which there is no dispute, in order to bring pressure to bear on Company B, with which there is a dispute.

Consumer boycotts, such as the successful ones held by the United Farm Workers over lettuce and grapes, have generally been allowed because they did not ask retail patrons to refrain from patronizing the store, against which there was no labor dispute; they asked only that shoppers not purchase a particular item. Store employees were not asked to stop selling or handling any product. As in other areas of labor law, boycotts have seen legislative and judicial interpretations that are not always clear or consistent.

The lengthy and highly contentious battle between J.P. Stevens, the large fabric manufacturer, and the Textile Workers (which later merged into the Amalgamated Clothing and Textile Workers Union) saw the development of a new and controversial weapon—the union's "corporate campaign." This weapon successfully sought to penalize the company, which the union asserted had repeatedly refused to recognize and negotiate with it by isolating it in the financial community. Other large companies were urged to sever connections with J. P. Stevens in the area of appointments to the board of directors. Thus, officers of other corporations were urged to leave Stevens' board, and the chairman of Stevens was pressured not to serve on other companies' boards. This pressure took numerous forms, such as shareholder letters and campaigns as well as threatened consumer boycotts of noncooperating companies such as Avon, the cosmetics firm that sells much of its product door to door in neighborhoods with many union supporters.

Many in the corporate financial community vehemently opposed the union's "corporate campaign" because they believed it was an improper intrusion into the operations of companies and fell well outside the pale of employee relations. The union and its supporters argued that normal weapons, such as strikes and picketing, were not successful because of the company's size and dispersed location. Further, administrative and judicial relief had not proved satisfactory. In any event, the "corporate campaign" was successful in that it propelled the settlement of a dispute that had dragged on for well over 17 years and had cost both sides a great deal, perhaps the least of which were the enormous sums of money expended by both parties.

Certainly a comprehensive discussion of the weapons of conflict must in the very least make reference to administrative and judicial approaches. Administrative tribunals such as the National Labor Relations Board (NLRB), or a public sector employee relations board, provide mechanisms for relief from unfair labor practices committed by either side. Unfortunately, due to often enormous case backlogs, as well as numerous appellate procedures, a complaint, such as a union's claim that the employer failed to bargain in good faith, may take a number of years to be resolved administratively. Then, judicial appeals are possible through various levels of courts, which in turn can add even more years to the final resolution of the complaint.

In the meantime, the dispute is unresolved and the parties have uncertainty added to their already conflict-filled relationship. Many union supporters argue that these great delays are, in effect, a management weapon against unionization and the exercise of statutory rights. Although the union does not have to pay legal costs (the NLRB or other agency bears the cost), the time delay and uncertainty are said to undermine union support and strength, the result being that even if the union's position is ultimately upheld, the victory is hollow because the employees, having seen no final positive results for so long, are no longer behind the union.

Employers argue in turn that they are only exercising *their* statutory rights. To do so may often involve extremely expensive legal assistance. If they are willing and able to fight for their rights, such actions should not be condemned but praised, and, if their challenge is successful, it only proves the correctness of their position. Finally, employers contend that, if during the exercise of their statutory rights union support erodes, that is a natural consequence of the shallowness of support for the union, not because of any antiunion behavior on their part.

Be that as it may, administrative and judicial procedures meet the test of a weapon of conflict, to wit, imposing a cost, financial or otherwise, on the other side in an attempt to effectuate a change of position. One expects, of course, that the cost one imposes on the other side is higher than the cost being borne, but this is not always easy to calculate.

For example, if the Marks Plastics Company takes a hard position in bargaining with its unionized workers, who are represented by a plastics workers union, the union may file charges with the NLRB alleging that the company is not bargaining in good faith, as statute demands. There may be a strike, picketing, a lockout, replacement workers hired or even a consumer boycott launched, but the administrative processes may continue to move forward. Long after the immediate dispute is resolved and a contract reached, the NLRB may find the union was correct and the company guilty of not negotiating in good faith. If the company appeals to a federal court, it may cost the employer much money and cost the union great uncertainty and instability. These are real costs to each side, but the employer may conclude that to continue the union's uncertainty may be worth the legal costs because the union is paralyzed, members are no longer paying dues, and it is possible the union may lose much support. The union may no longer be a viable entity and may risk decertification, and so regain for the employer unilateral decision-making.

Certainly in the example above the employer must bear some uncertainty and instability in the workforce that could, in turn, lead to morale and turnover problems as well as lower productivity. The union may also have to bear financial burdens from declining dues income as well as higher administrative and unit support costs during this period. These combined pressures on each side could lead to a joint settlement that includes withdrawing of the unfair practice charge, a not uncommon phenomenon. (The effect of the use of all weapons described in this section will be more thoroughly discussed in the material that follows on the subject of bargaining power.)

The Employer's Weapons

Management's weapons have typically been defensive fighting the strike, picket line or boycott—but there is certainly more the employer can do. Under certain circumstances, a private sector employer may lawfully lock out the unionized workforce, especially during a dispute in which economics is the sole issue. A lockout occurs when the employer unilaterally ceases operations to put economic pressure on its employees through the withdrawal of employment and compensation. Some employers counter a strike by seeking to hire replacement workers. Many times, this can lead to hostile and potentially explosive confrontations with strikers, who see their jobs being taken by "scabs." Also, there is usually some efficiency lost in seeking to introduce a new or largely new workforce, and then there is the question of the status of the old and new workers when an agreement is finally reached.

Other employers openly encourage employees to cross the picket line and return to work. While each of these approaches may be at times successful, they raise the level of hostility; often the striking employees retaliate by acts of vandalism, sabotage or violence against those working employees or managers.

In anticipation of a strike, where possible, some employers build inventory and then lock out employees when the contract expires, but before employees can strike. Depending upon all relevant facts, such preemptive action may be a legal action, or an illegal, unfair refusal to bargain in good faith.

Some union leaders have raised the issue of the employer in effect locking out employees by contracting out work previously done by members of the bargaining unit. Such work-task areas as plant and facility maintenance and custodial, janitorial, security and transportation services have been contracted out in order to save money and reduce the size and bargaining clout of the workforce.

Many employers argue that, if the work can be done satisfactorily and in a more cost-effective manner, it should be contracted out. If no contractual provision is violated, employers argue that the union has no ground for complaint, and, further, that all employees have a meaningful interest in the continued success and viability of the enterprise.

The public sector has not been immune from these issues. Some agency heads argue that, if money can be saved by contracting out certain services, taxpayers are better served. Public sector union leaders contend that, not only is no money saved by contracting out services, but the work is of inferior quality, and good, long-service employees are needlessly cast aside.

Lately, a new wrinkle has emerged in the public sector, called a "fund-out" by irate union officials. In this maneuver, it is alleged that the legislature is encouraged to reduce or withdraw funding from an agency or bureau as punishment for either the militancy of union members or the incompetence of the employees, or both. When the funds are reduced or removed entirely, operation and employment are obviously directly affected dramatically. On the other side, it is argued that government must be flexible in meeting the will of the electorate and the total budget taxpayers can support. If an agency no longer has a viable mission, it should not be maintained.

Privitization

Many free-market advocates urge privitization of a number of governmental services and this will likely be an increasingly contentious issue in the next decade. For example, it is argued that jails could be run on a more cost-effective basis if for-profit, private entrepreneurs ran them; the same argument has been raised concerning delivery of first-class mail. Union supporters counter that to privitize governmental service would be irresponsible in that the profit motive may lead to cost-cutting steps that could mean prison inmates would not be appropriately cared for and that those who live in remote areas would have to pay higher postage rates for reduced services. It is also assumed that entrepreneurs would preferably wish to operate with non-union employees or, at the least, pay lower wages and benefits than unionized workers receive.

Finally, these opponents of privitization argue that inherent in these institutions is a public purpose which cannot and should not be met by privately owned businesses. For example, the U.S. Postal Service monitors the mail for consumer fraud and pornographic materials; correction officers have law-enforcement powers which should not be given to private individuals. Given the diminishment of public resources amidst escalating and conflicting demands, conflict over this issue will only be exacerbated in the future.

Undoubtedly, future years will see the development of newer weapons of conflict and responses to them; nonetheless, this section has sought to provide a basic understanding of each side's weapons and responses. It should be remembered that every weapon, like a sword, cuts both ways, and there are costs imposed not only on the other side but on the side wielding the weapon. As discussed in the next section, any dispute presents each side with the actual and perceived *cost of disagreeing* with the other side's position and the actual and perceived *cost of agreeing* with the other side. A party, acting rationally, will generally do that which costs the least. Thus, if a brief union strike will present enormous cost to the employer, but only slight cost to the union and its members, the union has greater bargaining power because the cost of disagreeing with the union is simply too high. Hence, the employer will agree to the union's proposals. Conversely, if the employer, through use of automated equipment and supervisory employees, can withstand a lengthy strike, it will have greater bargaining power and then the union will agree to the employer's proposal. This assumes rationality and clear computation of cost.

It is not uncommon to witness disputes in which both sides are bearing and imposing enormous costs by utilizing many of the weapons discussed earlier, and appearing more concerned with winning a principle than resolving a dispute. These situations do not invalidate this analytical framework—rather they enhance it by demonstrating both the potency of the weapons of conflict as well as the emotional and philosophic character of the disputants and the difficulty of attempting to compute costs solely in monetary terms.

For example, consider a four-month strike at Addison Chemical Corporation's main plant. The chemical workers' union is adamant in its opposition to the company's proposal to make key personnel decisions, such as promotion and layoff, on the basis of the employer's new "skill assessment ratings program." To the union, this proposal represents a system of playing favorites, disregarding length of loyal service, and introducing a large, unknown element of subjectivity as well as uncertainty into an individual's employment status under the guise of a "merit" program. To the company, this proposal represents a meaningful attempt to improve productivity and job performance while affording it the flexibility necessary to meet competitive pressures.

To the union and its members, the cost of the strike, picketing and organizing a consumer boycott of Addison products is enormous for the strikers and their families in terms of lost wages, financial insecurity, unpredictable future, bitterness and animosity among striking employees and supervisors who are now performing the employees' tasks. For the union, there are lost dues, enormous administrative and logistical expenses and skepticism about the union leadership's ability.

To the company, the cost of the dispute is staggering. There is interrupted production, overtime premiums for working supervisors, potential recruitment and training of virtually an entirely new workforce, bad will in the community, the antagonism of striking employees, the problem of dealing with striker replacement workers after a settlement is reached, lost sales and revenue and a blunting of new market growth.

Thus, each side is wielding its weapons and engaging in publicity and propaganda while bearing and imposing great costs. An outsider may justifiably ask, "Why not settle and end all this loss?" But each side may argue that its cost of agreeing with the other side's position is simply too high, and it is less costly, especially in the long run, to make a stand "here and now" on very critical issues.

Union leadership might argue that to concede now to the company would substantially call into question its judgment in initiating and conducting the strike in the first place. Already having borne great costs by wielding their weapons, to stop now with no gain would make it all in vain. To accept the employer's position would undermine the union as a viable entity representing and advancing employees' interests. At stake, they conclude, is the very existence of the union.

To the company, concession to the union now would be an enormous error. Having borne great costs by exercising their own weapons while operating under the barrage of the union's weapons, much has been invested in the dispute. If they were going to let the union force them to maintain such an inefficient personnel system, why not have conceded four long months ago? If the union wins, the company will never be able to operate as efficiently as it must, and so will sooner or later go out of business. At stake, they conclude, is the very existence of the company.

On this rather unsettling note, then, it is appropriate to conclude this section on the weapons of conflict. As the following sections detail, the use, abuse and nonuse of one's bargaining power, as well as the use of another's bargaining power, are methods to effectively manipulate the weapons of conflict.

Bargaining Power

Bargaining power is a term many people understand instinctively and, therefore, fail to analyze closely. If we examine an extreme situation, the dimensions of bargaining power become clearer. Assume a large fuel oil distributor, Ace Oil Company, has a union contract that expires at midnight, January 15. After this time the drivers are free to strike legally. If the drivers are seeking a nine-percent increase and the company is offering seven percent, we can see that the union has greater bargaining power than the company because it is more likely that the cost of disagreeing is lower to the employees, who can withstand a short strike more easily than the company, situated as it is in a competitive market in a time of high fuel oil demand. Thus, the union is more likely to gain a settlement on its terms than the company. In other words, it is cheaper for the company to come to terms with the union at nine percent than to absorb lost business and customer displeasure by holding out for a two-percent-lower settlement.

The dynamics of the above situation would be radically altered if the agreement's date of expiration were July 15, a time of minimal demand for fuel oil. In this situation, the company would be enjoying greater bargaining power and the union less. Any strike, to be at all successful, would have to be so long that the employees' lost wages would be far greater than the employer's lost revenue. Here, the cost of agreeing with the union is higher than the cost of disagreeing with the union, and in a rational society a party will do that which costs less—in this instance, disagreeing. The company thus will resist settling on the union's terms and hold out until the union accedes to the company's lower offer.

In the dynamics of the collective bargaining process, bargaining power is subject to numerous factors, internal and external, that can alter the balance of power. Internal factors are those such as political and financial pressures, which can be very potent indeed. If the owners of Ace are negotiating to sell their interests to a large national firm, a strike, even in July, could make the proposed sale less attractive to acquiring investors, and, thus, it might be worth it for Ace to settle on the union's terms, even if the threatened strike is not truly a viable possibility. Similarly, if local union elections are February 1, the leadership may be very concerned that no one be on the picket line when it is time to vote. Thus, the union, even with greater bargaining power, may settle on the company's terms.

The dynamics are so fluid that the two illustrations above, with only slightly changed circumstances, could result in vastly different outcomes. In the first example, involving a proposed sale of the company, it is possible that prospective purchasers would find a collective agreement providing for a nine-percent increase so unappealing that they would reduce their price (or not acquire the company). Thus, company owners would especially resist the union's position. In the second example, involving an upcoming union election, if there were employees who claimed union leaders were too easy on the company, the union incumbents might feel pressured to maintain the nine-percent position and call a strike to achieve their goal of reelection to office.

External pressures can also alter the balance of power between the parties. Consider the Belair Hotel, a large convention resort whose employees are represented by a union. The Belair pays the highest wages in the rural area in which it is located, and always has a large file of applicants eager for a job. It would seem the Belair has superior bargaining power because its resources are far greater than those of the employees, who are already the highest paid in the area. However, two days after the current agreement expires, the Belair has scheduled its largest convention, the 3,500 delegates of the Amalgamated Garment Workers Union, whose president, Jacob Schuster, calls Robert Belair, president of the hotel, and informs him that, if there is a strike, his union will have to cancel their reservations and relocate its convention because they cannot cross a picket line. And, Schuster adds, his union must know within 72 hours whether or not they will have to move their convention. An external event has thus transformed the balance of power between the parties and increased the union's bargaining power.

In other situations, the outside pressure can reduce the union's bargaining power. For example, the Maldon Manufacturing Company is a small firm employing 60 workers who produce seatbelts. Over 95 percent of Maldon's sales are to General Motors, which has told Maldon that, if there is any interruption of delivery, General Motors will consider its contract breached and obtain seatbelts elsewhere. The large union representing Maldon's employees knows a strike would put the small company out of business and all its members would lose their jobs. Therefore, while it would appear that the union, with its large resources and membership, would have greater bargaining power, it may not be the case, especially inasmuch as the owner, Jerry Maldon, who is in his 60s, often mentions how much easier his life would be if he just closed up shop and retired to Florida, leaving the employees to fend for themselves in a high-unemployment labor market.

In most situations, bargaining power is approximately equal, and each party will take steps to increase its power at the expense of the other. There should be no mistaking the adversary and emotional aspects of these disputes. The parties are in a crucial struggle, and often the very existence of one side hinges upon the outcome.

Consider a community-college faculty organization that has been unable to achieve a satisfactory agreement through months of fruitless negotiation with the college's board of trustees. John Toole, a teacher of economics, argues at the faculty association meeting that the only way to pressure the board into conceding to their position is by threatening to strike and being willing to strike if their demands are not met. Stephen O'Brien, who teaches philosophy, answers that, as professional educators, it would be morally wrong to interrupt the educational process simply to advance the teachers' demands, which, while certainly justified, are intended only to promote the financial security of the teachers. "And what's wrong with that?" counters Toole. "Don't we all have families and financial responsibilities to look after?"

Marlene Nichols, a foreign language teacher, asks if the strike is illegal, and Barbara Gill, a law teacher, says yes, a strike might be illegal in this particular jurisdiction if held during school time, but not otherwise. Mike Hoffman, a physical education teacher, comments that it would be a waste of time if they struck when school was not in session. He asks, "If we struck over a vacation, who'd even miss us?"

Renee Francis, a psychology teacher, suggests that they strike at the most critical time—when grades are due at the end of the semester. "That way," she says, "we'll have met our classes and marked our final exams, but we won't submit the grades until the board agrees to seriously negotiate with us. How does that sound?"

O'Brien leaps up and says that if they don't submit grades, the students won't be able to graduate, and he cannot do that to his students. "But that's just the point," argues Toole. "To enjoy any real bargaining power, we must force the board to make hard decisions and face enormous pressure from students, employers and parents."

Analyzing this situation, many points are apparent. First, each participant has his or her own set of perceptions and makes judgments and decisions based on all sorts of factors, some factually based and some based upon underlying personal assumptions. The opinion of the law teacher is accepted, although many would argue that withholding grades by a teacher is indeed a form of work stoppage and as such illegal.

Second, whatever is decided by the group will not be a decision agreed upon by all. If the will of the majority is a strike or job action, perhaps many will choose not to participate, thereby seriously weakening the bargaining power of the majority, and thus shaking the resolve of those who are uncertain about their commitment to the job action or strike.

Third, to be effective, the threat of a job action must have the potential to do serious harm to the employer, yet many employees are not willing to make that choice. Be it concern about professionalism, their commitment to students, loyalty to the employer, concerns about personal economic security or a combination of these factors, there is often a reluctance to engage in confrontation and participate in inflicting harm by a withdrawal of their services, the very heart of bargaining power.

Similarly, many employers are unwilling to lock out their employees to gain bargaining power because of their concern for the welfare of the employees and their families, as well as a concern about customer loyalty should their product or service be unavailable. Certainly, a lockout runs the risk of creating enormous ill will among all employees, but especially among those not in the bargaining unit. While they do not participate in collective bargaining, they will be laid off because of the dispute. This group could often include clerical, secretarial and lower-level managerial employees, who may face severe financial hardships. Customers, be they commercial or retail, are often caught unprepared for the interruption caused by a lockout, and their response is generally negative.

If the owners of Friendly Brewing Company lock out their employees, other breweries will usually seek to obtain Friendly's share of the market, and retail outlets will fill their shelf space with competing beers. After the dispute is over, even if Friendly obtains the terms of the agreement it sought, it may have permanently lost some beer customers, and not all of its former shelf space may be restored. Customers tend to be creatures of habit. Once they get out of the habit of consuming a certain product, if only for a brief period, some will acquire new habits and ignore a product when it is once again available.

Special attention must be directed toward the unique dynamics in the public sector. As noted in the community college example, a strike is usually illegal and the employer, such as a police or fire department, cannot lock out employees because of the enormous potential for public harm. There are no competing firms that can fill the gap.

Although strikes by government employees are generally unlawful, they occur with some regularity, as is well known. The union calling the unlawful strike can expect decertification, loss of dues check-off, and possibly a stiff fine unless amnesty can be negotiated with the employer as part of the settlement, as it often, but not always, is. Unions having the bargaining power to shut down an essential public service often have the clout to demand and get amnesty for their unlawful strikes. Conversely, the union that launches an unlawful and unsuccessful strike will not only be unable to achieve a desired settlement but will be unable to command amnesty for its members and itself. Indeed, it sometimes appears that blues singer Ray Charles made a sage observation when he sang, "Them that got is them that gets."

Nonuse of Bargaining Power

In the discussions of interest arbitration, it will be noted that, in replacing the right to strike or lock out with a final and binding quasi-judicial process, society is telling both parties that bargaining power will be factored out of the settlement equation in the public interest to avoid any inconveniences or harm to the public. Conversely, in fact-finding, while the parties may not legally utilize self-help techniques of bargaining power, they *are* permitted to seek public support through persuasion. This is an opportunity some groups, such as teachers, nurses and firefighters, often use to great advantage, engaging many of their sometimes formidable resources to win over the public. Informational picketing, leafletting, ads in various media and political lobbying are used to gain union objectives while, on the other side, the public employer and political leaders court taxpayer backing for their position.

And, finally, some groups of employees seek to gain public support by surrendering, as a matter of organizational policy and philosophy, the use of the strike, even when not unlawful. Many state nurses' associations, constituents of the American Nurses' Association, are on record as declaring their absolute opposition to the use of the strike weapon. This declaration is based upon a concept of nursing as a vital service, the withdrawal of which is so dangerous and unprofessional that it cannot even be seriously contemplated, much less attempted. Some argue that this prior surrender of the strike weapon, which would appear to diminish bargaining power, actually increases it by assuring public support and placing a moral burden upon the employer to deal fairly with the nurses, who have voluntarily disarmed themselves before entering combat. Others argue that this is too idealistic an approach to the harsh realities of the negotiation process. This is probably a subject area in which hard-and-fast pronouncements are difficult, if not impossible.

Gerald Nierenberg, a lawyer who has written and lectured extensively on the subject of negotiation, was quoted as offering the following approach to the settlement of the strike by the National Football League players: have the games played as scheduled but with neither side taking any salary (players) or profits (owners), only expenses. The money would be placed in escrow and then, when the first party capitulated, there would be a payout from escrow proceeds. If this approach had been followed, Nierenberg noted that fans would not have been deprived and the football season would not have been disrupted.

Assuming Nierenberg's approach would have resulted in no disruption of scheduled games, why didn't the parties choose to do this? Is it possible that both sides saw some strategic benefit to be derived from the pressure of angry fans, television and advertising executives local officials and media commentators once no games were played?

What would the players' and owners' bargaining power have been had the strike not actually occurred? If there were no public inconvenience due to the strike, would there have been any external pressure to settle what may have otherwise been perceived as purely an ideologically abstract dispute?

Abuses of Bargaining Power

Some observers of labor–management relations note that, in certain instances, one group with vastly superior bargaining power has been able to achieve contract concessions, which, in their long-term operation, serve to diminish or even destroy the other party. For example, certain construction unions representing employees with skills not easily found are said to have achieved contracts so generous in wages and benefits, and with work rules so restrictive, that they have destroyed smaller construction companies because they cannot afford to operate profitably. Similarly, it is alleged that certain large industrial corporations dealing with small independent unions are able to achieve such favorable agreements that the union is simply not a substantial factor in operational decisions, and employees enjoy very few contractual benefits and protections.

Others argue that, while the above situations may well occur, they are all part of the process of free collective bargaining. While it is true that most parties are equally matched in terms of bargaining power, there will inevitably be instances in which one side enjoys a clearly superior position. It is argued that, if superior bargaining power is to mean anything, it must be utilized or else it is of only academic interest.

An opposing school of thought argues that the party enjoying this superior bargaining power has an obligation not to abuse it because it could irrevocably alter the balance of power between the parties. This might therefore lead to some governmental interference to redress the imbalance of power, and such interference would be in no party's best interests.

Those opposing this idea claim that the dynamics of bargaining are such that the balance of power usually does not stay grossly out of equilibrium for too long. If a union is too aggressive, and some employers cannot afford the contract, then, to save members' jobs, concessions will necessarily occur, or nonunion employers will spring up and prosper. Similarly, if a powerful employer abuses the weaker, smaller union too much, employees will select a larger, more powerful union to advance their interests. All of which means, it is argued, that no government intervention is necessary to restore the balance of bargaining power.

What is especially interesting about this debate is that both sides seem to agree only on the undesirability of government intervention in collective bargaining, and seek ways of avoiding it. Both sides appear to agree that government intervention leads to greater problems, and solves, in the long run, very little.

Whipsaws and Parities

A whipsaw is a maneuver in which a party is bested both ways, or pushed to the left and pulled to the right simultaneously. In collective bargaining, the phrase provides numerous examples. In the early days of craft unions, a local union committee would approach Company A with its list of demands and tell a reluctant employer that its main competitor, Company B, had agreed to those terms. The trusting folks at Company A would therefore agree to the terms, believing, falsely as it later turned out, that Company B had agreed. The union committee could now approach Company B and gain their agreement because Company A, having agreed, would pose no competitive disadvantage to Company B in agreeing to the terms.

In the early days of public employee collective bargaining, a variant of the whipsaw was developed by certain unions that negotiated with a large city, county or state. Union A would negotiate first and reach an agreement, which provided for a six-percent wage increase and one additional personal day. Union B would then agree to a seven-percent wage increase and no personal day. Then Union C would hold out for a seven-percent wage increase *and* one additional personal day, the best of both agreements.

If the employer granted both demands to Union C, then in the next round of negotiations Unions A and B would demand and argue that they also deserved the one-percent extra pay increase and the additional personal day in order to catch up with Union C and then add additional demands to make certain it would not be surpassed again by Union C. And Union C, in turn, would demand it deserved the best of the contracts that Unions A and B reached because a precedent had been established; their members expected the same or better contract.

Many large public employers became concerned that not only were they being whipsawed, but the various unions were unhappy with whatever settlement was achieved, no matter how generous, regardless or because of what another union signed for. To compound this problem, fact-finders and interest arbitrators, in their awards, were accepting the unions' arguments, resulting in institutionalization of relationships originally founded in a haphazard, casual manner in the heat of negotiation.

To rationalize these relationships, and to minimize the bad feelings and escalating price to the employer of increasingly costly settlements, systematic studies of jobs and compensation were undertaken. The results were the establishment of formalized, fact-based wage relationships, or, as they came to be known, parities.

For example, the Gotham Police Union may have its contract as the standard, or 100 percent. Firefighters would be at 90 percent, meaning they would receive 90 percent of whatever the police negotiated. If the firefighters settled first, the police would get 10 percent more. Other relationships were established with sanitation and public transit employees, teachers, noncertified school personnel, and so on. Often there would be refinements; police sergeants would get seven percent more than police officers, and police lieutenants five percent more than sergeants, etc.

This parity system, by no means perfect, has been helpful in many public sector relationships and has removed much of the fear of an early settlement by one group. In the following section, we turn to an examination of how smaller and less powerful parties are able to utilize the superior bargaining power of larger and more powerful groups.

Uses of Another Party's Bargaining Power

What does a small union do when it represents 225 employees, and all other employees, more than 20,000, are represented by a larger union?

What does a small employer do when a large employer, dealing with the same union, secures significant contract concessions?

The answers are varied, but certain discernible patterns have emerged in practice. As noted earlier, most unions seek uniformity and oppose any significant differences in wages or benefits because they can cause internal dissension. In the first example, the small union seeks parity or equality in wages and benefits with the contract secured by the larger union. It may do this by building into its agreement a protective clause commonly called a "me too" clause. This clause stipulates that the smaller union will receive the same or similar benefits and wages secured by the larger union. Thus, the smaller union can settle early with the employer and not fear that its settlement will be too low compared with what the larger union settles for.

Similarly, the small employer may secure a clause in its agreement with the large union stating that whatever concessions are given to some other employer will be given to them as well. This clause is called a "most favored nation" clause, a term derived from international trade and tariff negotiations providing that one country's import duties on certain items will be applied to all importing nations, and the duty charged will be the least any other country pays.

In both of these illustrations, what is occurring is the constructive use by one party of the greater bargaining power of another party on the same side, a not uncommon phenomenon. One might ask why the stronger adversary, the large employer in the first example, or the large union in the second, would consent to such a provision. A number of valid answers are possible and only a few can be described.

First, the stronger adversary may well believe that the agreement negotiated with a large union or company will not be too generous, or the concessions given by the large entity will be either nonexistent or insignificant, and so there is little risk in such an agreement. Another reason for such an agreement might be the stronger adversary's thinking that it should treat the weaker party equitably because not to do so would be an abuse of superior bargaining power. Third, there may be a tradition of equitable treatment in the industry, and it may be well accepted by all parties, big or small. And, fourth, as previously discussed, a parity relationship may have been established.

Costs of Agreeing and Disagreeing

It should be clear by now that each side can manipulate the costs of agreeing and disagreeing. In the simplest illustration, if the union drops its proposal for any wage increase and agrees to the company proposal for a wage freeze, the union is not likely to bear any costs of agreeing—or is it? While there may not be a strike or any union weapons exercised, the acceptance of a modest wage offer may undermine support for the union, causing many members to become disenchanted with the union. All this could lead to membership decline, apathy or even decertification.

Similarly, when the employer agrees to a generous union wage proposal, there will be no costs of disagreeing, such as a strike or interruption of production. However, an excessive wage settlement could lead to noncompetitive product pricing and a loss of market, progressively less production, and, ultimately, cessation of the enterprise, a rather high cost of agreeing indeed.

The key is to make the cost of agreeing lower and, therefore, more attractive to the other side than is the cost of disagreeing—but not too much lower and more attractive than necessary. The trick, of course, is the last phrase—what is that *necessary* margin? If your side's position is too appealing to the other side, this may mean your own interests are being jeopardized. If your side's position is not sufficiently low and appealing, then the cost of disagreeing is lower to the other side, and conflict will continue.

If the employer's offer is deemed too low, the union will likely decide the cost of disagreeing, high as it might be, is still lower than the cost of accepting an insufficient offer. If the union's offer is too high, the employer will decide that it is less costly to continue disagreeing than to agree to accept an expensive offer.

To return to the example given earlier concerning the Addison Chemical Corporation and its union, the four-month strike has engendered great costs on both sides. Each party must find some way of reducing the cost of agreeing so that it is lower than the cost of disagreeing—yet at the same time not reduce the cost so drastically that its previous position is undermined and appears abandoned. It thus falls to the mediator, Geoff Gastworth, who has no power to compel agreement, to come up with a compromise proposal acceptable to both sides. He considers the costs of disagreeing borne by each side and attempts to reduce the areas of disagreement. The union as an institution is in desperate financial and organizational peril; its members have been out of work for four difficult months and are seeing their jobs performed by supervisors and an increasingly larger cadre of newly hired replacement workers. The mediator is certain the union wants a settlement, but it must be a compromise that does not look like a total defeat for the union and its leadership.

The company is also in a difficult financial position. Production is down because its new workforce is not yet as efficient as the regular workforce, and the supervisors who have been doing production work for four months are exhausted physically and complaining of disruption of their personal lives. Much ill will has been observed in the community, and many personal friendships (and families as well) have been subjected to great stress due to the continued strike. There have been six acts of vandalism, the most serious of which resulted in costly damage to the warehouse and loading dock. And the International Union is launching a consumer boycott that the company fears may hurt sales of its major household product, a bug spray. Given all the above costs, the mediator is sure that the company wants a settlement, but it must be a compromise that does not look like a total defeat for the company and its leadership.

The mediator meets with each side privately and determines the most serious costs to each side. To the union, at this point, the greatest cost is the continuation of the strike; a settlement and a signed contract would reduce that cost. To the striking employees, returning to work is the highest priority; the replacement workers represent a barrier to achieving that goal.

To the company, disruption of production represents the greatest cost; resumption of orderly and efficient production by settlement of the strike would reduce that cost.

The mediator suggests that the parties end their dispute by jointly agreeing to the following proposal, which would reduce drastically the inventory of loss on each side: the strike and boycott are to be terminated effective 7:00 A.M. and all strikers are to be returned to their previous jobs; all newly hired replacement workers are to be put on layoff, with preferential hiring status given them when employment expands. Concerning the controversial issue of seniority/skill assessment ratings, the issue is to be handled in the following manner: for the term of the two-year contract, each employee will be given an individual rating on a 100-point scale, with length of company service credited as 85 percent of the rating. The company's skills assessment is to carry a maximum of 15 percent of the rating; each employee's score will be controlling in making personnel decisions.

The compromise not only ends the strike but gives each side something to show for its loss. The company has established the principle that each employee shall be rated individually, and that seniority is not the sole variable in making personnel decisions. The union has established seniority as the controlling variable in making personnel decisions, retaining the right to grieve any rating or personnel decision believed unfair.

As so often happens in labor–management disputes, the final resolution does not satisfy either party completely. Rather, each side has achieved a settlement with which it can live for the duration of the contract. Neither side reaches its optimum or maximum goals. Instead, to adapt Professor Herbert Simon's phrase, each side "satisfices," that is, comes to terms with the other side at some compromise position in order to end the costly strike. This settlement is reached at the point at which the cost of agreeing is lower than the continued cost of disagreeing.

Points to Ponder

Regarding the above example, consider the following point: why, if the parties were ultimately to reach a compromise settlement as they did, could they not have resolved the dispute without such a long and costly strike, with such heavy losses to both sides?

On the other hand, perhaps one might contend that the parties had to take the dispute as far as they could because the stakes were so high for everyone. Perhaps it was only the four-month strike, with its high costs of continued disagreement, that led each side to finally accept the mediator's compromise. Before that point, high as the costs of disagreeing were, they were lower than the costs of agreeing to the other party's proposal.

The Table Process Examined

*"You can't always get
what you want."*

—THE ROLLING STONES

*"At the dark end of the street
is the place we always meet."*

—JAMES CARR
The Dark End of the Street

IN THIS SECTION we examine the interactions across and around the bargaining table.

Three Dimensions to Every Team in Bilateral Negotiations

To the novice, it appears that collective bargaining involves negotiating between two teams—union and management. In fact, however, each team can itself be divided into three components: stabilizers (S), destabilizers (DS) and quasi mediators (QM).

Stabilizers are those team members committed to the table processes and oriented toward reaching agreement, sometimes at any cost. For example, consider Joe Smith, a newly elected member of the school board entering his first collective negotiation with the teachers' association. To him, the worst situation that could occur would be a strike by the teachers. At the bargaining table and in private school board caucus sessions, he may comment on the need for settlement and advocate acceptance of the teachers' association position. He fears the negative effects of a strike on the students, teachers, community and educational mission of the school board.

In the private sector, sales managers are often especially concerned with the ill effects a strike might have on market share or a competitor's position. When in caucus, Violet Green, vice president of marketing, may opine that, if a strike comes, she can foresee lost sales that may never be regained and ill will generated among customers that can never be redressed. For those reasons, she is all for accepting the offer the union made, now, before it is too late.

Destabilizers often lack a commitment to the table processes, may feel more comfortable with self-help techniques, engage in disruptive behavior, and may be unwilling to settle at any price. For example, consider Jim James, a veteran member of a school board that has participated in numerous negotiations with the teachers' association. He believes that teachers make too much money for too little work. He is committed to keeping the school budget where it was last year and avoiding a tax increase. At the bargaining table and in private caucus sessions, he very loudly states his position to all. As far as he is concerned, if teachers do not like what the school board offers, they can work somewhere else. And if the teachers' association calls an illegal work stoppage, he will see to it that the strike leaders are fined and jailed.

In the private sector, company financial analysts are frequently concerned with long-term ill effects of a settlement they feel is too generous. When in caucus, Pearl White, vice president of finance, may aver that, if the company accedes to the unreasonable demands of the union, it will price itself right out of the market; competitors, especially nonunionized and foreign companies, will permanently take away customers. It makes more sense to take a strike now than to agree to such outrageous demands, she says.

Quasi-mediators are usually the team leaders who are charged with the responsibility for the success of the negotiation and who see their role as harmonizing the interests of the stabilizers, who may too readily concede, and the destabilizers, who may adhere to extremely impractical positions. Although clearly an advocate, the quasi-mediator is interested in achieving a settlement that is workable, one that both sides can live with. The quasi-mediator is therefore often the ally of the outside neutral, such as a mediator, sharing with that neutral a deep commitment to the table processes. Not surprisingly, many neutrals with backgrounds as advocates consider their former roles to have been that of quasi-mediators.

The question is sometimes raised as to whether in fact the team leader is usually a quasi-mediator. The answer is yes, and that is based upon both theory and experience. If the team leader is a stabilizer, then that party tends to settle too quickly and easily. This in turn leads to severe consequences. The union leader who is all too eager to settle will be seen by dissidents and discontents as one who "sold out" too fast, as a "patsy" for the employer, and can expect serious opposition in the next union election. Indeed, the negative feeling generated by the insufficient settlement may even lead to a movement to decertify the union and/or a raid by another union that inevitably will promise to "deliver more" for the employees. Union members are constantly engaged in "coercive comparisons," that very human process of comparing one's wages, benefits and working conditions with those of others. Are other locals of the same union getting a better pension plan? Are the wages just won by a nearby local of another union appreciably higher? Do the teachers in the next county receive a larger increase for earning a master's degree?

Similarly, the employer team leader who wants to settle in the worst way usually does. He is not buying peace, as he may believe, but instead only buying more trouble. First, the lavish settlement may well price his or her product or service out of the market, or, at the very least, cause an increase in the cost of doing business or an erosion of profit or surplus, or both. Additionally, other employers will register their objections because their employees in turn will demand what was given to their peers. And, of course, there is the effect of a big union "win" on the climate of day-to-day employee relations. Some union stewards may feel so encouraged by the generous settlement—and some managers so discouraged—that the union may effectively gain control of the workplace, imposing such burdensome work rules and personnel practices that employers are no longer able to effectively manage the enterprise. The ultimate results of this are bankruptcy for the private sector company and taxpayer revolt and withdrawal of funding for the public sector agency.

The results are no more salutary when the team leader is a destabilizer. The union leader who is out to "destroy the filthy capitalist who is exploiting the toiling masses" by striking and taking intransigent positions may succeed all too well, and in the process destroy the jobs of all the members. As noted elsewhere in this manual, American unions have not widely sought the broad-based societal transformation that unions in Europe have, preferring the pragmatic course of dealing within the existing system for tangible material goals for their members.

Employers who seek to annihilate the union their employees have chosen also run great risks. By locking out the union, or seeking by intransigence to bring the union to its knees, the employer may well succeed in that goal only to have created a highly unstable employee relations climate, one full of bitterness and recriminations. It is also undeniably true that hostility on one side only serves to raise the other side's level of hostility, thus creating a vicious cycle of charges and countercharges, action and reaction. The employer who puts the union in a position in which it has nothing to lose may be sadly dismayed by acts of desperation, such as sabotage and rioting; after all, union supporters may argue, we weren't getting anywhere before, so what have we to lose by vandalism?

To sum up, it is in the long-term interests of each side—and ultimately both sides—to have each team led by a quasi-mediator. The experience of most labor relations professionals is that, indeed, most spokespersons and leaders are quasi-mediators.

It should be noted that the roles of S (stabilizers), DS (destabilizers) and QM (quasi-mediators) can and often do change over time during the negotiating process. On certain issues, all three components may be transformed into destabilizers. An example might be the union team's response to a management proposal to have employees contribute to a previously noncontributory health insurance plan. This proposal may strike the union as such a backward, negative move that all negotiating team members may agree that a strike, if necessary to defeat the proposal, would be totally justified.

Similarly, as a result of a lengthy strike that completely closed company operations, management negotiating team members may undergo an alteration of position. Those ardent foes of the proposed agreement (the destabilizers) may, after seven months of a strike, become more settlement oriented, if only out of desperation, and a previously unacceptable position may now be embraced. For example, the company's proposal that employees contribute to their health insurance plan may simply not seem worth seven months of lost production and sales, even to those who proposed it initially. Indeed, after 206 days of a strike, everyone on both sides may well be classified as a stabilizer, in that they wish as rapid a settlement as possible. The price of continued strife is seen as too high, whatever the settlement cost.

Four Bargaining Configurations

1. Horizontal (H) Bargaining

To the novice, there appears to be only one bargaining configuration, that of across-the-table, or *horizontal*, negotiations. It is depicted in Chart 1.

In "horizontal bargaining," negotiations occur across the table and may often be highly structured and formalized. To the untrained eye, it may appear that a great deal of bargaining occurs across the table. This is not necessarily so. In fact, in difficult negotiations, very little actual bargaining occurs in this horizontal configuration. What does occur across the table is by no means unimportant. While often the activity itself is not negotiation, it may set the tone for future negotiation. The activity across the table may include information sharing, posturing, education, oration, yelling, cursing, begging, wheedling, emotional catharsis, threats, crying, etc. Where then does most of the real bargaining occur? It occurs mainly within the bargaining teams themselves, away from the table, in caucus, where the decisions are made about what to promise, when to promise, and who shall promise.

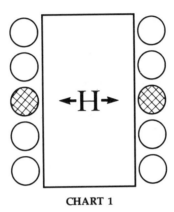

CHART 1

2. Internal (I) Bargaining

Within each team, active negotiations are constantly being conducted. As previously noted, there are three components to each team and they are often very adamant about their respective positions (see Chart 2). In addition, it must again be considered that team members' positions may well vary from issue to issue (Chart 3).

Thus, away from the bargaining table, in caucus, each team must deal with the questions of what movement, if any, to make, how much of a

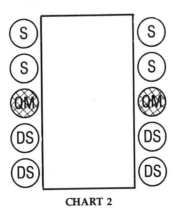

CHART 2

movement, when to make the movement, and how to make it. Predictably, the destabilizers resist movement, the stabilizers encourage movement, and the quasi-mediators facilitate the making of the decision, implement it and seek to keep the team unified.

For example, when the county nurses are in caucus, Judy Brand may argue that the hospital board is not seriously negotiating and does not begin to appreciate the enormous contribution registered nurses make to the delivery of health care. "Only three percent! What a terribly insulting offer!" she exclaims.

Becky Anders, a stabilizer, says, "Yes, Judy, it's a low offer but it's just bargaining. You know, they say three percent but they'll come up. I think we should make a move now to show them we're serious. We never really thought we'd get 12 percent for one year, so why not see how they'll respond to us if we go down to 10 percent, which is still a mighty hefty increase. What do you think, Karen?"

Karen Roberts, the team's spokesperson, is the full-time representative from the state nurses' association and is an experienced negotiator and quasi-mediator. She says, "Yes, Becky, I think it's time we made a move to show the hospital board we want a contract, but I don't think we should drop down to 10 percent without making sure they understand we must get movement in return."

The team then discusses the open items and reassesses its priorities. Once a consensus is reached, Karen Roberts summarizes what the team will do and how it will be done.

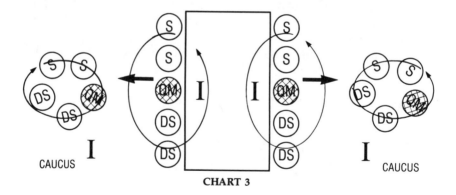

CHART 3

3. Vertical (V) Bargaining

Each team must not only bargain among itself; it must bargain with its own hierarchy, its constituencies and those whose interests they present. This configuration of bargaining is also called "constituencies bargaining'' (see Chart 4). The plural is used intentionally because each party is comprised of numerous subgroups of constituencies with unique interests that must be served. For example, in the 1980s when the United Auto Workers negotiated a new master contract with General Motors, it had to pay attention to the skilled and unskilled workers, males and females, younger and older workers, and Americans and Canadians, to name but a few groups. And surely there were those in multiple constituencies: consider how the interests of a 25-year-old black female unskilled worker at a GM plant in Georgia might differ from the interests of a 55-year-old white male skilled worker at an Ontario, Canada, GM plant. The two employees would have different and yet similar interests. The union negotiating team must consider their interests plus those of so many other members who could be put in numerous categories.

Indeed, the Canadian Auto Workers ultimately felt they needed to disaffiliate from the UAW group in the United States to pursue what they saw as their uniquely Canadian concerns. This only underscores the complexities of dealing with the demands of multiple constituencies, always a highly challenging task for negotiators.

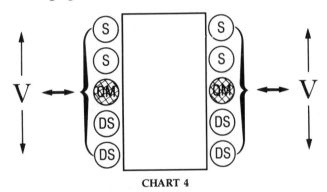

CHART 4

This constituencies, or *vertical*, bargaining can be of enormous importance, especially when the proposed agreement is to be voted upon by the membership. It is not uncommon to find that the proposed agreement reached and recommended by the union negotiating team is voted down by the membership, sometimes overwhelmingly. This negative ratification vote may be caused by a failure of the negotiating team to convey the reality of the bargaining situation to the membership, and most especially to the opinion leaders, such as shop stewards and other union activists, or perhaps because the union negotiating team simply misread its constituencies or overlooked the needs of a key subgroup.

The same sort of danger can also be found on the management side of the table. When Jason Payne, the hospital director of employee relations and chief spokesman, is faced with making a move from the five-percent limit he was previously given to six percent, he cannot simply take a caucus and decide to increase the hospital's offer. He must contact Richard Crane, president of the hospital board and a leading figure in the community, and secure his agreement on the change. President Crane is clearly a member of the hierarchy, and a most powerful one.

After getting a full explanation of the rationale for the increased offer, Crane tells Payne it is all right with him to make the move, but he suggests that Payne should also call Clara Burch, chairperson of the hospital board, to get her agreement. Burch is an active businessperson who has numerous employees, many of them female, and she expresses concern that if Payne grants the largely female nurses group a six-percent wage increase, this will bring pressure from Burch's own employees to achieve a six-percent wage increase also. Payne persuades Burch that the situation of the nurses, who are professional and organized, is far different from Burch's generally unskilled factory employees, who are not represented by a union. At length she acquiesces, but strongly states that under no circumstances is Payne to go over a six-percent wage increase.

While this procedure of calling on key members of the hospital hierarchy may seem time consuming and somewhat cumbersome, it is a very necessary part of Payne's job, for if he were to move to six percent without the authorization of Crane and Burch, he might well find that the hospital board would not approve the negotiated agreement and he would be put in a highly untenable position. He might price his product or service out of the market, or, at the least, cause an increase in the cost of doing business by agreeing to something with no reservations. He then might have to back away from a firm agreement.

This bargaining within the vertical hierarchy can be expressed using this diagram:

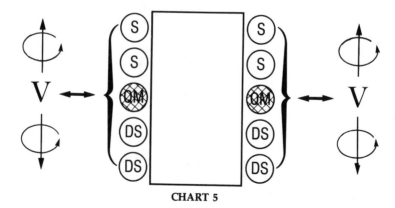

CHART 5

4. Shadow (S) Bargaining

The phrase "shadow bargaining" describes the informal negotiating that occurs away from the bargaining table, formal caucuses or official constituent meetings. The negotiating may not necessarily occur in the "shadows," but it often does. The principals of each side may meet privately to see if a deal can be reached, and frequently they are successful because, with no observers, neither person has to engage in rhetoric or publicly expound on the virtues of his or her side of the table (see Chart 6).

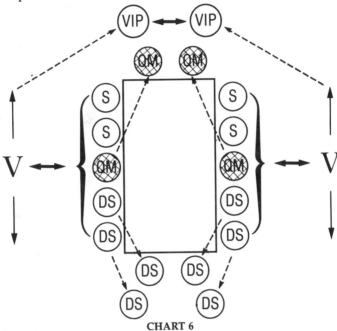

CHART 6

Sometimes the shadow meetings are fully authorized by team members or key hierarchy members, and sometimes not. There are many dangers in unauthorized shadow meetings. Any deal reached may not be embraced by the constituents, who may fear a "sellout" or the like, and then the credibility of the principal is obviously seriously undermined. This in turn may create additional barriers to reaching agreement.

To continue the hospital/nurses case begun previously: when the hospital board's Burch meets Karen Roberts, the nurses' representative, at their common college alumnae function, neither passes up the opportunity to discuss the last remaining unresolved item, the nurses' proposal for tuition reimbursement for college courses. Burch states that she does not understand why the hospital should pay for courses taken that will benefit the nurses. As they sit and chat, Roberts tries another approach. "The courses will benefit the hospital in two ways. First, they will help the nurses give better care, which I know concerns you, and, second, they will make it easier to recruit new nurses, and, Clara, you know how serious a problem that is. And this is something that really doesn't concern the women who work at your factory, does it?" Burch agrees to think it over. A few days later, she calls Payne and tells him that she thinks the nurses should have some program of tuition reimbursement. At the next negotiating session, Roberts and Payne, with the aid of their respective committees, are able to reach a mutually satisfactory agreement on this issue.

Perhaps the most famous incident of shadow bargaining at the VIP level is recounted by Frederick Lewis Allen in his book *Only Yesterday*, in which he discusses John L. Lewis, the legendary leader of the United Mine Workers and the Congress of Industrial Organizations. Myron Taylor was the chairman of the board of United States Steel Corporation, a company that had resisted all efforts to gain recognition by the CIO's Steel Workers Organizing Committee, headed by Lewis' then most trusted lieutenant, Phillip Murray. As Allen recounts, Lewis met secretly with Taylor, one on one, at Taylor's suite in Washington's Mayflower Hotel and at Taylor's house in New York. Ultimately, the two men were able to come to an agreement upon "a formula by which the Steel Corporation would recognize and sign contracts with the Steel Workers Organizing Committee" (page 233). Robert Goldston, in his book *The Great Depression*, notes that the agreement also provided for "a 10-percent wage increase and a 40-hour week" (page 216). Saul Alinsky, in his unauthorized biography of John L. Lewis, notes that what Lewis achieved was incredible, given the fact that the union could not have won an election and gained recognition (page 149).

When the Lewis–Taylor agreement was announced to the public on March 1, 1937, following the U.S. Steel board's ratification of it, the union leadership was taken as completely by surprise as were the members in the plants. Perhaps because the agreement was so obviously advantageous to the fledgling organizing committee, which badly needed a victory, and because John L. Lewis was such an imperious and charismatic leader, the agreement reached in the shadow bargaining sessions was accepted by the union. Because of the unique circumstances, Lewis succeeded, but it is not recommended that anyone else seek to replicate his feat. Unauthorized and secret shadow bargaining presents too many risks and is not often utilized successfully today.

Sometimes a well-intentioned individual may take it upon himself or herself to meet with a similarly inclined individual from the other side in an effort to facilitate agreement. Unless each person's mandate is clear and their authority agreed upon in advance, the fruits of such meetings are more likely to be misunderstandings and bad feelings than viable, workable agreements.

Structure of the Teams

While most negotiations are conducted between one employer and one union local for a contract covering one work location, there are numerous other possible bargaining structures.

First, there may be a number of work locations of one employer, and this, in turn, may involve a number of locals of the same union (e.g., General Motors' 25 automobile plants and 25 different locals of the United Auto Workers), or different locals of different unions (e.g., General Electric's 25 plants and locals of the International United Electrical Workers, the United Electric Workers, and the Machinists). In this latter structure especially, the internal, vertical and shadow bargaining possibilities are especially hazardous and may often lead to deep schisms as each union seeks to advance its goals, interests and objectives.

Second, a number of different employers may negotiate together with one large local union (e.g., the Gotham Building Contractors' Association, comprised of 25 different building contracting companies and the large Gotham area carpenters local), or the employers' association may negotiate with a coalition of local unions that bargain together (e.g., the Gotham Building Contractors' Association and the Gotham Building Trades Union Council, which represents 12 different construction unions, such as those representing painters, electricians, plumbers and carpenters).

Third, there may be any number of permutations of the above structures, such as two employers that bargain together with one union local, which represents all the employees of both companies (e.g., Aida Fashions and Leah's Dress Company, the only two such firms in the area that negotiate with a large local of the Garment Workers' Union), or three employers that negotiate contracts with one large union and a coalition of smaller unions. Three newspapers in Gotham's area bargain together with the Newspaper Guild, which represents all editorial and clerical workers and then, in separate negotiations, with the Printing Trades Coalition, which represents all the graphic department employees, such as typographers, printing pressmen and the like.

And then there are special coalitions, such as an area employers association, which can negotiate for all employers dealing with whatever union structure is appropriate—single or multiple employer, specific industry or narrow skill specialty (e.g., electricians who may work in construction or maintenance). This latter sort of coalition seeks some level of employer uniformity on wages and benefits. In the unionized public sector, there may be special arrangements; in Gotham City negotiations, each particular union may negotiate wages and conditions for its members separately (police, firefighters, sanitation workers, etc.), but on issues of pension, health, welfare benefits and the like, in which the city seeks uniformity for ease of administration and lower cost (through having one plan with one insurance carrier), all unions must bargain together in a coalition with the city.

Regardless of the structure of the negotiation relationship, however, each team possesses three sides and engages in the configurations of bargaining discussed earlier.

"All Together Now"

The bargaining configurations were set out above as discrete processes for better illustration and comprehension. In reality, however, what occurs is often not by any means so discrete and orderly. An analysis of the hospital nurses' example discussed earlier would reveal not only the four configurations, but also such permutations as a splinter, or "rump," meeting of the nurses' negotiating committee, led and dominated by Judy Brand, the destabilizer; an informal session of the hospital negotiating committee that met without Jason Payne and discussed not only contract negotiations but financial concerns, such as a new Medicare reimbursement policy; and a chance meeting at an airport lounge between hospital president Richard Crane and Veronica Charles, the executive director of the state nurses' association, at which time they discussed the current status of negotiations at the hospital.

Judy Brand, a forceful and active individual, calls her fellow nurse negotiating committee members together to meet informally at her apartment. She does not invite the nurses' chief negotiator, Karen Roberts, nor fellow committee member Becky Anders, both of whom she feels are too tame and pliable at the table. As she pours coffee for her two fellow negotiators, she argues that hospital negotiators must be pushed harder for more concessions. "I think we've been too easy on those guys, really. Our nurses are counting on us to get something really good. Otherwise, we're wasting our time. They pay such low salaries and then wonder why there's such a shortage of nurses. Last night, Margie told me how she could have used at least two more RNs on her floor. Imagine, short two nurses! We've just got to force those guys to the wall."

Her remarks are well received by John Dennis, who is of the same frame of mind, but Linda Clarke is not persuaded. She is upset that her friend Becky Anders was not invited, and she has a great deal of faith in the nurses' association representative. In fact, Clarke is vital to the balance of power on the negotiating committee, and when Becky Anders learns of the meeting, she will tell Karen Roberts, who will in turn chide Brand for her actions and keep an extra-sharp eye on John Dennis. As an experienced negotiator, Roberts well knows that, if she loses control of her bargaining committee to a destabilizer like Judy Brand, she will be impeded—and possibly prevented—from achieving her goal of a satisfactory contract with no strike.

After the hospital administrators concluded their meeting to discuss changes in the Medicare reimbursement formula and its attendant ramifications for the institution's finances, the conversation turned to the negotiations with the nurses. Bradley Manning, the vice president of finance, said that he thought now was the time to "hang tough, not give an inch," but Simon Norwalk, the director of the hospital, immediately said, "Brad, the last thing we should do is play hardball. Do you know what a nurses' strike could do to us? Our image in the community would be ruined, and this place would never be the same again. When I was associate director at my last hospital, we had a nurses' strike. Let me tell you, it was pure hell. We ended up giving the nurses more than we could have given without the strike. And the way the community sided with those nurses, it was terrible! The strike cost us terribly—and money was the least of it. The residents wouldn't admit new patients. Do you know what it's like for a hospital to have to turn away ill people? No, I will not, absolutely not, be a party to a negotiation that ends in a strike!"

Jason Payne, the hospital's chief spokesperson, will have to be careful that director Norwalk does not try to buy peace at any price, for he has learned that a badly negotiated agreement can be worse than not having a contract and taking a strike. Although Payne wants a contract with the nurses, a few days later he tells Norwalk that "negotiators who want a contract in the worst possible way usually get a contract that is worst in every possible way."

When Richard Crane, the president of the hospital and the leading real estate broker in the community, spots Veronica Charles, the nurses' association executive director, at the airport, he engages her in conversation. They first met a number of years ago when they both served on the governor's task force on health policy and since then have met periodically. Crane, who admits he knows nothing about the issues in the nurses' negotiation, tells Charles, "All negotiations are the same, labor or real estate. If the parties, both of them, want to cut a deal, they can always find common ground. Listen, if things get sticky, you and I will work out whatever problem there is. We want to do right by our nurses, if you know what I mean, but we've got our limits on what we can give. Veronica, you of all people know what the state Blue Cross and Blue Shield posture is on reimbursement for wage increases, so we've got to toe the line, don't we?"

Charles agrees that reimbursement guidelines are a factor that must be considered, but she says pointedly, "Richard, you know how valuable the nurses are, and you've often said yourself that the hospital couldn't run without them. Well, I've met with these nurses and I can tell you just how very determined they are to get a good contract. It's good to know I can call you if I need to, and I just may have to. Richard, this is a very serious situation."

In many bargaining relationships, there are numerous channels of communication available to each side. The relationship between Richard Crane and Veronica Charles is one example of this. Often, these lines of communication can be very valuable should an impasse develop. However, there are potential problems as well if either party loses control of one participant who utilizes a private communication channel, and may, in so doing, send a false or misleading message to the other side.

Additionally, mention should be made of the following interactions growing out of the negotiations and, in turn, affecting their conduct and outcome: a lengthy conversation between Mike Brecker, an employee relations manager at a nearby hospital that also negotiates with the nurses' association, and Jason Payne, the hospital's director of employee relations; a meeting between the nurses' chief negotiator, Karen Roberts, and Millicent Sherman, the business agent for a union representing hospital employees other than the registered nurses; and a chance encounter at a bar association meeting between Neil Eisen, the nurses' association attorney, and Brenda Heath, who serves as general counsel to the hospital.

At the first meeting, the one between Payne of the hospital and his long-time friend Mike Brecker, who has a similar position at a nearby hospital, the concern was expressed by Brecker that if Payne settled too generously with the nurses, he in turn would be under pressure when the organized nurses at his hospital came to the bargaining table in three months. "You know, Jason, whatever you give them, they'll try for more from us, and we just can't afford it," he said.

When Karen Roberts had lunch with Millicent Sherman, the same topic was discussed, though from a rather different perspective. Representing as she does nonprofessional and paraprofessionals, Sherman is well aware that the settlement the nurses make with the hospital will have a material effect upon the contract she must negotiate in four months when they go to the table.

At the bar association meeting, Brenda Heath, the hospital's general counsel, is most interested in the negotiations, as is her opposite number, the nurses' attorney, Neil Eisen. There may be unfair labor practice charges filed by either side, especially if a failure to bargain in good faith, as stipulated by law, is perceived. Also, these two attorneys will participate actively in drafting the contract once an agreement is reached.

Though neither sits on the negotiating team, they are good conduits for information and may be used on short notice to ascertain the legality of a proposal.

Points to Ponder

Consider one contract negotiation with which you are familiar or, if not appropriate, use a bargaining simulation which you either participated in or observed.

On the union side, who were the stabilizers, the destabilizers and the quasi-mediators? What actions or comments demonstrated their orientation? Did that orientation change during the negotiations? If so, how and when?

Analyze the employer side the same way. Who was the team leader? Was he or she a quasi-mediator? Did one team leader deal with the other side's leader? If so, how and when?

Did shadow bargaining occur? Was it fruitful? How did each team respond to it?

Multilateral Bargaining

"Stand by me."

—BEN E. KING

IN THIS SECTION we consider bargaining configurations in which more than two parties are involved.

Trilateral Bargaining

Having examined the bilateral bargaining model and noted some of its inherent complexities, it is now appropriate to begin a consideration of some negotiating models of greater complexity, starting with the trilateral, or three-sided, model.

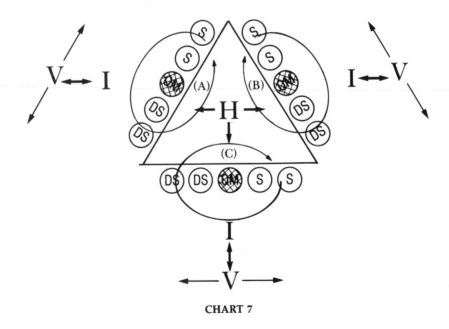

CHART 7

Although a diagram of the trilateral model may not appear especially intricate at first, such is not the case. In fact, the bargaining configurations discussed earlier—the horizontal, internal and vertical—increase geometrically rather than arithmetically when only one additional party is added. This is demonstrated by Chart 7.

One dramatic differential the trilateral model presents is in the reaching of an agreement by two sides. In the bilateral model, of course, that is the goal of the negotiators, and, should their assistance be sought, they are neutrals as well. However, in the trilateral model, if two parties reach agreement, it may threaten the interests of the third party, as seen in Chart 8. Concerning the first issue, wherein teams A and B coalesce against team C:

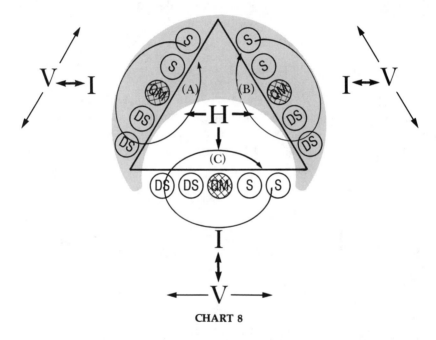

CHART 8

However, on issues 2 and 3, the alignment of the parties may change so that now teams B and C coalesce against team A (Chart 9).

And, on issues 4 and 5, teams A and C may unite against team B (Chart 10).

This trilateral model is not merely theoretical. Rather, it was actually utilized to resolve conditions that nearly caused a riot at a large state maximum-security prison. The three teams were "A," unionized correctional officers; "B," organized prison inmates; and "C," the prison administration.

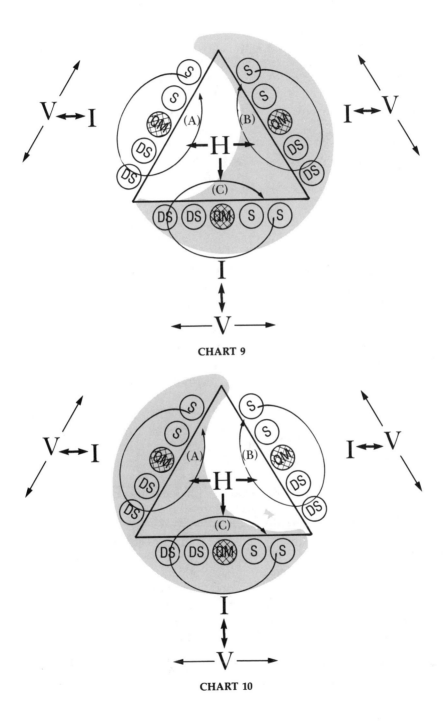

CHART 9

CHART 10

Consider an issue, such as the nature and frequency of spousal visits. Inmates wanted unlimited visits and no physical barriers to embracing spouses. Correctional officers and administrators were concerned about the logistical problems that unlimited visits could afford, as well as the possibility of the passing of contraband (weapons or drugs) that might occur if there were no physical barriers. One way to deal with this contraband problem would be to subject each spouse to an intense personal "strip search," a procedure spouses find degrading. These subjects were thoroughly discussed by all three parties, accommodations were made to each party's interests, and agreements were reached.

The dynamics of reaching those agreements were most interesting, and a bit unexpected. As issue after issue (and subissues) was identified and discussed by the three parties, there emerged not a permanent two-team coalition, but rather coalitions that were formed issue by issue (or subissue). Nonetheless, full three-party consensus was the stated goal of all teams and was reached on a large number of issues. It turned out that what seemed the major problem and fundamental weakness of the trilateral process, the coalescing of two parties against the third, was ultimately the basic strength and saving grace of the process.

As each party sought to build bridges and achieve a two-party coalition to control a vital issue, sensitivity to each other's needs developed, which in turn facilitated the achieving of true three-party consensus. Indeed, it developed into a living model of the old British diplomatic maxim: "We have no permanent allies, nor permanent enemies, only permanent interests."

Shadow bargaining, the informal negotiating that team spokespersons or others may conduct away from the table (discussed earlier), is even more difficult here because a party must continually question whether these informal off-the-record discussions should be held between just two parties, or whether a representative of the third party should also be included; whether to meet first with one party and then the other; and, if so, whether to inform each party of a meeting with the other—and how much of that discussion to share. As with any shadow bargaining, there are the additional potential problems of someone from one party meeting without authorization from that team and making commitments or gaining concessions on his or her own. Here, because there are more players, there are increased chances of this sort of behavior occurring. The building of trust and good faith, so very critical to the exchange of promises, is extremely fragile and not easy to achieve between two parties. Between three parties, it is not only more difficult, more fragile, and more unstable, it is also more easily threatened by shadow bargaining, even if—and perhaps especially when—it is well-intentioned but unauthorized.

Quadrilateral Bargaining

The quadrilateral, or four-sided, model of bargaining is, in turn, even more complex than the trilateral model just discussed. In this configuration, not only are there the intricacies of four parties engaging in horizontal bargaining across the table, four sets of internal negotiations, four relationships to hierarchies and constituencies, and countless shadow bargaining possibilities and permutations, but there are opportunities for coalition building in geometric quantities. Initially, before trust is established, it is not surprising to find four different positions on one issue; then a "two versus two" syndrome develops. On still other issues there may be three teams united against one, or any other permutation, such as two teams united, with two other teams having their own individual positions. Some of these possibilities are pictured in Chart 11.

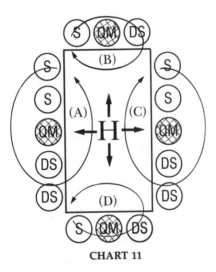

CHART 11

Consider the earlier illustration of the trilateral model, which was utilized at a state maximum-security prison. But now add the fourth party, the unionized correctional supervisors who have a bargaining unit different from the guards they supervise. On certain issues, this fourth team may coalesce with the prison administration, the guards, or the inmates, or any combination of the three parties, or quite possibly none. Especially in the public sector, many groups of lower- and middle-level supervisors have become interested in collective bargaining and often are permitted to unionize under law. In the private sector, this has been im-

Three against one—B, C and D versus A.

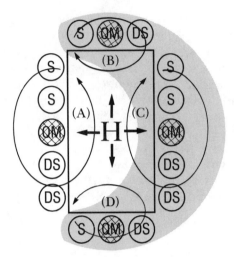

CHART 12

Two united, two independent—A, B united; C, D independent.

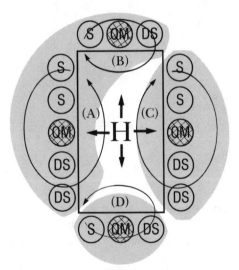

CHART 13

peded, it not completely blocked, by statutory language, the NLRB and judicial decisions that have generally held that those in a supervisory capacity are not covered by the Wagner Act.

Hydralateral Bargaining

Rather than go through the numerous other possible configurations, such as five-, six- or seven-sided bargaining models, it is perhaps more instructive to consider that form of multilateral bargaining called hydralateral, after the nine-headed serpent of Greek mythology, which, when one head was cut off by Hercules, grew two heads to replace it. Sometimes it appears to be the case that when one party is scrutinized closely, it quickly becomes two (or more) subtleties, making the determination of who should be at the table a crucial and controversial issue that in itself may be the subject of intense bargaining.

Consider the state maximum-security prison discussed earlier. Now assume the subject of controversy is prison overcrowding and how best to deal with it. There is one suggestion to expand the prison, which is located in the distant suburbs of the state's major city, while another idea is to construct a large facility within the state's major city. The prison administration, unionized guards and unionized supervisors, as well as many in the local community where the prison is a major employer, favor expansion. The inmates and their families and friends favor an urban location because most of the inmates are from the city and travel for visita-

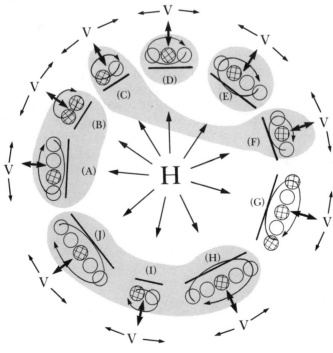

CHART 14

tion is not easy, especially because few have access to private automobiles and must instead use public transportation.

However, many of those who live in Gotham Center, the residential community where the proposed new prison will be built, oppose the prison, arguing that it will depress property values and present a threat to the safety and security of the neighborhood, especially because the possibility of escapes from a maximum-security facility in which hardened criminals are housed is a particular hazard. Politicians from the two areas are brought into the fray, as are the governor and state legislative leaders. Contractors and construction workers are also heard from, as are judges, social workers and members of the prosecutors and defense bar.

When the state correctional commissioner seeks to resolve the conflict through multilateral negotiation, the first issue to be resolved is who shall be at the table and what shall be the powers of each party. Given this uncertainty, horizontal, vertical and internal bargaining may well be highly emotional and volatile. The possibilities for shadow bargaining, especially given the participation of politicians, are enormous, as are the potential pitfalls and abuses.

Points to Ponder

The hydralateral model discussed above would appear to have great relevance to many disputes in our society and in the world. Consider negotiations to achieve peaceful racial integration of a city school system with a majority of black students and a county school system with a majority of white students. How many groups would have a stake in the outcome? Should a group that is opposed to racial integration be allowed to participate in the negotiations? Who functions as "gatekeeper" in this negotiation and from where would they get power?

The Table Process Analyzed

"And in the middle of negotiations
you break down."

—THE BEATLES
You Never Give Me Your Money

IN THIS SECTION we analyze the dynamics of the table process and examine the essence of what goes on at the table.

Ritual, Game, Catharsis and Problem-solving

Collective bargaining is simultaneously a ritual, a game, a catharsis and a problem-solving process. It is a ritual in that it is customarily performed the same way on different occasions. Just as ritual is an integral part of religion, so is it an integral part of the collective bargaining process. We all take some comfort in the familiarity of ritual, and this is especially true in tense negotiation sessions. We know the union may begin by announcing its initial demands, which are unrealistically high. We can then expect management to react negatively and make exceedingly disparaging remarks about the probable outcome of negotiations, given the unreasonable posture of the union. Thus, the union may begin by proposing a 33⅓-percent increase in wages for a one-year contract. While no one on the union team seriously expects to receive so high a settlement, management will respond with great dismay, pointing out the severe economic consequences of such a settlement. It is a ritual, one with which most participants are quite familiar.

Collective bargaining is a game in that it is an activity pursued according to certain rules. The rules are both of the written statutory variety and the unwritten behavioral type. For example, we expect the parties, upon reaching agreement, to execute a written agreement. Indeed, the refusal to commit the agreement to writing is an unfair labor practice in the opinion of the National Labor Relations Board. Conversely, the usual practice of the union presenting its demands first is a standard, unwritten rule that seems universal.

In conflict situations, the presence of rules of the game channels the parties' behavior into predictable and safer courses. It should also be noted that there are playful and amusing aspects to games, and many veterans of negotiations will recall past situations with humor and fondness. For example, negotiating committee members recall how seven years ago they bargained for 37 hours straight until they reached agreement, and, although at the time it was probably irritating and fatiguing, now it is fondly remembered the way one recalls a championship football game. It is not coincidental that the word "team" is used to describe each side.

A catharsis is an emotional release, and clearly the negotiating table provides an opportunity for this. Under generally accepted rules of employment and decorum, it is grounds for discipline for insubordination should an employee verbally castigate his or her supervisor without some unusual provocation. But at the collective bargaining table, such rules are suspended. Now, in his or her role as negotiator for the union, an employee is free to say whatever he or she feels with no fear of disciplinary retribution. Similarly, management personnel are generally expected not to verbalize any negative feelings about employees as a group; but now such restraints are gone.

Psychologists report that bottling up one's emotions is unhealthy. The bargaining table provides a safe outlet for these feelings. Often, the outsider, the company attorney or the international union representative, will be the most vocal and outspoken. This appears to be a paradox because as an outsider that person might have the lowest emotional investment and, therefore, the least motivation to release emotion. However, it must be stressed that the parties must live together after negotiations are over. Harsh words said in a heated moment may never be forgotten. It is often best, therefore, for such words to be said by one who does not have to live with them. This may be termed "vicarious catharsis."

For example, at Village Manufacturing Company, production manager David Norman and chief union steward Carl Travis have a highly contentious relationship. The company has sent Norman to various training programs at which good human relations techniques have been emphasized, and Norman has been instructed repeatedly never to denigrate the workforce because of the bad feelings and low worker morale such comments generate. Chief steward Travis has been cautioned on numerous occasions to curb his tongue by the local president and other officers, but this advice has not always been heeded.

As both men are on their respective negotiating teams, no one is surprised when the following interchange occurs during a discussion about the union's proposal for voluntary overtime. Norman, who is not the company spokesperson and has been keeping his own counsel, finally explodes. "Damn it, how the hell can I run my machines on weekends if I have to beg people to work? And I'm lucky if I get four hours of halfway decent work from these slackers anyway! Voluntary overtime, my foot! This is the most ridiculous thing I've ever heard in my life! It's not like anyone's dying from overwork as it is! Not one of them is worth a damn!"

Travis pounds the table and jumps to his feet. "That's right, Norman, nobody works, according to you, do they? You just want everyone to be your slave, like some kind of trained dog, but we're *people* and we're entitled to our own lives, aren't we? If you weren't such a tyrant, you'd find plenty of people who'd work overtime if only you would treat us like real people! You're the coldest bastard I've ever seen in my life. I'd love to see you rot in hell with all your damn production schedules and speedups, you no good S.O.B.!"

If such negative feelings are to be expressed, it would perhaps be less destructive to have outsiders, those who do not have to live with one another, express these sentiments. Long after the contract is reached and the problems solved, the harsh words between these men will be remembered and will be a constant source of friction.

Hostility

Our hesitation about endorsing the expressing of hostile sentiments across the negotiating table is not based on our cherishing polite, cool behavior. Of course, no one wants to have someone yell at them or repeatedly use abusive or derogatory language. But fundamentally, hostile behavior, unless one can predict with deadly accuracy the results of such behavior, is usually not productive. Very few professional negotiators are at all cowed by such actions (and usually do not behave that way themselves at the table) and the negative phrases are shrugged off as meaningless. While it is true that author Robert Ringer enjoyed a brief moment in the spotlight by urging us to *Win by Intimidation*, such behavior is simply at cross purposes with what a negotiator's real goals are: reaching agreement and having those on the other side advocate to their ratifiers the agreed upon settlement. Hostility, therefore, needs to be examined in its full context.

First, is it expected and accepted as part of the negotiating process between the parties? If so, it can be an appropriate channel to both release hostility and, as a catharsis, move the process of reaching agreement forward.

Second, if hostility is expected, acting hostile can be a predictable form of behavior which will meet the expectations of the other side. Remember, acting in a predictable manner increases the chances of your being able to accurately predict the behavior of others.

Third, even though hostility clearly has its negative consequences, it can have its positive aspects as well. As noted elsewhere, each table team is composed of those individuals who have the deepest emotional commitment to their side. These strong emotions need to be dealt with if the negotiations are to move toward agreement, and verbalizing hostility is an excellent way of doing that.

In sum, like any other aspect of the collective bargaining process, whatever you say or do must be placed in the overall context of what your ultimate goals are. Expressing hostility, therefore, can be, in the final analysis, either constructive or destructive, depending on how and why it is used and your ability to predict resultant behavior.

Exchanging Information

Amidst the often emotionally charged atmosphere in negotiations, it is easy to undervalue the important role of information exchange between the parties. The negotiating table presents the parties with a unique opportunity for face-to-face communication and for clarification of positions, policies and proposals for change.

For union negotiators, especially rank-and-file employees who may sit on the bargaining team, this is a rare opportunity to communicate with management officials, many of whom they would never meet but for their participation in negotiations. Often, union negotiators find that, once they are given a clear, logical, face-to-face presentation about the rationale for a management policy, they are better able to understand it, and perhaps even not oppose it. For example, when the vice president of finance explains that the company must now bid on contracts for work that will not commence until three years hence, perhaps the union team may begin to appreciate the company's proposal for a three-year agreement so that labor costs can be more accurately forecast for that period. At the very least, such an instructional opportunity serves to personalize that vague, amorphous entity called management, and provides a different view of a negotiable issue.

Similarly, management negotiators, some of whom may be removed from the day-to-day workplace, are given a chance to learn what employee concerns are, and how their policies are viewed by those on the receiving end of memos and procedural bulletins.

For example, in one urban teacher/school board negotiation, a key emotional issue was the reading of board memos (which had been previously distributed to teachers) at after-school faculty meetings. At the end of a hectic teaching day, the last thing most teachers wanted was to have the meeting extended by having the school principal laboriously reading aloud a memo already received—and presumably read—by the teachers. Some teachers found this professionally degrading, as if they lacked the ability and/or wisdom to read a memo. To others, it seemed a needless extension of a meeting at which their attendance was compulsory. When the assistant superintendent who had promulgated the policy of reading distributed memos was personally confronted by the angry teachers, he was able to reassess his position on the matter, and a new policy was negotiated that was satisfactory to all.

In the following illustration, numerous opportunities are present for misconceptions and negative feelings, but note how the parties are able to deal constructively with the situation.

The teachers proposed the following language: "No teacher shall be required to be present when students are not in attendance." When board negotiators received this proposal, Jerry Carstairs, assistant superintendent for instruction, became quite upset. He noted that, historically, teachers have always had about eight days each year before, during and after the teaching year to perform various clerical and reportorial tasks, as well as for attending orientation meetings and the like.

In the board caucus, Carstairs took an antagonistic attitude toward not only the proposal but the teachers' representative in general. As a destabilizer (DS), he was willing to view the proposal in its most negative light. "Don't these damn fools realize those days are a very necessary part of the instructional process? I swear, all these teachers want is to do as little as possible!"

Jane Porter, the principal of the largest high school in the district and a team member, viewed the proposal more charitably. She was very settlement oriented, as stabilizers (S) are. "Perhaps we ought to query the teachers on exactly what they really mean. I'm sure, Mr. Carstairs, that the teachers are well aware of the importance to the instructional program of these nonteaching days."

Bill Brandon, team spokesperson and director of staff relations, is a team harmonizer, one who serves to bring the conflicting interests of the team together, acting as a quasi-mediator (QM). He speaks up, "Jerry, I think we ought to ask them what they're really after in that proposal."

At the next joint conference, when Brandon asks the teachers' spokesperson, Mary Clark, what she is seeking, he does it in an open, nonaccusatory manner. This gives her the chance to reply in a clear, open, undefensive manner, which she does. She says, "Our concern here is that a situation might occur, such as a school closing due to a problem like a broken furnace, and the students are sent home for the day or even the next day. We don't want our teachers to report to work in a cold, empty building and have to stick around with no students to teach.''

Brandon asks Clark whether in fact that has ever occurred. Clark turns to Fred Hunt, the teacher who authored the proposal, and asks him to respond to that question. Hunt says, ''Well, no, it never has occurred here, but it could. If we get the needed language, it won't happen to us.''

Brandon sees Carstairs throw up his hands in despair. Brandon responds very firmly to Hunt, ''No agreement can ever hope to cover every possible contingency that might arise. Your language, which seems far too broad for your purpose, does not really address the possible situation you describe. I would suggest, with all due respect to your proposal, that we really have other, far more important issues to be resolved, and our time should be spent on these.''

Hunt nods in agreement and says, ''Yes, I agree with you, Mr. Brandon, but I think it's important to know the board policy on this matter. Are you saying that, in a situation such as I described, where the students are sent home because of a problem at a particular school, the teachers at that school will not be required to report to an empty building?''

Brandon says that before he makes a pronouncement on official board policy, he wants a caucus. In the board caucus, Carstairs is relieved to learn that the teachers' proposal is not what he first feared. He is, however, upset that the teachers do not seem to trust the board.

Principal Porter asks why the board cannot agree to commit to a policy they have always followed. Brandon expresses concern that the board not agree to language that might restrict operational flexibility. ''What about a situation like the one we had at Snow Hill Elementary School? The boiler was out and it took three weeks to get it fixed. We used the facilities at the local YMCA until the repairs were done, and I certainly don't want to limit our right to have teachers working outside their usual building under those kinds of emergency circumstances.''

By the time the board team returns to the table, it has reached an internal consensus on what they will—and will not—agree to. By posing a situation like the one that occurred at Snow Hill, Brandon is seeking not only the teachers' position but their understanding of his concerns.

The teachers, who have also caucused while the board caucused, have their position clear. Clark again asks Hunt to respond because it obviously is an issue he is deeply concerned about. ''Mr. Brandon, I know you're talking about the Snow Hill situation that occurred last year, and I want to tell you that what the board did was fine with us. We want to teach, and we're not just looking for a dodge to avoid teaching. What we don't want is the board making us go to an empty building when there are no students to teach because of a temporary emergency situation. Now I know, in fact, that Miss Thomas, who is the principal there, sent everybody home that day and the next day, and nobody had to report to the school. The following day, they made arrangements with the YMCA, and everybody—students, teachers and administrators—showed up at the Y. I'm just concerned about whether, if the same or a similar situation occurred, the board would handle it in the same way. Can you give me that guarantee?''

Mr. Brandon, who has discussed the matter thoroughly with his team, nods and says ''yes.'' The matter is resolved and the parties move on to other issues.

Trust and Integrity

It is important to note here the vital role of trust and integrity in labor relations. As has been mentioned earlier, it is the continuing close daily relationship of the parties that distinguishes collective bargaining from many other negotiating relationships. It not only means the parties must reach agreement, they must live up to those agreements, not all of which are by any means reduced to writing.

In the illustration above, note that the parties reached an oral agreement concerning a policy matter and did not reduce it to writing. As one of the speakers correctly observed, no agreement, no matter how large, can possibly cover all potential situations. Ultimately, certain matters must be left to the parties' trust and integrity.

Certainly, should the matter go to arbitration, the handwritten notes from negotiations, as well as the parties' oral testimony about their recollection, would be most germane. In fact, most grievance matters never reach the arbitration stage because the parties usually stand by their oral agreements. The negotiator who lies or bends the truth and cites the absence of a written agreement may well emerge victorious—once. Because labor relations is an ongoing process, he wins the battle but loses the war. Henceforth his word is valueless and his reputation may be damaged beyond repair.

It is not true that people in the field of labor relations are necessarily any more virtuous than people in other fields. What is true is that premaritally, as well as ethically, the system is based upon integrity, predictability and trust. To lose one's integrity, and the trust of others, is as shortsighted as it is impractical if one intends to remain in the labor relations profession.

''Sunshine Bargaining''

In the aftermath of the secrecy and closed atmosphere of the Watergate era, and as a reaction against the negative feelings it engendered, legislators began to enact open-meeting laws providing that all deliberations must be conducted within public view.

The idea underlying these laws is a basic one, and one which many citizens support: government, which belongs to all the people, should make its important decisions in the open, where taxpayers and voters can observe that process and the dynamics behind it. Decisions must not be presented as *faits accomplis*. Governmental decisions of great significance and importance should evidence how they were reached.

While these laws originally applied only to meetings of governmental boards and regulatory bodies, the state of Florida applied this law to all meetings at which collective negotiations for public employees were being conducted. (Florida, known in travel and tourism as "The Sunshine State," called their open-meeting laws "sunshine laws," and negotiations conducted under them thus became known as "sunshine bargaining.")

Many other jurisdictions have adopted sunshine laws for governmental meetings, and a few have adopted sunshine bargaining laws with the best of intentions. Since public monies are used to pay public employees, it is argued that the public has a right to observe the process by which labor–management contracts are reached. People will more likely support these contracts if they are free to observe the negotiations as opposed to agreements produced at closed or secret negotiations. Public officials who negotiate agreements can have their performance more easily evaluated; thus, a better assessment of their conduct can be made by the electorate, their "employers."

This latter point is also said to apply to union members, whose economic welfare is so seriously affected by negotiated agreements, but who rarely can observe their elected and paid leaders in action. In a land cherishing freedom of the press, sunshine laws allow access to the media, whose representatives can convey the essence of the proceedings to readers, listeners and viewers. The result of all this access and openness, it is argued, is that the parties will assume more responsible postures and negotiate reasonably and fairly, making the bargaining process more mature and less emotional.

Indeed, no union negotiator will demand such a large wage increase that the city or county will go bankrupt. Similarly, if such demands must be publicly presented and defended, no public employer negotiator will wish to appear unduly miserly or unfair in his or her treatment of public employees. Thus, the process of reaching an equitable agreement will be expedited, saving time and money while avoiding abrasive confrontations, which are as unseemly as they are counterproductive.

Opponents of sunshine bargaining argue that it creates more problems than it solves. While it is true that the media enjoy unhindered access to the negotiation sessions, they neither understand the process nor convey an accurate portrayal of the parties to their respective audiences. Although the union may initially request a wage increase of such proportions as to cause a doubling of the current tax rate, and the city negotiator may predict dire consequences for the municipality's financial condition, these are merely postures and hyperbole, a preface to real negotiations.

To have such statements taken seriously by the public, which may either be in attendance or receive the information through a news report, is to unfairly prejudice the process and the parties. Perhaps worse is the effect of public declarations on the parties themselves. Having taken a stand publicly, one is often hard-pressed to abandon such a position, no matter how untenable, for fear of losing face. Thus, if the union moves from its initial position, as indeed it always intended, the spokesperson can be seen by the members as having retreated or surrendered, which is something dissidents will not let the membership forget. Similarly, when the city, despite earlier pronouncements of financial collapse, does agree to a wage and benefit increase, political opponents and taxpayer-revolt leaders may argue that the jurisdiction's very existence is being compromised by inept bargainers.

Although contract negotiations are not usually the place to resolve grievances and personal problems, these matters sometimes come up at the table. An open meeting under a sunshine law would appear to be a particularly inappropriate place to discuss such sensitive matters as the allegedly poor classroom performance of one special-education teacher, or the outside commercial off-duty activities of two firefighters, matters which often do arise and are usually disposed of at the bargaining table.

The physical presence of crowds of partisans is said to transform the atmosphere and make real bargaining more difficult, with each side making speeches, not deals. Who, in reality, attends these public negotiation sessions? They are union members, spouses and other supporters on one side, and taxpayer groups, whose concern is lower taxes (through lower salaries and benefits for fewer public employees). Rarely do nonpartisan, disinterested citizens attend these sessions. When they do, it is argued that they lack a real understanding of the issues and the parties' respective positions.

Certainly, the presence of the public changes the process. Whether the changes are positive or negative, they ultimately result in value judgments. Yet, there are certain unseated assumptions behind sunshine bargaining laws that must be identified. First, sunshine bargaining assumes that horizontal, or across-the-table, negotiations are the key to reaching an agreement. Presumably, internal and vertical bargaining are not covered by these sunshine laws, and, as we have seen, they are vital

parts of the negotiation process. Perhaps, especially in the highly publi-
cized atmosphere of public sector labor relations, shadow bargaining by
powerful members of each side is often the means by which agreements
are reached. It would appear that this type of negotiating is barred by
sunshine laws, and must be done, if at all, in complete secrecy, which
paradoxically appears to negate the entire purpose of sunshine laws.

And what of the cathartic release of the horizontal negotiation process? It would appear that true emotional release is hampered by the audience, which may overreact to customary bargaining table rhetoric. The
normal give and take, the floating of possible settlements, is hindered
by the presence of a large and boisterous audience, or even by the presence of one reporter. Candor is inhibited and posturing encouraged.

For example, the union may be presenting a proposal vigorously sponsored by one group of employees that insists on its inclusion in the list
presented to the employer, even though the union negotiating team does
not really believe the proposal is reasonable or justified. In the usual type
of negotiations, the union spokesperson may well dismiss the proposal,
or, by verbal intonation or body language, convey its low priority to the
employer. Were members of the sponsoring group allowed to be present,
the union would not be able to respond that way, and the proposal could
well receive far more attention than it deserves.

Observers point out that nowhere in the private sector has this open
negotiation format been tried with the presence of a mass of union
members and/or shareholders, two groups which obviously hold a large
stake in the outcome of negotiations. Also, much energy has been directed
at circumventing these laws in the public sector, developments that appear to indicate the impracticality and unfeasibility of the laws.

And, finally, critics note that the very legislators who enact sunshine
bargaining laws do not themselves negotiate "in the sunshine." Indeed,
one of the authors of this manual often says he would readily support
any sunshine bargaining law enacted completely in the sunshine and not
"made in the shade," behind the closed doors of a legislative caucus
session.

It is enough, many seasoned negotiators conclude, that the agreement be made public and subject to scrutiny once reached; the process
itself need not be opened up. Closed negotiations are not sinister, evil
or contrary to the public interest, per se. They are often more effective,
efficient and equitable than open negotiations.

Points to Ponder

Herb Cohen, the author of *You Can Negotiate Anything*, discusses what
he terms the pre-Perestroika Soviet style of negotiations. Such an

approach involves the following six elements: (1) extreme initial positions —outrageously high demands or low offers; (2) limited authority—negotiators themselves have little or no authority to make any concessions; (3) emotional tactics—getting red-faced with anger or exasperation; (4) adversary concessions viewed as weakness—any concession you make will probably not be reciprocated; (5) stingy with concessions—delay as long as possible in making any concessions and, when concessions finally are made, let them only reflect a minuscule change in position; and (6) ignore deadlines—have endless patience and act as though time is of no significance.

Is such an approach appropriate in a labor–management relationship where the parties must live together on an ongoing basis? To continue this line of discussion, in negotiations such as U.S.–Soviet arms limitation talks, why have agreements historically not been easily reached? Does it have any relation to the issue of trust and integrity? To promise-checking?

Preparing for Bargaining

"Are you ready?
Yes I'm ready!"

—BARBARA MASON
Yes I'm Ready

"Viva Las Vegas!"

—ELVIS PRESLEY

IN THIS SECTION we discuss how each team prepares for and approaches the bargaining table.

Preparation for Bargaining

If, as the old adage goes, the race is to the swift, success in negotiation lies in diligent preparation. All the material in the following sections presupposes adequate preparation; the importance of this point cannot be overdressed. Too often, overworked union representatives and employer representatives do not have the time, due to the press of travel and other duties, to fully prepare for negotiations—and the results can be catastrophic. Each side's spokesperson must have the time and information to be completely knowledgeable, not only about the team's own goals and objectives, but about the other team's goals and objectives.

As an ongoing process, contract administration must be monitored. This is sometimes called a "grievance audit," but, to be truly effective, it must go deeper than simply reviewing cases that went to arbitration or even written grievances. This is because problems often arise that may be informally settled, and no one above the working employee or first-line supervisor may learn about the issue. While it is certainly good industrial relations to resolve all grievances as quickly as possible and as close to the source, there may well be some underlying problems needing resolution at the bargaining table.

Similarly, while each side will undertake a "contract review and analysis" before going to the table, that process must also be approached with some depth. Problem areas—both actual and potential—must be identified, together with proposals for their change.

Hard data must be developed on items such as wages and benefits by both sides. Compensation costs and related personnel data, such as accidents, illnesses and absenteeism, must be compiled in a form both reliable and useful. In the heat of negotiations, when one side makes a proposal, the data must be readily available for costing out and analysis. Because of time and pressure constraints, the table is not the place to develop data.

For example, when the Food Workers Union drops its wage proposal from an 18¢ per hour increase to a 15¢ per hour increase, the Ace Food Store negotiating team must be able to calculate quickly that each penny per hour costs the employer $21,635, and thus the union's concession represents a movement of $64,905. Hence, when the union argues that the employer should grant the new optical benefit because the downward three union move saved the company enough to pay for it, that figure, too, must be available. (There are numerous books and manuals detailing how to cost-out an agreement. For that reason, it will not be covered in this manual.)

Each team must also establish its communication infrastructure. The union must determine how much and in what way members will be informed about the progress—or lack thereof—in negotiations. Many unions utilize a system in which general information flows only from the bargaining committee to the shop stewards, who in turn inform the members. Similarly, many employers provide information to top-level managers, who in turn inform their subordinate managers. As a general rule, rumors and misinformation are rife during negotiations and may cause severe problems. It is far better to provide in advance for an orderly—and limited—information flow than to run the risks of grapevine gossip.

Contingency planning in the event an agreement is not reached must also be done. For the union, it may mean building a large strike fund and having staff and logistical support for a job action should one be deemed necessary. Companies often seek to build inventory or plan for supervisors to staff essential functions should employees strike. These plans must be both detailed and flexible on both sides of the table, and must be updated to allow for conditions that may have changed over time. Put simply, it is not enough to have created a detailed contingency plan in 1972 if that plan has not been updated in 1982; an outdated plan may often be worse than no plan at all.

In the public sector, where job actions may be illegal, increasing emphasis has been placed on contingency planning, and wisely so. Unions and employers often need to have a legal staff, communications people and operations capability at the ready in the event of a strike. What will the teachers' union do when arrest warrants are issued against its five negotiating team members? What will the school board do when only 25 percent of the teachers show up for class? Again, it must be emphasized that the best time to deal with these situations is well before they occur, and, indeed, being prepared for these situations often ensures that they will be less likely to occur. If they do, their impact may be greatly reduced because adequate damage-control steps have been taken that lessen the threat, which thereby makes the action less potent.

For example, if the teachers' union will not be crippled if its five negotiating team members are jailed, there is perhaps less likelihood that the school board will seek their incarceration. Similarly, if, by the utilization of supervisors, administrators and substitute teachers, classes will be covered, there is perhaps less likelihood of the teachers' union calling for a job action.

In conclusion, then, while it is probably impossible to prepare for every eventuality that may occur in the course of an upcoming negotiation, it is wise to plan thoroughly and seek to anticipate problem areas. When the unexpected occurs, as it inevitably seems to during every negotiation, prepared advocates, if they do not immediately have the answer, have positioned themselves so that they may react quickly and effectively.

Proposal Formulation

The key in preparation for successful collective bargaining is the formulation of team proposals and the anticipation of the other party's proposals.

Employee Proposals

Most unions and employee associations seek to involve as many of their members as possible in formulating negotiation proposals. Certainly, this must be the case if an employee is to meaningfully participate in the collective bargaining of his or her contract, given the impracticality of a large negotiating committee and the societal predilection for industrial democracy.

Indeed, despite cartoons and television comedies, most employees in our society do not enjoy individually negotiated salary agreements. Whether or not there is a union present, most large employers pay according to predetermined wage plans, and the individual usually has little say in the matter. A high school English teacher with an M.A. and six years of experience will be placed on the seventh step of the salary scale no matter what his or her personality or other individual factors may be. What this means is that, for employees who are represented in collective bargaining, this process is their only means of both economic advancement and individual input into the process through which their compensation is established.

It is no wonder, then, that many employees wish to actively participate in formulation of bargaining proposals. Add to this the union's encouragement of participation, plus the union's wish to promote itself, and we come to the "Las Vegas Mentality."

Las Vegas Mentality

At the McCarren Airport in Las Vegas, planeload after planeload of gamblers land. Do any of these hundreds of thousands of people come to the casinos of Las Vegas hoping to lose their money? Of course not. They all hope to win, an outcome which, rationally, they all know is impossible, or at least highly unlikely. Nonetheless, each one believes and hopes *he* or *she* will hit the jackpot.

The comparison to collective bargaining is especially relevant, particularly for the union members. While they may rationally know all their lofty goals cannot conceivably be achieved, they nonetheless believe and hope the settlement will be as generous as the demands.

Just as casinos seek to promote the ambience of opulence, luxury and wealth, so unions seek to increase membership by escalating the expectations of those they represent. For, in truth, who would want to join, support and pay dues to an organization that does not promise very positive benefits?

As will be discussed in the section on contract ratification, sometimes the high expectations cause a great sense of disappointment with the proposed agreement. Thus, while some members might have been satisfied with and ratified a contract with a six-percent wage increase, they may feel acutely let down that they did not receive the proposed 16 percent, unrealistic as that figure may have been.

Employee Input

Some unions hold membership meetings where proposals are sought from the rank-and-file employees, while others may have a more informal process, such as asking shop stewards what they think the next agreement should contain.

In any event, the union obtains some input from members and mixes that with the experience of the union officials who have lived under the current agreement and thus are familiar with problem areas and subjects causing numerous grievances.

For example, many employers have rules concerning absences due to illness. Commonly, if an employee misses three or more days, he or she must provide, upon returning to work, a doctor's note explaining the absence and, sometimes, certifying that the employee can perform work tasks. Suppose an employee is treated for back pain by a chiropractor, gets a note, and returns to work. The employee's supervisor rejects the note, correctly pointing out that chiropractors are not licensed physicians, and only a note signed by a licensed physician is acceptable. It will not be surprising to then see the union propose that notes be acceptable when signed by a licensed physician or a chiropractor.

Similarly, local union leadership usually receives information and contracts from other locals containing provisions and language that may be of interest. Other locals have faced similar circumstances, or are dealing now with situations that may emerge at the local level in the future, providing the opportunity to benefit from other's experience.

Unions have institutional goals, such as union security and dues check-off, which are of great importance to the continued operation of the union as an entity. And, while it may perhaps be true that many employees are not overly concerned with these issues, those who are concerned are local leaders most involved in collective bargaining and who care the most about the continued existence of the union. It is *they* who will propose and support such proposals as the union shop or agency shop, where legal.

As noted above, once the union's proposals are formulated, they are usually disseminated to the membership verbally and/or in written form in circulars or union publications. While this obviously makes public the union proposals, and thus removes any element of surprise, most union officials believe dissemination is worth the cost. The feeling of participation in the decision-making process is important, especially when the decisions concern an individual's economic welfare. Certainly, the opportunity for participation serves to strengthen the union and the individual's commitment to the union, two goals union leaders must achieve.

There is a further benefit from such participation in the process, one often observed when the negotiations either reach impasse or an agreement is obtained. If the latter occurs, employees will be more likely to vote for ratification because they feel it is *their* agreement, one in which they participated, at least to some degree. If an impasse occurs, employees are more likely to support the union in whatever action it might take to achieve its goals if the employees believe in and are committed to those goals. The employee who has to ask, "What are we striking for?" is going to be the least committed to the strike, and likely the first one back to work, even if it means crossing the picket line.

Employer Proposals

Too often it appears to novices to the negotiating process that only the union takes the lead and makes proposals, and that the employer only reacts. In truth, many employers approach negotiation with proposals and goals of their own. For the employer to put proposals on the table is neither illegal nor an unfair labor practice. Often, employer proposals are in effect reactive in nature and in keeping with the maxim that "the best defense is a good offense." That is to say, in an effort to blunt the force of the union's proposals, the employer may promulgate proposals of its own solely as a countermeasure to the union. For example, when the union at Decker Corporation proposes a 24-percent pay raise for one year, the employer proposes that employees will pay half the cost of the previously company-paid optical plan. The company is not in truth seeking this, nor do they realistically expect to achieve it, but it has placed an item on the bargaining agenda that must be dealt with. The employer's goal is simply to trade away in the process of negotiation this item for a substantive union concession.

This type of employer proposal should not be confused with a counterproposal, or a proposal one makes in response to the other side's proposal. For example, to continue the illustration above, the Decker Corporation may respond to the union's 24-percent wage increase proposal by making a counterproposal of a 10-percent wage cut. In the early phases of bargaining, it is not uncommon to have this sort of posturing, with each side exchanging unrealistic numbers, proposals and counterproposals.

Our real focus here is the employer's serious proposal, one arrived at after careful research and analysis. As the parties' relationship matures, one sign of that maturation is the increase in the number of serious affirmatively made employer proposals.

For example, if first-line supervisors have been complaining to the production manager that they are having staffing difficulties on weekends because the contract provides for only voluntary weekend overtime, this may well lead to a company proposal for mandatory weekend overtime.

Many employers provide for periodic input from managers concerning the collective agreement and any problems arising under it. This input may come in the form of written submissions or from questionnaires from the industrial relations department. Another source of employer proposals comes from arbitration decisions or grievance settlements that have occurred during the life of the agreement. Often, large corporations or agencies dealing with many different unions or locals of the same union will seek to share information about various problems encountered. For example, many employers who negotiate with the United Steelworkers

Union note that the union's proposals concerning prohibitions against contracting out are phrased in the same language. Therefore, if one employer has a problem, a grievance or ends up going to arbitration over that language, other employers similarly situated may propose language to deal with that issue before it becomes a problem at their own company.

Thus, while the employer's proposals may be compiled by the employee relations manager, they are in reality the product of numerous inputs. When the city school board comes to the negotiating table, for instance, its six proposals may fall into two categories: the defensive (reactive) ones, which are bargaining ploys, and the affirmative (active) ones, which represent goals the board seriously seeks. The first three proposals falling into the first category provide for the elimination of planning periods for middle-school teachers, an increase in the rate of employee contribution for health insurance and a reduction in tuition reimbursement for graduate courses taken by teachers. The other three proposals about which the board is sincere provide for a restriction in teacher political activity, a limit on the number of sick days that may be accumulated and a change in the current procedure concerning teachers who wish to transfer school assignments.

Although the latter three proposals may be couched in language far broader than what is actually sought, their intent is clear, and the board is committed to achieving at least some favorable changes in each. Additionally, it must be noted that the desired changes may not all be achieved in this year's negotiations; indeed, some issues are so entrenched on both sides that they will be subject to intense negotiation for many years. It is almost invariably true that an issue the employer feels strongly about will evoke similar passions on the opposite side of the table.

Separate consideration must be given to that category of employer proposals generally called the ''give back,'' wherein the employer is aggressively and seriously seeking a reduction in an existing benefit or contractual right. While it is true that unions do not readily agree to such proposals, they will do so when certain circumstances prevail. If the management can prove to the union's satisfaction that the continued viable existence of the employer is imperiled unless certain changes occur, often the union will accede to the request.

In the late 1970's, when the Chrysler Corporation was fighting off suppliers and banks and struggling to avoid bankruptcy, the United Auto Workers union was convinced that the situation warranted the union's negotiating away certain contractually mandated wage increases in an effort to keep the company alive. To be sure, the union sought and received certain promises in return for its concessions. The union president was elected to the company's board of directors, and employees were promised certain financial considerations should the company regain profitability.

Many governmental entities have also sought concessions from their unions in the face of reduced revenues and tax limitation legislation. In many cases, the unions have agreed to concessions—albeit rather reluctantly—in an effort to avoid massive layoffs of members.

The reluctance of a union to surrender a contractual right won at the bargaining table in return for employer promises of future benefits and job retention for its members is not hard to understand. Employees look to their unions to win benefits and salary increases, not to participate in reduction of existing benefits. Traditionally, the position of unions was clear: the employer must abide by the contract, and, if this meant layoffs, so be it. The union was confident that layoffs would be fewer in number and shorter in length than the dire prognostications of the employer, which was not especially to be trusted anyway. And, in a short while, when the employer's condition improved, all those working *and* those called back would work at the higher contract rate, not some lower figure the union had foolishly agreed to in a moment of employer-induced panic. Finally, the union would not have to renegotiate for already-won benefits at the next bargaining session.

Evidently, that scenario is rapidly changing, and unions are more willing to accept concessions than ever before. In part, it is due to employers' willingness to open their books, and the evolving labor law making it more difficult for a company claiming diminished financial capacity to keep its books closed to the union. In the public sector, where books and financial records, as part of the public trust, have traditionally been accessible, the well-publicized taxpayer revolts and tax-limitation legislation have made it clear to unions that, if widespread layoffs (reductions in force, or RIFs) are to be avoided, the union must agree to measures that reduce the cost of employment to the government.

As a final point of clarification, "give backs" must be distinguished from "buy backs," in which the employer often compensates employees in a lump sum for concessions made. Typical examples can be found in the newspaper industry, where there have been rapid and far-reaching technological changes in how a newspaper prints its editions. At some newspapers, the new technology has reduced the need for printing pressmen, and companies have bought certain rights the employees once held. For example, when a contract provided "manning schedules" which set the minimum number of employees for certain functions, newspaper management would pay each employee a one-time, lump-sum bonus in return for agreeing to abolish the schedules. In establishing many of management's proposals, one may assume that the "Las Vegas Mentality" is not in the sole purview of the union.

In sum, then, employers frequently approach the bargaining table with an agenda of their own, doing far more than simply saying no to a union's proposals. The most well known, and controversial, management strategy is called Boulwarism, after its founder, Lemuel R. Boulware, a General Electric official, and this is the next topic to be examined.

Boulwarism

To many observers and participants in the collective bargaining process, especially persons favoring management, the haggling, homesteading and posturing over terms of a new agreement can seem rather silly and time consuming. Why, they wonder, can't the whole process be approached more scientifically, more rationally and more like businesspeople than bazaar traders?

Additionally, and even more fundamentally, many management officials have often expressed despair over not only the way negotiations themselves proceed, but over the way in which negotiations are portrayed and perceived by employees, the community, opinion leaders and the general public. It always appears to them that the union *wins* concessions from the employer, and the universal conclusion is a feeling that the employer was being unreasonable or stingy, and that the union was justified in its demands and conduct up to and including a work stoppage. Succinctly phrased, then, if the union won, then the employer must have lost, and nobody enjoys losing.

As noted earlier, there are often underlying fundamental philosophic differences between union and management. In the private sector, many union leaders have expressed deep doubts about the essential equity of the capitalistic economic system and a belief in the greater equity of a socialistic system wherein employees own and/or control much or all means of production.

Lemuel R. Boulware was a vice president of General Electric Company, and had responsibilities in community and employee relations, two areas he came to see as closely and inextricably related. Alarmed with what he perceived to be an anticapitalist bias, not only on the part of the unions with which GE dealt, but among government officials and opinion leaders, he launched in the late 1940s and 1950s an integrated program that came to be named after him. After his retirement, he wrote a book called *The Truth About Boulwarism* (Bureau of National Affairs, 1969), in which he sought to provide an in-depth explanation of his program. It is accurate to describe Boulwarism as highly controversial, with staunch supporters and equally adamant detractors. In fairness to all, it must be noted that the term is often misused, as when a union official exclaims that a hard-bargaining management is engaging in ''Boulwaristic bargaining.'' There is, in fact, far more to Boulwarism than merely hard bargaining.

In his book and numerous speeches, Boulware was careful to explain himself as advocating a comprehensive system of employee and community relations that goes far beyond hard bargaining at the table with the union.

First, his approach was grounded in marketing concepts, such as determining consumer needs and satisfying them. Instead of selling a product, he was concerned with selling ideas to a number of "markets," some of which overlapped. He was concerned that a company meet fairly the needs of, not only its employees, who as a unionized group usually can most aggressively seek satisfaction, but also the shareholders, the customers and those in the community in which the company's facilities were located. He called this the "balanced-best-interests" approach. Boulware established a two-way communication network wherein the company could both ascertain employee needs and have those employees learn the company's needs as well as its efforts to meet employee needs.

Second, supervisors were given extensive training in better human relations, as well as a grounding in the fundamentals of the capitalist system, so that they could not only effectively satisfy employee needs but could also answer questions about shareholder dividends, company profits and government tax and regulation matters.

Third, and perhaps most noteworthy, instead of engaging in high/low bargaining, in which the employer would be pushed and pressured into making a fair offer to the union—which began by making exaggerated and overblown demands—Boulware advocated a radically different approach. The company would engage in extensive research to determine what wage increase it could afford, given the product market, productivity, improvement and a fair return to shareholders (the "balanced best interests" of all). Next, the company would determine by surveys what employees wanted and expected. Then, the company would formulate a fair package and present it to the union at the bargaining table, simultaneously conveying its offer and rationale directly to the employees as well as the community at large. The company then would not alter that offer unless it could be shown to be factually invalid. For example, if a seven-percent wage increase was deemed equitable, the company would present seven percent initially, ignoring the union's proposal of 14 percent, and simply hold to the seven-percent position instead of beginning at a zero-percent wage increase and ultimately meeting the union halfway at seven percent. Further, the company stated that neither a threatened nor an actual strike would alter its position.

Fourth, the company would seek support for its position among prominent members of the academic, religious, civic and business communities. Special attention was directed at the media, which Boulware felt had previously given undue and undeserved support to the union's position. He reversed the usual company posture of "no comment" and instead vigorously sought to convey the company's position and rationale to reporters, as well as taking out paid advertising in which the company would clearly and fully state its position.

An interesting part of General Electric Company's energetic community outreach program, and its staunch support of the capitalist system, was to choose as its public spokesman a motion picture actor with strong antisocialist tendencies. He had been president of the Screen Actors Guild, and vigorously opposed those he felt were communists or socialistically inclined in that union. The actor's name—Ronald Reagan. His efforts and speeches on behalf of the company and its procapitalist, antisocialist philosophy deepened his political consciousness and led him to a political career.

To say that unions opposed Boulwarism is putting it mildly. Boulware's name became an epithet, and his catch phrase, "trying to do right voluntarily," was parodied in numerous ways, most of which cannot be mentioned here. In his book, he listed the charges unions levied against Boulwarism:

> that we [Boulwarists] were trying to separate the members from their Union officials, that the offer had been made so good because the Union officials then could not get the members to strike for more: that both our statement that we did not regard strike threats as convincing and our implication that we would take a strike were unfair tactics; that we were "playing God" in all the talk about the balanced-best-interests (of customers, shareholders, etc.): that we could have offered lots more out of our "swollen" profits without having to raise prices; . . . that our new program was just a slick device to butter up employees and get a "speed up" which would yield still more unwarranted profits; that we were in a "capitalist plot against labor gains"; that we had no business talking over their heads to their members but should communicate only through them (Union officials); that we would wreck Unions if we could ever "get away with" the idea that we were both willing and trying to do right voluntarily.

Ultimately, Boulwarism and General Electric ended up before the United States Supreme Court, which upheld the Second Circuit's finding that Boulwarism was not compatible with the statutory duty to bargain in good faith. As often occurs in major labor law cases, the adjudication of Boulwarism took almost a decade of protracted litigation before the National Labor Relations Board, the Federal Court of Appeals, and, finally, the Supreme Court.

An NLRB trial examiner, after extensive hearings, found that General Electric had not bargained in good faith with the union, and, when the company appealed to the board itself, the NLRB agreed with all the examiner's findings.

The company appealed, and the Second Circuit Court of Appeals issued its split (2-to-1) decision, which basically sustained the NLRB's condemnation of Boulwarism. When the U.S. Supreme Court denied *certiorari*, in essence deciding not to decide, the Second Circuit's decision became the law of the land.

The Second Circuit's Judge Kaufman's decision thus represents the ultimate judicial determination on Boulwarism. His key findings are that the company negotiated

> to the greatest possible extent, by ignoring the legitimacy and relevance of the Union's position as statutory representative of its members. . . . The aim, in a word, was to deal with the Union through the employees, rather than with the employees through the Union. . . .

But Judge Kaufman was careful to delineate what the court was *not* condemning:

> We do not today hold that an employer may not communicate with his employees during negotiations. Nor are we deciding that the "best offer first" bargaining technique is forbidden. Moreover, we do not require an employer to engage in "auction bargaining" or . . . compel him to make concessions, "minor" or otherwise . . .

What the court did hold was that

> an employer may not so combine "take-it-or-leave-it" bargaining methods with a widely publicized stance of unbending firmness that he is himself unable to alter a position once taken. . . . Such conduct, we find, constitutes a refusal to bargain "in fact." . . . It also constitutes . . . an absence of subjective good faith, for it implies that the Company can deliberately bargain and communicate as though the Union did not exist, in clear derogation of the Union's status as exclusive representative its its members.

It appears then that, by examining the "totality of the circumstances," Boulwarism violated the law, although, perhaps, individual aspects of the company's conduct would not have violated the law. Yet, as noted earlier, Lemuel Boulware was most adamant in his depiction of Boulwarism as an integrated and interrelated campaign of activities, and so, perhaps, it is fair that it be judged on its totality and not on its several components.

Concurrent with this 1969 decision was a rather bitter 122-day strike against the company. Gradually, and somewhat reluctantly, General Electric appears to have abandoned its strict adherence to Lemuel Boulware's program, although the company still believes in two-way employee manager communication and a "rational" approach to bargaining, although it no longer pursues its one-firm-and-fair-offer policy.

In sum, then, the law has apparently condemned the integrated program of Boulwarism, but many employers practice at least certain of Lemuel Boulware's ideas. Beyond legal opinions, Boulwarism calls into question many basic tenets of the process of collective bargaining. In its research and in making but one offer to the union, it is alleged that a company engages in an act of unilateral determination no matter how scientific or enlightened. There is clearly no room for rituals, games or catharsis, those important elements of emotional satisfaction so necessary for a satisfactory conclusion of negotiation.

Boulwarism thus leads to a very fundamental controversy in collective bargaining. What is a "fair contract"? Some answer that a fair contract is one that both sides *perceive* as fair. This perception arises from the relationship between the parties and the negotiation of the agreement. If there is no such negotiation, then where will the perception of fairness come from? It should be remembered that unions initially arose to counter employer unilateralism; Boulwarism would appear to make unions largely superfluous if it prevailed. Thus, we return to the fundamental dilemma posed by Boulwarism: while the employer may be as fair as possible, this cannot be expected to satisfy unionized employees, who look to their union to compel the employer to act equitably. Put simply, if the employees believe their employer will do right voluntarily, they would have no reason to join and support unions, and there would be no need for collective bargaining and Boulwarism.

Others argue that, once employees choose a union, the employer should be fair and not seek to penalize them for unionizing. They argue that Boulwarism is an honorable way to deal with employees, whether unionized or not, and that it is grossly prejudicial to assume an employer cannot or will not be fair to its employees. Further, it is an unnecessary and unrealistic burden to place upon an employer in that, in addition to being fair to employees, the employer must put on a show with the union and wrangle endlessly in seeking to satisfy some amorphous psychological need of union members and their leaders. These advocates argue that not only will employers be fair, but society is stopping them from being fair and placing employers in a "no win, always lose" position.

In conclusion, it is clear that this controversy still rages despite decisions by the National Labor Relations Board and the federal courts, and will no doubt continue to rage. If it has not yet been resolved, surely this manual is not the place to attempt a resolution, and no such effort will be essayed.

Points to Ponder

Boulwarism appears to challenge the basic assumptions of collective bargaining. The NLRB and federal judges who considered the legality of Boulwarism have not had the benefit of the analytic tools now available. Having read this far, you are now able to bring to bear analytic tools to examine and analyze Boulwarism. You, the reader, may find it useful to ponder how those who passed judgment on Lemuel Boulware's approach to collective bargaining might or might not alter their opinions based on these and other current analytic tools.

Perhaps it would be helpful to consider the fundamentally bilateral nature of collective bargaining and the essentially unilateral nature of Boulwarism.

Participation and Democracy

"If we think them not enlightened enough to
exercise their control with a wholesome discretion,
the remedy is not to take it from them,
but to inform their discretion."

—THOMAS JEFFERSON

"So long as we remain a democracy,
the judgment of the people must prevail."

—SENIOR CIRCUIT JUDGE DAVID L. BAZELON
Science and Uncertainty: A Jurist's View

IN THIS SECTION we consider the important issues of participation and democracy in negotiation on both sides of the table.

Democracy in the Caucus: Union

Most unions tend to make caucus decisions in a democratic fashion, asking the opinions of various team members and often taking votes to determine the team position on a proposal. These discussions are usually spirited, to say the least, and cliques are formed of like-minded individuals. For example, on the issue of employer-provided work uniforms, not all team members are as concerned as Jack Marsh and Sue Kelly, two people who are expected to work in uniform on the maintenance crew and cafeteria staff, respectively. The other five on the committee see themselves as representing clerical and office workers, none of whom work in uniform. When the employer makes a proposal to institute an optical-care plan and states that in return the union should drop a number of proposals, including employer-provided uniforms, the team must engage in what we term internal bargaining to determine priorities and positions.

On this issue, Sue Kelly is adamant; this is *her* issue—this is what her coworkers at the cafeteria elected her to bargain for and she will not be dissuaded. To her, this is a strike issue, and she is willing to do anything to obtain this benefit. Unless the agreement contains employer-provided uniforms, she will oppose it, no matter how beneficial it might otherwise be. In short, she is a destabilizer (DS).

Jack Marsh views the uniform issue more flexibly. He would like free uniforms, but he is interested in other aspects of the agreement. To him, especially because of his three children, all of whom wear glasses, the optical plan is most appealing. He is inclined toward settlement; he is a stabilizer (S).

It is up to the chairperson of the negotiating committee, the union president, Carole Mann, to act as a harmonizer of these disparate interests. As a quasi-mediator (QM), she must consider what is best for all employees. She is committed to reaching the best possible agreement.

She might take many approaches to reach her goal. One is to examine the real concern of the destabilizer and seek accommodation. This process begins with a straightforward nonjudgmental inquiry. Mann asks both Kelly and Marsh to review the entire uniform issue, starting with current practice.

Marsh responds by saying that the employer pays an allowance of $10 per month for employees to clean their uniforms. He says that, given the dirty type of work they do in maintenance, frequent cleanings are needed, a sentiment Kelly echoes, citing numerous food spills in the cafeteria.

Kelly points out that, with current clothing prices and cleaning costs, $10 per month is ridiculously low and totally inadequate. She also says that she has done some research on the subject; Apex Uniform Company, a new concern eager for business, will provide uniforms and cleaning for only $35 per month per employee. Kelly adds that, when she sought to report this to Thomas Anderson, director of purchasing, he did not appear at all interested.

Now Mann can begin to develop parameters for potential settlement. If the employer is already paying $10 per month, and the cleaning bill would be $25 more per month for the 75 employees involved, it will cost $1,875 per month, or $22,500 per year more, to have cleaning provided. While this is by no means insignificant, given the size of the entire bargaining unit and the estimated cost of settlement, the cost for uniform cleaning is manageable.

Mann asks both Marsh and Kelly whether they can reasonably expect the employer to make such a large increase in benefits to all employees, such as an optical plan, as well as a 250-percent increase in uniform benefits. Marsh says, "I guess not. That's kind of expensive when you put it that way, and that optical plan sure seems nice."

Kelly says that the company can afford it, and more. She read in the paper that the company president gave $350,000 to his college, so why can't he give money to his own employees?

Mann is concerned lest Kelly launch an emotional diatribe against the company and its president. That would get the discussion off objective data and into emotional issues, which will only further becloud negotiation. She therefore begins the "what-if" process, a hypothetical testing of potential settlements.

"What if I proposed to the company that they take the Apex uniform plan and, for the first year of the contract, have the employees split the cost with the company, and, then, say, next year the employees pay only $10. How does that sound?"

Marsh says immediately that he would welcome any improvement. Whatever they can get would be acceptable. Kelly is not pleased, yet senses that others on the team are not terribly sympathetic to her position. When Dick Moore, who represents the largest group in the bargaining unit, says, "Sue, I know you have a legitimate concern, but, hell, we can't get everything at once," she accedes.

Before going back to the joint conference, Mann will carefully review the uniform proposal. "Okay, I'll ask the company to pay the full $35 per month for uniforms as an opening position. We know they'll never buy it, but we can come back with the company paying $25 and the employee paying $10 and then we can drop to a split of costs if we have to. Is everybody agreed?" At this point, Kelly concurs, knowing that the entire group would vote against her if she did not.

Ultimately, through the give and take of the bargaining table, the company offers to adopt the uniform plan and pay $15 per employee for the first year, and $17.50, half the cost, for the second year. The company's chief negotiator tells the union team across the table that he cannot and will not go any further on that issue.

In the union caucus, Kelly expresses her regret and disappointment at the company's proposal, but eventually accepts it, lacking team support for her position. Mann tells her, "You did your best for your people, Sue, you really did. The rest of the company's offer is very good, the best we've ever gotten. You can tell the cafeteria people you did your best. Listen, this bargaining process is like that—you don't always get what you want."

Note that, if Mann had taken an antagonistic tone, she would have encouraged Kelly to continue to oppose the proposed settlement. This would have put her in a position wherein if the proposed contract were accepted, she would have lost face.

In fact, the first-year settlement on the issue was below the bottom fall-back position of the union. This is not uncommon in bargaining.

Often, a party must give more and get less than anticipated. This can present problems in the ratification process, discussed next.

Employee Ratification

Union negotiation committees are either empowered or not empowered. If empowered, the committee may give the employer a binding commitment on acceptance of a contract. Most usually, the negotiation committee is not empowered and must present a proposed agreement to the membership for approval before it is binding.

Only in rare circumstances, such as a bitter and costly strike, is a committee empowered. In today's sociopolitical climate, union members expect to be given a voice in the negotiation process because it is their economic welfare and working conditions that are being determined. Gone are the autocratic days when a single individual, such as John L. Lewis of the United Mine Workers, could bind union members on his personal decision. The potentialities for poor judgment and corruption abound under such a one-man decision-making system. Today's better-educated employees will not readily accept that behavior. Indeed, union organizers often tell prospective members that theirs is a democratic union and promise employees they will never have to work under an agreement they are not given a chance to vote on.

Concomitant with the increase in employee demands for participation has come a rising number of contract rejection votes by irate members. There are many possible reasons for this increase, such as the "Las Vegas Mentality" mentioned earlier, caused by parties asking "for the moon" and then being disappointed and angry when the proposed contract is not all they hoped for, either because of the increased bargaining sophistication and intransigence of the other party and/or the proliferation of union dissident groups who urge rejection of the proposed agreement as a means to repudiate union administration and advance their own political ambitions. Some argue that, for certain employee groups, contract rejection may be their own means of venting deeply felt hostility toward employers *and* their jobs, and that no agreement could be generous enough to overcome these negative feelings. Still others contend that contract rejection is merely a successful ploy by both members and leaders to achieve an even better contract.

Be it a preconceived ploy or merely the way employees truly feel, the process works something like this: The union negotiation team tentatively accepts the agreement at the table and agrees to put it to a membership vote. If the majority of members accepts the agreement, the contract binds the union. If a majority rejects the agreement, the union is not bound. What occurs then is dependent upon the parties. If the employer is willing, negotiations may commence, attempting to find an agreement employees will find acceptable, and it will again be put up for a vote.

Sometimes, however, the employer may argue that the rejected offer was its best and there simply are no more concessions that will be made. The employer's fear is that, if more is offered, the union will never ratify an agreement the first time out. This will only add immeasurably to the difficulties of reaching agreement, for who will believe an employer who says, "This is my last, final and best offer," when it is later significantly improved in the face of a union rejection vote? If, as often occurs, a contract rejection is accompanied by a job action or strike, the pressure on the employer may be so intense that unanticipated concessions will be forced.

In an effort to avoid this kind of problem, some employer negotiators demand that the union negotiation team recommend membership ratification, although this does not always guarantee the result sought. As noted, sometimes union dissidents will oppose the tentative agreement in order to build political capital for themselves. Or, there may be some employees who do not fare as well as they would like, and so will oppose the agreement until they are assured their needs will be met.

In other situations, the union negotiation team may seek to use this as a lever to achieve additional concessions from the employer. Thus, they may say, "We won't accept or recommend this contract to our members unless we get two percent more on wages and a better dental-care plan."

Further complicating this situation is the possibility that, no matter what union leaders recommend, members will vote as *they* deem best. For example, one financially strapped school district set a final wage increase offer of four percent, a sum too low to satisfy the teacher union's leadership. The school board was adamant that union membership would accept it if put to a vote. To prove to the school board that it was wrong, union members were given a chance to vote. Surprisingly, they overwhelmingly accepted the agreement despite strong objections from their leaders. One can conclude that many members believed the school board's assertions that more money than what was offered would result in teacher layoffs and program cutbacks. Interestingly, union leadership, although surprised and repudiated, was not turned out at the next union election. Many members apparently wanted these leaders because they were hardworking and aggressive, but that did not mean that they would blindly follow them down a path to confrontation and possible job actions.

Conversely, often when the negotiating team recommends settlement, the members will vote down the proposed contract. The leadership's future is dependent upon what occurs next. If additional concessions are obtained, the leadership may redeem itself in the members' eyes or they may be seen as too passive, requiring the impetus of a membership vote to spur them to be more aggressive at the bargaining table. But if union leaders can obtain no additional concessions, they will likely be seen as too weak, and there will be pressure to replace them with leaders who will deal more forcefully with the employer.

Another possible scenario should be mentioned, that of a face-saving change in the contract, making it more palatable to members while not costing the employer any more than the previously rejected contract. For example, when union members voted down a proposed contract at Martin Products because the first day of deer-hunting season was not made a holiday, negotiators went back to the table and agreed that employees could, with advance notice to their supervisors, take that day off instead of, say, the employee's birthday, an in-place contract holiday.

Of course, it is not always possible to find such a ready adjustment that satisfies both sides when a proposed contract is rejected. Indeed, a negative ratification vote often causes increased bitterness between the parties.

Given this litany of problems attendant upon membership ratification votes, many raise the fundamental question, why have them? Surely, they argue, industrial relations would be far simpler and more efficient if all bargaining committees were empowered. An employer would know that, if the union negotiating team accepted an offer, it would be binding, with no escape clause and no additional demands. Under such circumstances, an employer could make its final offer its most attractive and not fear having to increase it under later pressure.

Finally, it is argued that most business deals are concrete when made and not subject to later alteration, and virtually all private sector employers are bound by table agreements. Public sector employers are not so bound, as has been described, and this has lead to numerous problems regarding uncertainty and politicking (the ''end run''), which are said to undermine the integrity of the process of collective bargaining. All this leads to the conclusion that ratification votes are both premaritally and philosophically wrong.

What then are the arguments in favor of membership ratification votes? First, there is the fundamental equity argument. If employees are to be bound by an agreement and are expected to live and work under an agreement, does not fairness demand they have at least some say in accepting or rejecting terms? After all, in a very real sense, it is their contract, not just the negotiators'.

Further, employees who have an opportunity to participate in the acceptance of an agreement will feel more committed to that agreement, and will be more inclined to obey its terms. This in turn provides for a better, more orderly climate of industrial relations, which is the goal of negotiations in the first place. There will be less resort to "street-and-field processes" if employees have some stake in the success of the contract. The way to give them that stake is to have them vote on the agreement.

Additionally, ratification votes afford employees protection against corruption and incompetence by union negotiators. The "sweetheart contract," an agreement more beneficial to the employer than employees due to some illegal payoffs, is made more difficult (if not rendered impossible) by having members vote on the proposed agreement. While it is sometimes alleged that full-time union negotiators may lose touch with the workplace, ratification votes provide some insurance that employee needs will be met and union officials will be compelled to stay attuned to employees' concerns.

One of the harshest criticisms of ratification votes is that members may make an uninformed, unintelligent emotional choice in placing their vote and, in so doing, may undo the careful and laborious efforts of both union and employer negotiators, who bargained the agreement over many hours. In response, an equally compelling line of argument is offered. First, if employees are uninformed about the agreement, it is the fault of union leaders and not the process. Union leaders should take steps to ensure that everyone knows *what* the terms of the proposed agreement are, and what they *mean*. Second, why shouldn't employees make an emotional choice on such a vital matter as their union contract when so many of their other choices, such as the choice of a spouse, purchase of a home or car, or the decision to vote for one political candidate over another, are at least tinged with emotion? And, finally, in making these and other important decisions, who shall judge what "sufficient knowledge" is? In national elections, we do not demand that voters be capable of distinguishing one candidate's economic views from another, or that they give a comprehensive discourse on Keynesian economics.

In sum, ratification votes are a permanent fixture on the industrial relations landscape, and it appears unlikely that they will disappear. As with many techniques, they have their defenders and detractors. It does seem clear that at least some of the more grievous problems can be avoided, or at least minimized, if steps are taken to ensure that employees are fully informed about a proposed contract.

Democracy in the Caucus: Employer

It may appear that there would not be too much democracy in a management caucus because neither business nor government is run by principles of participatory democracy, but such a view is both shortsighted and inaccurate.

In a small manufacturing company owned by the president, Jerry Jackson, he makes the final decision on negotiations with the union but cannot make an informed decision without consulting his production manager, financial manager and marketing director. Because he relies on these people in the day-to-day operations of his enterprise, he also wants their input while negotiating a contract with the union, and would ignore their advice at his peril. Thus, even if ultimate decision-making responsibility is on Jackson's shoulders alone, he would not make a decision without at the very least consulting these valued members of his staff. More likely, he would encourage their active participation in decision-making.

In a large corporate setting, the chief company spokesperson may be a vice president of industrial relations who enjoys considerable power and authority within the company. Nonetheless, he or she likely gets parameters for settlement from the executive committee of the board of directors. While there may be some flexibility within those parameters, authority is clearly not unbounded. Additionally, at the negotiating table, input from line operations would be necessary because of technical issues, such as appropriate staffing to run a particular piece of machinery. Certainly, input would also be appropriate from those with financial, legal and marketing expertise, especially if, as is often the case, the local situation possesses some unique elements. If there are unusual problems or contract provisions, a negotiator from central office would need the counsel of someone with a background in the particulars of the local situation.

Similar problems are presented when an employer uses the service of a "hired gun," often an attorney or negotiation consultant who may not possess a detailed operational background and is brought in to deal only with the current contract negotiations. While many such outsiders are highly skilled and extremely competent, unless they have been involved in prior negotiations, they will often lack a detailed operational background and have to rely on those with that information and experience in order to negotiate intelligently with the union.

Many local governmental entities, such as school, hospital and library boards, utilize hired negotiators as well as full-time staff to negotiate and administer agreements with employee representatives. Because many of these service-oriented organizations are operationally unique, the negotiator must understand intimately the operational side and, equally important, the legal environment in which the organization exists and negotiations occur. Often, each subdivision, city, county or state may operate under its own collective bargaining law, as well as having its own personnel rules and practices. Given this complexity, the negotiator ("hired gun") must consult in great detail with the negotiating committee, comprised as it is of individuals with extensive knowledge in the numerous areas so vital to successful negotiations.

In all of the above situations, for one reason or another, the chief spokesperson must use others effectively, and cannot make decisions on his or her own. This usually leads to at least some semblance of participatory democracy in the employer caucus room. Add to this the philosophic and sociocultural changes of the past decades, and one finds an increased unwillingness on the part of many high-level managers and administrators to let decisions be made for them. Put simply, today's better-educated executives will not easily tolerate unilateral decision-making by the chief negotiator; they demand participation. While it is still true that decision-making power and authority are more hierarchically assigned on the management side than on the union side, there is increasingly less of the dictatorial style of decision-making. Most likely, this trend will become more pronounced in the future.

On the management side of the table, the greatest participatory democracy is found in coalition or trade association bargaining, wherein a group of employers bands together to negotiate with either one large union or a group of unions. Although smaller employers often seek to negotiate together for greater bargaining power, size and financial strength vary considerably, and therein lies the problem.

Consider an association of 10 leather-tanning companies in one geographic area who negotiate with one large union representing all the production and maintenance employees at each company. While each company has much in common with its fellow association members, there are significant individual differences. Three companies, Alpha, Booth and Charm, are the largest and most secure financially; four are medium sized; and three are small and struggling. Additionally, all 10 are competitors, sharing many of the same customers.

The three big companies are able to afford the most generous settlement, and are concerned that there be no interruption of service, which would jeopardize their lucrative, long-term contracts with large glove manufacturers. The medium-sized enterprises are less capable of paying a large wage increase, and the three smallest companies are caught in the dilemma so common to financially insecure businesses. They can neither afford generous pay increases nor a strike, which would probably put them out of business.

When the union presents its wage and benefit package, the association splits three ways as indicated previously. How can this be resolved?

The association usually has a set policy for decision-making procedures in the event of a conflict of opinion. A vote is taken, and each member of the association votes either according to the number of employees or each has one vote regardless of size. Some associations provide that on nonlabor negotiation issues, such as administration of the organization, election of officers and the like, each member has one vote, but on labor negotiation issues, each member votes according to the number of employees on the payroll. Because Alpha has 350 employees, and Booth 250, the two alone can determine policy inasmuch as the entire association employs only 1,000 workers.

Interestingly, however, the wishes of all association members, even the very smallest, are often given full and serious consideration. The reason is not only the democratic impulse, but also a more pragmatic one. If the interest of the smallest members is constantly given short shrift, they will leave the organization and seek to bargain either individually or as a new, splinter association. This could undermine the larger associations by settling upon lower wage and benefit increases based on the smaller companies' limited financial ability. Smaller companies could underbid work and steal business from their larger competitors based upon lower labor costs. In the event of an association strike, the smaller nonmembers could still operate and might take valued customers from the bigger companies.

Thus, in a desire to keep the association together and continue to present a unified front to the union and avoid whipsawing, many employer associations are run rather democratically, with a great deal of negotiating taking place between and among the members.

Participation and Democracy

As discussed in the earlier section on Vertical Bargaining, each team must bargain with its own hierarchy, its constituencies and those whose interests they represent. Each team at the table must always maintain some level of communication with those in its "vertical" world, since the vertical hierarchy may be engaging in its own internal bargaining. Managing expectations is obviously crucial to having a proposed agreement accepted. Whenever an agreement is reflected, those acting negatively do so because their expectations are inconsistent with the proposed agreement.

Points to Ponder

Given the advantages to the employers of engaging in coordinated or association bargaining, why don't the three major auto manufacturers (General Motors, Ford and Chrysler) bargain together with the United Auto Workers Union, which represents the production and maintenance employees of all three companies? Would the UAW benefit, and if so, how? If not, why not? What about the manufacturers? Why or why not? And what would the effect be on the economy and/or society and on foreign trade and competition? What are the implications of the UAW members in Canada splitting from the UAW in the United States?

The Framework for Bargaining

"Come together right now."

—THE BEATLES
Come Together

IN THIS SECTION we examine the framework for bargaining, those statutory and administrative rules and procedures society has created to assist parties in resolving disputes by negotiation.

Meet-and-Confer: Precursor to Collective Bargaining in the Public Sector

We now examine employee relations wherein a group of employees chooses a representative to meet-and-confer with the employer on the employees' behalf. This interaction occurs usually under a statute in the public sector, and is often a precursor to collective bargaining, which will be discussed next. The final resolution under meet-and-confer is often one-sided, with the employer having final decision-making power.

Example: Arizona permits public employers to meet-and-confer with employees, but only if the employer so desires.

Typical statutes permitting meet-and-confer arrangements may preclude written agreements between parties. Usually the employee group may make a presentation before a legislative body, but that body has unilateral decision-making power.

These laws are generally viewed by unions in the public sector as being precursors of true collective bargaining, which involves bilateral determination of critical issues, such as wages, hours of work and conditions under which that work will be performed. Therefore, even though employee representatives are opposed to such laws on both philosophic and pragmatic grounds, they will support meet-and-confer laws as a temporary bridge between complete unilateralism and true bilateralism, collective bargaining.

Collective Bargaining: Making Promises

Collective bargaining is that process through which representatives of employees and management have an opportunity to exchange promises about their future relationship. Each side negotiates by giving up something in order to get something. In the early phases in a collective bargaining relationship, it is common to observe only the employee representative making demands. As the relationship matures, the employer representative may well make demands on employees for such items as longer hours or sharing some fringe-benefit costs, as noted elsewhere.

Collective bargaining differs from meet-and-confer in at least one very significant way: There is no commitment to agree under a meet-and-confer arrangement, while collective bargaining implicitly or explicitly provides for reaching a bilaterally agreed upon resolution. Under a typical meet-and-confer arrangement, the final decision-making power rests unilaterally with one side, the employer.

"R–U–I"

Every labor relations system in all sectors must make provisions to deal with three major subjects: representation (R) (who represents whom?), unfair labor practices (U) (what happens if a party does not follow the rules?), and impasse (what happens when the parties cannot resolve disputes through negotiations?). Under our private sector labor relations laws, the National Labor Relations Board (NLRB) is empowered to make decisions concerning representation and unfair labor practice matters; impasse resolution is left to the Federal Mediation and Conciliation Service's efforts. Various public sector arrangements often vary this pattern considerably.

Most, but not all, collective bargaining relationships are founded on a statutory base. When the negotiation process is superimposed on a labor–management sector (private, federal, state and local), it is referred to as collective bargaining. Collective refers to the employees as one group and negotiating through one representative. These collective bargaining laws usually detail who may bargain over what, where, when and how. Often, an administrative body is established to govern the conduct of collective bargaining. Most of these administrative bodies are modeled after the National Labor Relations Board, which exercises jurisdiction over private sector parties engaged in interstate commerce.

The process of collective bargaining is governed and controlled by many pressures external to the parties themselves. Society, speaking through the legislative, executive and judicial branches of government, has sought to define and shape the process of collective bargaining.

The National Labor Relations Board and other similar agencies in the private and public sector begin by defining the parties and proceed to supervise the process of collective bargaining. Thus, the determination of the appropriate bargaining unit, and which employees may be eligible to vote, are two important decisions such boards customarily make. The NLRB will then conduct the election, often paying close attention to the parties' conduct and statements during the campaign, and will decide upon the validity of any objections to the conduct of the election.

Once a bargaining agent has been certified as a result of the election (or through other board procedures), the parties must bargain "in good faith," the latter term the subject of endless attempts at board and judicial definition. Should one party not bargain in good faith, the board will entertain charges of an unfair labor practice. Since the Taft–Hartley Act of 1947, both employers and unions may be held guilty of committing such unfair labor practices by either party, such as restraining or coercing employees in the exercise of their statutorily granted rights.

Society engages in such regulatory actions because, as stated in the preface of the National Labor Relations Act of 1935:

> Experience has proved that protection by law of the right of employees to organize and bargain collectively safeguards commerce from injury, impairment, or interruption and promotes the flow of commerce by removing certain recognized sources of industrial strife and unrest, by encouraging practices fundamental to the friendly adjustment of industrial disputes arising out of differences as to wages, hours, or other working conditions, and by restoring equality of bargaining power between employers and employees.

Thus, it is clear that society, seeing great benefit in "friendly adjustment of industrial disputes," is not going to stop at merely setting public policy. It is going to take very definite steps to implement that policy. How this is accomplished will be more fully discussed in the sections following a discussion of impasse.

Definition: Collective Bargaining Contract

A collective bargaining contract is the medium through which the parties formalize and list their promises to each other in writing. They will usually provide a mechanism to ensure that the other side lives up to its promises—usually a grievance procedure terminating in binding arbitration, discussed in greater detail later.

The point to emphasize here is that, because the parties to a labor agreement have constant daily interaction, there must be some means or mechanism to achieve two objectives: one, reaching agreement, and, two, ensuring the other party's performance under that agreement. The first objective is usually achieved through extensive reliance on external pressures, most usually statutes, ordinances, and governmental assistance and/or support. The second objective is achieved with a greater reliance on internal pressures, by forces the parties themselves create and/or control, such as grievance arbitration, discussed later.

"Cutting a Deal"

Despite the rhetoric and publicly taken positions, each side has its range of acceptable settlements. For example, although the union may begin by proposing an 80¢-per-hour increase, it may realistically expect a settlement of between 35¢ and 45¢. Similarly, a company may begin at an offer of a five¢ per hour increase but realistically anticipate a settlement in the vicinity of 35¢ to 45¢ per hour.

It can be seen here that the bottom of the union's acceptable range of settlement overlaps with the top of the company's range of acceptable settlement. If the parties are able to communicate their true positions to one another, a mutually acceptable settlement is possible. (Later we will consider interpret communication, techniques and pitfalls.)

If, however, the parties are not able to communicate their true positions, or if there is no overlap, we may be at an impasse situation. For example, if the lowest the union will accept is a 40¢-per-hour increase, and the highest the company will pay is a 30¢-per-hour increase, the parties, no matter how good their communication skills, will be at an impasse.

Points to Ponder

As noted earlier, there is no federal law that mandates collective bargaining for employees of state and local governments. Each jurisdiction has been free to adopt whatever arrangements, if any, it deems appropriate for public employee collective bargaining rights and responsibilities. Consider your home state. Which government employees have the right to negotiate and what subjects are covered? You may wish to compare your findings with others to better understand the variation among jurisdictions.

The Continuum of Peacemaking Table Processes

*"Peace will come
(according to plan)."*

—MELANIE

IN THIS SECTION the "arsenal of peacemaking weapons" is explored and contrasted.

Impasse

An impasse occurs at that point in the collective bargaining process when either or both parties make the determination that no further progress toward reaching an agreement is possible. It must be noted that often one party believes that negotiations have reached an impasse while the other party may not. As Section 8(d) of the Taft–Hartley Act states, the obligation to bargain in good faith "does not compel either party to agree to a proposal or require the making of a concession." Thus, hard bargaining—taking and strongly adhering to one position—may not be acting in bad faith or creating an impasse per se.

As noted in the previous section, society, interested in stability, is vitally concerned that the parties reach contract settlement and thus will not let an impasse continue when the consequences to society of industrial strife are too severe. To end an impasse, society calls forth what has been termed "an arsenal of peacemaking weapons"; that is, a variety of dispute resolution techniques that will be utilized until the impasse is resolved and the parties have reached an agreement.

The "weapons" society calls forth may be placed on a continuum, with the variable being the increasing power of the neutral. At any one time in any one impasse, power may be viewed as being finite. This power comes from the parties themselves, and they usually guard it zealously from outside interference.

As the neutral's involvement increases, the procedures often become more formal as greater decision-making power flows from the parties to the neutral. In the sections that follow, we trace this progression from conciliation, in which the neutral's power is slightest and the procedures least formal, to interest arbitration, in which the power of the neutral is greatest and the procedures the most formal.

Historically, the usual way an impasse was broken was by one party overwhelming the other. The strike by the union or the lockout by the employer were the traditional weapons of industrial conflict. As society has increasingly come to view these weapons of conflict as unacceptable, however, most especially in the public sector (protective services, i.e., police and fire), greater emphasis has been placed upon peaceful dispute resolution. Simply put, these weapons of conflict are seen as too awesome to be used. The inventory of loss—not only to the disputants themselves but to society as a whole—is seen as too great.

As the economic and political pressures of the weapons of conflict build upon the disputants, their perceptions begin to alter, and one side may decide that what was previously unacceptable is now acceptable as an alternative to prolonging the conflict and bearing the costs of continued disagreement.

Conciliation and Mediation

Conciliation and mediation are somewhat similar and are considered "soft" approaches, because they involve low levels of outside pressure on the parties to resolve their dispute.

Conciliation consists of a neutral nonparty to the dispute lending his or her "good offices" to the parties by almost literally providing a neutral physical space for them to meet and resolve their differences. The conciliator takes a relatively active role in encouraging settlement but usually does not get deeply involved in the substantive issues between the parties. The conciliator is often a government official who may publicly admonish or warn the parties of possible dire consequences should they not resolve their dispute.

For example, the governor of a state where a certain employer is a major economic factor may well be concerned about the severe consequences a strike might cause. The governor, who might in fact have little or no legal power over such a dispute, may summon the disputants to his or her office and publicly urge them to settle for the good of all citizens. The governor may then offer them the executive conference room as a neutral site for their negotiation sessions. It would not be necessary for the governor to be present—and politically the governor may well not wish to do so.

In mediation, a neutral third party is more active in bringing the disputing parties from impasse toward agreement. Typically, a mediator, like a conciliator, lacks authority to impose a settlement upon the parties; he or she may only suggest compromise solutions and/or alternative approaches to resolving the issues at impasse. If the parties do not like the suggestions, they may reject them.

Mediation is initiated by one or both parties and/or by statute. Under various statutes, an impasse may be declared by one or both parties, and with such declaration the process of mediation may be automatically begun.

In mediation, there is a tight grouping of the disputing parties and each team has a formal leadership structure. The mediator may meet with the parties jointly or individually. Often, the mediator meets informally with one side during its caucus and determines the actual power and leadership structure, which may well differ from the formal Leadership structure. Indeed, often those with formal authority lack real power. A well-trained mediator learns to make this distinction and must act accordingly if mediation is to be effective.

Viewed analytically, mediation involves the introduction of a third party into the bilateral bargaining process. The mediator is a neutral non-party usually appointed by a government agency. The Federal Mediation and Conciliation Service makes trained full-time mediators available free of charge to private (and in some cases public) sector disputants pursuant to their federally created mandate to assist in the peaceful resolution of employment disputes. Carrying appointments as commissioners, these men and women are often able to open channels of communication and suggest ways the parties may have overlooked to resolve issues or may not have wished to put forth as an offer.

For example, when the privately owned Leisure Bus Company is negotiating with its employees, represented by the United Bus Driver Union, the parties reach an impasse. The company has offered a four-percent salary increase, but the union's proposal is for eight percent. A casual observer might quickly suggest that the parties split the difference and settle upon a six-percent increase, but who will put that figure on the table? If the bus company moves from four to six percent without any guarantee that the union will accept, the company may find itself at six percent while the union stays at eight percent, thus shifting the dynamic of negotiation to a settlement between six and eight percent, possibly at seven percent. Similarly, the union would not reduce its proposal unless it had some certainty the company would increase its offer.

Enter the mediator, who by virtue of his or her position as a neutral nonparty can reopen communication channels and explore settlement possibilities more freely than either side. To complete the above example, the mediator may propose the six-percent figure to each side separately in caucus and find each receptive. The company may tell the mediator it will go to six percent but not a penny more; the union may say it can accept six percent but not a penny less. The mediator thus has served as a communication conduit and assisted the parties in resolving their dispute.

Many state public employment boards, especially in the public sector for state and local disputes, are also empowered to make mediator appointments. Although most of the mediations are handled by full-time employees, it is not uncommon to have some ad hoc appointments due to the seasonal caseload variations. Typically, as each state's budget deadline approaches, the number of impasses increases, often overloading state mediation staffs. It is rare, but not unknown, for public employers and unions to be empowered by state law or local ordinance to mutually select and compensate their mediator.

Each mediator tends to have an individual style, which will be adapted to the situation at hand to better catalyze the parties out of impasse and toward settlement. A mediator may be very passive at one point, very active in making suggestions at another point, and his or her demeanor will vary, depending on the participants in their process and their particular needs.

Mediators do not issue public reports on the dispute, and, indeed, are often statutorily precluded from issuing written recommendations. This serves to emphasize that communications with a mediator are confidential and will not be disclosed to the other party unless that party so authorizes. The mediator must enjoy the trust of both sides if he or she is to function effectively, and that trust must be earned.

If one were to eavesdrop on the private caucus being held by the Gotham Teachers' Union negotiating committee, one might hear this:

Robert Grey: "I've been teaching in this system for 22 years, and I've never known a time when the school board would really be unreasonable. Oh, sure, they talk tough, but if we come back to them with a reasonable proposal, I'm certain they'll accept it. And we certainly don't want a strike!"

Stanley Black: "The hell with them! They have to learn some respect for teachers and the teaching profession! That Mr. James, he'll learn how important professional educators are—and how powerful we can be! I'd love to see his face when we close down the whole system!"

Mary Tyler: "Now calm down, Stanley. Let's look at this latest board offer. They've come back with a four-percent offer and we're at eight percent. Now, let's ask the mediator if the board would accept six percent. I think a six-percent settlement is reasonable, don't you Robert?"

(The mediator is called into the caucus room and Tyler, the team spokesperson, asks him what he thinks about a six-percent settlement.)

The mediator: "Well, I think it's a fair settlement, one you can live with, one your committee can take to your members in good faith."

Stanley Black: "Only six percent! We're worth much more than that! I think..."

The mediator: "Yes, I'm sure you're all worth more than that. I'm worth more than I'm paid, too, but unfortunately ours is not a perfect world. Speaking realistically, I believe that six percent is the best you can do, given this school board and its posture. I believe they will go for six percent and I'll go over to them right now and see."

Note here how the mediator is seeking quickly and decisively to diffuse the destabilizer, Stanley Black, and is concerned with obtaining stability— and a settlement.

It must be emphasized here that mediators instinctively will support the efforts of quasi-mediators and stabilizers in undercutting destabilizers. Those who see mediators as simply genial messengers, shuffling from caucus room to caucus room, blandly conveying offers and gently proffering suggestions, are wrong. A good mediator is all of the foregoing and more a catalyst in generating settlements, though that catalytic action may be taken in any number of postures.

Numerous uninformed, naive observers of the process have written glowingly of "win-win" negotiations, wherein each side emerges with a victory. While this is certainly a laudable goal, practically speaking it is clearly not what collective bargaining is about. Mediators are settlement oriented and their definition of "victory" is a settlement, the same goal as the stabilizers and, with certain conditions as discussed earlier, as the quasi-mediators. Destabilizers on either side will oppose settlement, and, when one is reached, their goal is obviously not achieved. Thus, collective bargaining that is successful will result in a win-lose/win-lose settlement, which is depicted in Chart 15.

Mediator *avec Baguette*

While most mediators are neutral and bring only limited authority to the table, such as that of the federal or state government that appointed them, there is a special class of mediators we denominate as mediators

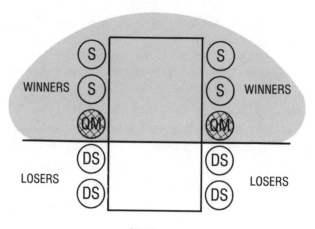

CHART 15

avec baguette. This phrase refers to both a style of gem as well as the French word for a style of bread. Put simply, the mediator brings something additional, and that something is often crucial.

When the Gotham Symphony Orchestra Musicians' Union strikes the symphony management, the issue is money. The symphony musicians are seeking a 10-percent wage increase, which they can demonstrate will put them in parity with comparable orchestras in cities of similar size. While the management does not deny that the musicians are certainly entitled to a significant pay raise, though perhaps not 10 percent, the problem is that the symphony has lost money consistently over the past few years and last year registered a deficit of $65,000. The management estimates that to eradicate the deficit and fund the pay increase will require $135,000 over and above all predictable revenue sources, subsidies and grants.

During the fifth week of the strike, which has already resulted in cancellation of eight concerts and put the entire season in jeopardy, Gotham Mayor Richard Ayres enters the picture. He is concerned that the city will lose a valuable cultural resource, which will harm the progressive image the mayor has sought to promote. He persuades Reginald Sanders III, scion of the city's leading family and chairman of the board of Sanders Products, Inc, the area's largest manufacturer, to assist in the settlement.

When Sanders enters as a mediator, it is with the permission of both sides. Everyone knows who Sanders is and what he represents in terms of wealth and prestige. As a businessman, he makes no pretense of neutrality or objectivity; he emphasizes his concern that the symphony play again and as soon as possible. He is able to convince the musicians to drop their demands so that the total cost of eradicating the deficit and giving the musicians a 6½-percent pay increase will cost $94,500. He then tells the symphony management that he will guarantee that, within four months, there will be a check for that amount delivered to the symphony's chairman.

Having achieved a settlement, Sanders then holds a series of private fund-raising dinners in his home, and many of his wealthy family, friends and associates contribute significant sums of money. Sanders has also promised to personally match any pledge over $500. On the agreed-upon date, Sanders is able to present a check for the necessary amount.

Note that this settlement was achieved by the intervention of a mediator with money, prestige, power, position and influence of his own. It is these latter factors that distinguish the mediator *avec baguette* from others.

Fact-finding, Advisory Arbitration and Special Masters

These are three terms whose distinctions are vastly outweighed by their similarities and, thus, will be considered as one. Generally, in the public sector, if mediation has not resolved an impasse, fact-finding will next be utilized to resolve any open issues. After mediation, there is often a winnowing of issues and a noticeable movement of the parties' positions on issues not resolved, setting the stage for the entrance of the fact-finder.

When the fact-finder enters the dispute, most underground communication between the parties has ceased with the dissolution of the main channel of communications, the bargaining process.

Fact-finding may be defined as the investigation of a dispute by a board, panel or individual, usually under the aegis of a government agency. Generally, if there is a board or panel (called tripartite) it will be chaired by a neutral. Often, there will be known advocates named to such a board or panel to provide informational resources to the neutral in addition to the data conveyed through actual fact-finding sessions. Some neutrals prefer to sit alone as fact-finder without advocate panel members, because it makes the process move more expeditiously. Other neutrals prefer to actively utilize the advocate panel members in assisting both in the fact-finding process and in any mediation that may occur.

Usually, a fact-finder will issue a report on the matters in dispute with recommended solutions. The fact-finder's recommendations are advisory only and do not bind either side. It is believed that the recommendations of a neutral will carry great weight with the disputants and cause them to reevaluate their respective positions under the glare of public pressure. It is indeed difficult for a party to maintain that its position is reasonable when a neutral has recommended otherwise.

In fact-finding, perhaps as nowhere else, there is a meeting of society's goal of peaceful dispute resolution and reliance upon the pressure of public opinion to assist in the resolution process. As Professor Tim Bornstein has pointed out, the fact-finder's report may provide some face-saving possibilities by allowing a party to gracefully move off an untenable position by hiding behind the recommendations made by the neutral. Also, the fact-finder, usually a skilled neutral, may be so "right" and "fair" in his or her recommendations that both sides see the light and choose to break the impasse by agreeing to the recommendations.

The term fact-finding is often said to be something of a misnomer because there are often strenuous disputes over what the "facts" in a dispute are. The union may present factual evidence clearly demonstrating that employees are underpaid for the work they do in their geographical location. The employer may present equally compelling "factual" argumentation demonstrating rather clearly that there is not enough revenue to maintain the current roster of employees and meet all their attendant fringe-benefit costs.

How then does a fact-finder make determinations as to what the recommendations shall be? The approach most fact-finders take is to avoid determining what the most factually accurate settlement would be. Rather, most take the approach of seeking equity under all relevant circumstances, giving due weight to such factors as the change in the cost of living, what comparable jurisdictions are paying for work similar to that done by the employees under consideration, and what the fiscal position of the employer is.

Often, many fact-finders will, with the parties' permission and cooperation, attempt mediation, believing that their primary mission is to resolve the dispute, not hear evidence and issue recommendations. Indeed, mediation will often precede and follow the formal process of fact-finding. Thus, experienced fact-finders will often successfully utilize their reported recommendations as a basis for further mediatory efforts.

Interest Arbitration

If the dispute has not been resolved through mediation and/or fact-finding and the controversy may have significant societal consequences, interest arbitration may be imposed by statute or adopted by the disputants voluntarily.

Interest arbitration is defined as a neutral (or panel), after hearing and weighing evidence and arguments by the disputing parties, issuing a decision resolving the open issues. The decision is binding on the parties and sets forth what the terms of the contract shall be.

For example, in New York state, if an impasse over new contract terms involving police or fire employees has not been resolved by mediation and/or fact-finding, a neutral, acting as an interest arbitrator, will determine what the terms shall be.

Interest arbitration may also be utilized voluntarily by disputants. The United Steelworkers of America and the large steel companies chose to agree contractually to utilize interest arbitration should their collective negotiations reach impasse. This private sector precedent-setting "experimental negotiating agreement" grew out of a realization by both parties that an impasse between them was too destructive and could create a high inventory of potential mutual loss. The threat of a strike or lockout was severe enough to drive steel customers to stockpile and/or make long-term purchase agreements with foreign steel companies, the result being that, even if there were no strike, many employees were laid off and the domestic steel companies lost enormous sums of money. Thus, it was seen by both sides to be in their own best interests to surrender their weapons of conflict and provide a mechanism for dispute resolution. Interestingly, perhaps because of their reluctance to use interest arbitration, these parties twice reached agreement on all issues through collective bargaining and never resorted to interest arbitration. The parties later agreed in negotiations not to continue this approach.

A question worth asking is why is there a reluctance to use interest arbitration? Americans have always wanted to "cut their own deals," that is, determine their contractual terms themselves. Perhaps it is a feeling that the disputants themselves are in the best position to know what terms will satisfy their own needs. Perhaps it is a distrust and dislike of "outsiders" imposing their judgments upon the parties. Or perhaps it is the dislike and fear of surrendering the traditional weapons of conflict.

The strike and the lockout are weapons whose utilization determines bargaining power, and traditionally the stronger party, the one that could outlast the other, was the winner. In the private sector, we see corporations with enormous assets pitted against large unions with substantial strike funds. The parties are not able to maintain indefinitely a power equilibrium. Perhaps the shareholders or customers of the employer bring forth irresistible pressure to settle, i.e., pay the increase the union requested. Or perhaps the families of striking employees feel the economic crunch when savings become depleted and the strike-fund balance is critically low. As Professor George Taylor noted, economic power provides the final arbitrament in most disputes.

When interest arbitration is utilized, bargaining power on both sides is minimized and its sway vastly reduced. The disputants do not persuade one another by economic pressure, but persuade an outsider, a neutral, by reason of their logically sound arguments and evidence.

Therefore, disputants used to settling conflict by superior strength must now utilize an entirely different approach, one in which the rules and results are vastly transformed. Perhaps this unfamiliarity explains its less frequent voluntary use.

Many public managers and politicians have also opposed the use of interest arbitration because they believe that the arbitrator, someone not elected to public office, is by his or her binding decision usurping the legislative authority and responsibility of the city or county council in establishing wages and benefits of government employees and, in effect, raising tax rates because the new, higher contract must be financed by increased revenue. In addition, these critics argue that the standards utilized by interest arbitrators in formulating their awards are often unclean, sometimes unrealistic, and sometimes simply wrong.

Others counter that interest arbitration is preferable to street-and-field processes such as strikes, slowdowns, or sickouts by essential government employees, and provides a finality to potentially harmful disputes. They conclude by noting that, if legislators and politicians are so concerned that their powers and prerogatives not be usurped by an outside neutral, they may avoid interest arbitration simply by engaging in good faith negotiations with the duly selected employee representative, and, in so doing, reach an agreement by utilizing their lawful powers at the negotiating table.

"Last Best Offer" Interest Arbitration

Given the parties' trepidation about giving the arbitrator too much power, the parties (and legislatures) have sought ways of reducing the arbitrator's discretion. One of the most interesting means of achieving this is through a process called "final offer" arbitration or "last best offer" arbitration. Definition: The interest arbitrator must accept the position of one party or the other; he or she is not free to make a decision that is a compromise or a combination of the parties' positions. The arbitrator must choose among the final positions of the disputants.

For example, in a dispute at impasse, the key issue was the salary schedule: the union sought an eight-percent pay increase and the employer offered four percent. These were the parties' final positions. The arbitrator had to select either four percent or eight percent; he was not free to compromise and decide upon six percent.

There are two well-known types of "last best offer" interest arbitrations in use today, especially in the public sector. The first is "item by item," wherein the arbitrator hears the arguments and decides on each item individually by selecting one side's position. In "total package," the arbitrator must choose between the positions of the parties on all items together; that is, decide to accept the final position of either the union or the employer based upon his or her judgment of the merits of each party's package.

This concept is founded upon a mixture of distrust of an outsider's unvarnished judgment and dislike of having a settlement imposed with little say over its content, added to the disdain of many neutrals to "cutting the baby in half," or compromising in an effort to find favor with each party. Perhaps there is also the feeling that the parties themselves will be more moderate, more realistic in their positions, if they know the other side is going to be equally pressured. If a party adopts too extreme a position, they realize that no neutral will select it, nor can the neutral temper it in a compromising effort.

Final offer arbitration is a means of resolving disputes, and the different forms that have emerged are indications of both the ingenuity of the parties and neutrals, as well as an effort to make the process of collective bargaining flow more smoothly. One can be certain that other innovative forms of dispute resolution will emerge in the future. One such example is med–arb, which will be discussed shortly.

Those who follow professional baseball will no doubt be familiar with a form of *last best offer interest arbitration* simply called "salary arbitration." The team owners and the union representing the players both realize that a major league career is a short-term commodity because of the enormous physical demands of training, playing and traveling. While it is true that a player dissatisfied with his team's salary offer may always elect to sit the season out, both he and his team suffer. For the player whose total longevity in the major leagues may only be six years, one lost year represents a significant portion of his entire career. For the team and its owners, the unavailability of a particular player may well hurt the team's overall performance for, after all, one key hit or defensive play can alter the outcome of a crucial game.

Therefore, it is in the interests of both parties to have a workable, *time-sensitive dispute resolution mechanism* available. There is only one issue, salary for the coming season, and each side presents its *last best offer* from which the jointly-selected arbitrator must pick one. This system avoids the extreme positions that may emerge during a heated dispute when the parties are "miles apart," because the arbitrator will select the most reasonable of the two figures, given salaries paid comparable players. Frequently, by the morning of the arbitration hearing, the parties realize how close their positions have become and negotiate a compromise settlement figure. This, then, is another illustration of the influence of the imminence of an arbitration hearing serving to bring closure to a dispute. Should negotiations fail, the interest arbitrator is of course available to bring closure by adjudication.

The "Hard" Approaches

In certain disputes in which the national defense, health or safety is jeopardized, the labor dispute may be subject to what is termed the truly "hard" approaches, wherein the remedy utilized is extremely severe and unusually hard on one or both sides.

The United Mine Workers Union, while led by John L. Lewis during the turbulent 1940s, demonstrated all the possibilities—and pitfalls—of these hard approaches. A judge may issue an injunction enjoining the strikers and their leaders under penalty of fines and even imprisonment if they fail to return to work. Even if the penalties are imposed, historically they have not compelled employees back to work. Lewis was personally fined $10,000 and his union fined $3,500,000 in 1946, but observers noted that the miners did not return to work until Lewis believed he had a satisfactory contract.

There is the possibility of government seizing the private employer's facilities and declaring it public property, and drafting employees into working, but while this is of dubious constitutionality, it is, more significantly, of little long-term effect. To put the matter simply, employees will generally not work unless they and their leaders believe they should; if they do not so decide, injunctions and imprecations are of little avail. This observation is most acutely relevant in the public sector, where employees generally lack the right to strike legally; indeed, for police and firefighters, no jurisdiction permits a legal strike. The customary effect of an injunction is only to raise the level of martyrdom among strike leaders. Imprisonment and fines only exacerbate the already hostile situation and actually create additional barriers to settlement.

This is not to condone illegal actions or to encourage flaunting of the law and judicial authority; rather, it is an acknowledgment of the realities of the behavior of unions and their members. For many, it appears that the right to withhold their services is perceived as a basic right, one which is seen as superior to other demands of law. It appears true, as has been observed, that injunctions or court orders do not end strikes. Employees do, and until and unless the employees are so inclined, much of the injunctive relief sought appears futile.

This is not to deny the persuasive pressure such action contains. Sometimes, striking employees may decide their interests are best served by obeying the court decree and returning to work, or perhaps the outstanding threat of a fine and/or imprisonment may convince the members that the dispute cannot be won by continuing their illegal action.

The fundamental point thus remains that the best means of resolving a dispute is to provide the disputants themselves with an opportunity to resolve the controversy. Strikes and injunctions may be successfully utilized as bargaining ploys but they do not—and cannot—replace negotiating as the preferred means of dispute resolution. It appears axiomatic that the more a settlement con.es from within, the greater its suitability to meeting the parties' needs and the greater their commitment to it. Conversely, the more an externally generated settlement is imposed upon the parties, the less suitable and the lower their commitment to it.

Thus, while some people dislike interest arbitration because they feel the settlement is being imposed upon the parties from "outside," they can also see that the potential loss to society is so great in a police or fightfighter strike that some alternative is needed. It is for reasons such as these that "med–arb," discussed next, has generated many supporters.

Med–Arb

Perhaps it was inevitable that someone would come up with a new approach to dispute resolution. Sam and John Kagel, experienced West Coast neutrals, are credited with combining some of the salient elements of arbitration with mediation, resulting in "med–arb."

In med–arb, the parties must repose great confidence in the neutral for they are endowing him or her with great power and flexibility. Under med–arb, the neutral first acts as a mediator, clarifying issues, suggesting solutions, catalyzing the parties in the impasse on as many issues as possible; then, acting as an arbitrator, he or she makes binding decisions on those issues remaining open. Obviously, with this potential power, the parties pay close attention to the mediator's suggestions, because his or her recommendations may well become the binding decision of the arbitrator.

For example, in a dispute between nurses and hospital administrators involving many issues, Sam Kagel first persuaded the parties to sign a binding agreement renouncing the use of the strike and lockout. The parties also agreed to accept and be bound by his decision as arbitrator on any issues unresolved by his mediation efforts. At the time this agreement was signed, there were some 40-plus open issues. Mediation was able to resolve all but four issues. On these four, Kagel issued a binding arbitration decision, thus completely resolving the dispute. It is interesting to note that the area of disagreement had been so narrowed that, even on the four open issues, the parties' final positions were not so far apart.

Med–arb is successful in large measure because of the element of voluntarism on the part of the disputants. Because they are selecting the neutral, agreeing to the ground rules and participating actively in mediation, they are in many ways fashioning their own settlement. This gives the parties input into the terms they are to work under, and it gives them a stake in the success of the med–arb process and in the continued success of the contract that results from this process. This is important because the parties must live together and interact constantly under their negotiated agreement.

The Power Pie

Chart 16 is a schematic representation of the effects of intervention by a neutral upon the power of the disputants.

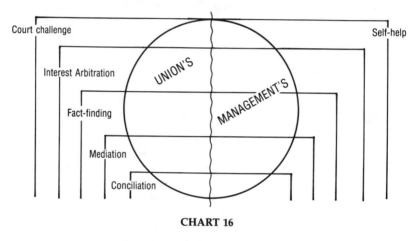

CHART 16

This schematic figure assumes that power between the parties is, at any one time, finite. As the outside neutral gains more power, there is increasingly less power in the hands of the disputants themselves. Also note that the scope of decision-making power of a neutral increases dramatically from the procedural (arranging a meeting as a conciliator) to the very substantive (deciding the size of a wage increase as an interest arbitrator). It is not, therefore, surprising that the level of disputants' resistance to neutral intervention increases concomitantly with enhanced power granted the neutral, because power is being yielded by the disputants to the third-party neutral.

Points to Ponder

On more than one occasion recently, the authors have heard the following unsolicited approach suggested for reaching satisfactory labor–management agreements. This unattributed quote is typical of the high-tech approach: ''Here we are, over 50 years after the passage of the National Labor Relations Act, and we're still bargaining in the same way today we did back then! Why don't we have bargaining by computers?

It would be faster, cheaper and better all around. Each side would feed its data into the computer, which would digest and analyze the data and then print out a binding decision. There wouldn't be strikes, I bet, and everyone would be happy."

In fact, we do not have computers making decisions in contract negotiations. Why not? What are the strengths and benefits of the current system of negotiating? Would computer decisions be acceptable to labor and management? Why or why not? To discuss this question intelligently, it is not necessary to have any advanced knowledge of computers. Focus, rather, on how the negotiation process works.

Table Manners

---

*"You've got to
know when to hold them,
know when to fold them...."*

—KENNY ROGERS
The Gambler

"Time is on my side."

—THE ROLLING STONES

IN THIS SECTION we examine what actually occurs once the parties are physically at the table. This is, of necessity, a general description and there may be variations. Nonetheless, most parties tend to follow the pattern discussed.

Ground Rules

Usually the first matters discussed are those pertaining to establishing ground rules for conducting negotiation sessions. If the parties have bargained with one another previously, this area will generally not require much discussion. However, if the parties are new to the process, such as those involved in a first contract, or if there was a strike or lockout during the negotiations for the prior contract, the parties may devote much of their early energies to this task.

Location

Many parties prefer a neutral site, such as a hotel or motel, because even though there is a rental charge involved (which is usually evenly shared), neither side will enjoy a "home court advantage."

Other negotiators do not seem as concerned with the location, and, in those instances, usually the employer provides facilities free of charge.

Most school negotiations, for example, occur on board of education property. Sometimes, once the parties reach an impasse, negotiations are moved to a neutral site. It is relatively rare to conduct negotiations on union property, though it has occurred.

Whatever the location selected, it should contain appropriate space to accommodate both teams and allow for at least one smaller room for use as a caucus room. The arrangements often have one large room for joint use and two smaller rooms for the use of the teams.

Access is important, but easy to overlook. If a government or office building is utilized, there may be limited access after normal business hours, and this may present great difficulties to negotiators who may need to come and go in the late evening and early morning hours. This is one reason why hotels and motels are used. Not only are they accessible at all hours, but they can provide food and beverage service as needed, again at off hours. And, finally, it is not uncommon for some negotiators, after a particularly lengthy session at the table, to take advantage of a hotel's sleeping accommodations to avoid a lengthy trip home, or to be fresh for resumption of negotiations at an early hour.

Seating

Generally, the parties are seated across from one another, with the team spokespersons directly across from each other. Sometimes, the spokespersons will sit at the head of their side of the table. Others prefer to sit in the middle, flanked by their aides.

The reason a team chooses to sit together is not only ideological or philosophical (demonstrating team solidarity), but also practical. Information may be more easily transmitted either verbally or in writing if all are seated on the same side. Recently, some parties are beginning to experiment with some success with no table, since the table, a physical barrier, is also sometimes viewed as a psychological barrier between the parties.

Confidentiality

Another concern of the parties is confidentiality of negotiations and news leaks. Not infrequently, negotiations may be of great interest to those in the community, and the media may avidly seek any information available. As noted earlier in our discussion of sunshine bargaining, often the media may distort the actual position of a party, or one spokesperson may make a public pronouncement he or she may later regret. Additionally, the parties at the table need to develop a relationship that must include some degree of rapport and trust. This is often quite fragile, and can be easily shattered if the media becomes involved. Usually, both parties will agree not to "negotiate in the press," and will give out only bland, general comments, such as, "We plan to meet again in two days and we're hopeful a settlement can be reached soon."

The horizontal negotiation process, as discussed earlier, is the most visible bargaining configuration and perhaps the most subject to leaks and distortions of statements and positions. Often, "trial balloons" (discussed later) are floated and possible settlements are discussed. In such a fluid process, it is vital that those at the table enjoy some rhetorical leeway so that they may more fully explore the issues and better determine where the other side's real priorities are.

For example, during negotiations at the Rawson Manufacturing Company in Ohio, Howard Rawson, company president and principal stockholder, mentions that he has been contacted by the Sunnyside Chamber of Commerce in Arizona and that they are most eager to have his plant moved there. This is a ploy by Rawson to convince the union that it should moderate its demands. In reality, as a lifelong resident of the Ohio town in which the plant is located, Rawson has no serious intention of relocating. When the confidentiality agreed to by the parties is breached by a member of the union negotiating committee, who mentions Rawson's remarks to a reporter for the town paper, unnecessary tension and anxiety may be created not only among all levels of company employees, but in the entire community, and some real barriers to an amicable and expeditious settlement may be created. It is therefore for rather good reasons that the parties agree to, and make real efforts to, maintain confidentiality during the negotiation process.

Inevitably, there may be leaks and rumors about the negotiations anyway, but they can perhaps be minimized if both parties stick to their agreement. As noted earlier, each team is in contact with its constituencies and, obviously, the more people who are involved, the greater the likelihood of a leak. For example, the Gotham teachers may have a special phone line established that any member may call to receive a recorded message about the current status of negotiations. Clearly, there is nothing to prevent an enterprising reporter from learning the number and calling to receive the message. Similarly, the Gotham schoolboard may issue and circulate to its many managerial and administrative people a confidential memorandum on the status of the negotiations. In these days of "xerox journalism," it is not difficult for an enterprising reporter to obtain a copy of such a memo. While it may be impossible to completely avoid leaks, if both parties are properly attentive to their communication with their constituencies, the damage may be greatly minimized.

Empowerment

It must be made clear at the outset of negotiations what authority each side possesses. This will not only avoid serious misunderstandings that can cause deeply negative feelings, but will focus the efforts of negotiators more equitably. As noted earlier, in the private sector, when negotiations were rather new, few employer representatives were empowered to make a binding commitment on an agreement reached at the bargaining table. Most union teams, conversely, were so empowered. Over the years, this situation has dramatically reversed itself, so that today it is the employer advocates who are empowered to make a binding commitment and the union negotiators who must submit the tentative agreement to a membership vote. This rise in the prevalence of membership ratification votes is a result of the democratization of both the labor movement and our entire society. Many unions tell prospective members during organizing campaigns that, if they vote to become unionized, they will never have to work under an agreement they did not, as a group, approve.

In the public sector, not only do the unions have membership ratification votes, but employer negotiators must seek approval of tentative agreements before they are legally binding. As discussed in the section titled "Clarity of Parties," many public employers, such as school boards, are not self-funding but must go to some legislative body to get money to pay for any contractual agreements made with a union or employee association. Thus, in sum, in the public sector especially, empowerment is very much alive as an issue that must be clearly understood by both parties before they commence bargaining over substantive matters.

Time Schedules and Frequency of Sessions

Concerning scheduling of sessions, time limits may be established, such as sessions to commence at 10 A.M. and end by 4 P.M., unless otherwise agreed. Usually, the length of the sessions will increase as the date of contract expiration draws closer and the pace of negotiations increases.

Many experienced negotiators note that a majority of the important issues get resolved in the last critical hours before a strike deadline, when each party is faced with the reality of an interruption of production or service and hard choices must be made. By contrast, in the federal sector, where strikes and lockouts are illegal, there is not the intense pressure of a deadline and so, not surprisingly, negotiations can and do drag on month after month. Observers note that there is little reason to make a concession here, and it is more attrition than bargaining power that triumphs.

In state and local government negotiations, where strikes are generally unlawful, the impetus to settle comes from the proximity of budget submission dates. In many jurisdictions, once a budget is officially submitted, it may not be increased, only reduced by legislators and the executive branch. This means that the union in question must reach a settlement before the budget is submitted, or else it must live for the next year with, perhaps, no wage increase. Similarly, as noted earlier, interest arbitration may be statutorily mandated if agreement is not reached by a certain date, and, given that most parties dislike that resolution process, they may reach a negotiated agreement shortly before the interest arbitrator arrives.

Topic Agenda

Once the parties have dealt with all the issues discussed above, they are ready to begin to bridge the gap between purely procedural and substantive matters. The bridge is the topic agenda, that is, what subjects will be negotiated and in what order or sequence.

As discussed in the section "Scope of Bargaining," the subjects of bargaining—mandatory, permissive and prohibited—vary according to the law applicable to the parties at the table. Within the mandatory and permissive subject areas, much leeway exists for the parties to decide what they believe best meets their needs, and most parties, in all sectors, have been both creative and pragmatic in fashioning their agreements.

The union usually begins by making its proposal to the employer, which customarily takes a caucus to digest the union's opening position. The employer then puts its initial package on the table, and, as discussed earlier, this can range from the purely defensive negative response to a creative package of its own proposals. By their opening salvos, the parties customarily thus define the topics to be negotiated, and very rarely will either side make a proposal or counterproposal on a subject not initially discussed. To do so would be a sign of bad faith and might even constitute an unfair labor practice in certain situations. The reason it is not done is more than legal, however; it goes to the heart of the parties' earnest efforts to resolve their differences by an exchange of promises. When a party is considering whether to make a change in position, many factors are weighed in the balance, but all of them are at least *terra cognita*, known subjects. If a new unknown element is added, it may necessitate total reassessment of all positions, which is both time consuming and counterproductive to reaching an agreement. The parties want to narrow the gaps, not increase them.

This leads to the realistic question of which proposals should be discussed in what order. Usually, less important topics are negotiated first. To better create a climate of compromise and agreement, emotional and critical subjects are delayed. Money is usually the key topic and, as such, is negotiated last. To be sure, money and other important issues are discussed early and often, but emphasis on resolving the dispute is delayed until other, less important matters have been handled and the timing, relationship and atmosphere are more appropriate.

Momentum

Each negotiation has its own rhythm, pace, texture and momentum. While no two are identical, some elements are common to all. The rhythm and momentum, the pace of give and take, vary not only from one negotiation to another, but from one session to another and even within one session. Often, neither side is willing to make a move for fear of looking weak, indecisive or foolish and so the parties simply may exchange unchanging positions and repeat rationales that persuade no one. At times like this, one party may withdraw an item of slight importance or agree to the other side's position just to ''get off the dime'' and start the process of meaningful give and take, of horse-trading, of real, substantive collective bargaining.

Consider the following situation: The contract between the janitorial and custodial employees and the realty management company that manages 15 major office buildings in the city is due to expire at midnight, at which time the union has announced its intent to strike if no satisfactory agreement has been reached. A strike will inconvenience the management company's prestigious tenants and embarrass the company; on the other hand, if the settlement is too generous, it will have an adverse impact in building operation costs that may lead to higher rents, and, in turn, may negatively affect profits.

At issue are wages and time off. The union is seeking a nine-percent increase and an additional paid holiday, each employee's birthday. The company has offered a five-percent increase and no increase in holiday time. At 11:40 P.M., the mediator is ready to make one final effort to assist the parties in reaching settlement. The time is right. The union does not really want a strike, because its members are not financially secure and are dependent upon a steady paycheck. The mediator senses that if some momentum can be created, a settlement is possible. All the other matters have been tentatively settled with the understanding, as is common, that, unless all items are agreed upon, any and all prior agreements are off.

The mediator convinces the management that they should make their best move now. She advises them that, if they will do something about holiday time off, the union will probably show some flexibility on its wage demand. She knows this from her conversations with the union in caucus, where she determined that the mostly black workforce wants not only a fair wage settlement, but also some recognition of their contribution. The management negotiators have told her they are unwilling to give the birthday holiday because it would be difficult to schedule by its varying nature.

At the mediator's suggestion, the company offers to make Dr. Martin Luther King's birthday a paid holiday. This offer is accepted by the union, which counters by dropping its wage demand from nine percent to seven percent. It is now 11:55, and management must act quickly. The momentum, the roll and rhythm of agreement, is present, the pressure to agree is unavoidable. The company, which might have preferred to counter with a six-percent wage offer, has run out of time. Unless it agrees to the union's seven percent, there will be a strike. The company agrees to the union's proposal of seven percent and the strike is averted.

This example also demonstrates the risks attendant in waiting too long to make a position change. If the move is made too early, on the other hand, the settlement dynamics may tilt against the moving party. As is true in so many pursuits, timing is critical, and yet so difficult to correctly gauge. Sometimes one party, sensing that it has waited too long, may wish to extend the deadline. Many times, a union team, sensing that a few hours could be decisive, will delay the beginning of a strike. A company in a similar situation may request from the union a delay of perhaps three hours before the announcement of a strike. To keep the pressure on, the union may grant only a two hour extension, expecting that, as that time grows short, the employer will be pressured to make an additional move.

Having established ground rules for conducting the negotiations and having introduced the subject of momentum, and after a discussion of critical moments, we will be ready to examine some table techniques and behaviors. Our discussion is intentionally selective and designed to give the reader a sense of not only the particulars enumerated but the larger possibilities of behavior at the table. The most experienced and successful negotiators will often remark that they are still learning, and often come across a technique or refinement of a tactic that is new to them. Similarly, good negotiators are creative and capable of inventing novel approaches, not only in substantive topic areas, but in procedural techniques, strategies and ploys.

Critical Moments

In each negotiation, there are critical moments when one side acts or does not act, and it changes the nature of the process. As noted in the preceding illustration, the realty management company perhaps waited too long before making its move. One critical moment probably occurred at 11:55 A.M., five short minutes before the start of a strike. The employer could have offered six percent, but decided to accept a seven-percent wage increase offer and thus avoid a strike.

Typical critical incidents, or moments, would be the acceptance or refusal of an offer to shadow bargain, creating conflict over a relatively minor item or readily agreeing to break a stalemate situation, or refusing or agreeing to delay the start of a strike or lockout. Often, it is not clear at the time that an incident was, in fact, critical; but experienced advocates cannot only identify critical moments when they occur, they may even be able to anticipate them.

Points to Ponder

Consider one contract negotiation with which you are familiar—or, if not appropriate, use a bargaining simulation which you either participated in or observed. What were the dynamics of momentum? Was there one (or more) critical moment(s) that had a significant effect on the outcome? What were the dynamics of that incident? In retrospect, did someone say or do something that was counterproductive? Remember that negotiating is a skill and one can often learn much from a mistake—especially one's own mistakes!

Table Talk

"Talk that talk."

—JACKIE WILSON

*"You got to me,
you got control."*

—NEIL DIAMOND
You Got to Me

*"I can't do what ten people
tell me to do."*

OTIS REDDING
Dock of the Bay

IN THIS SECTION we discuss the mechanics of team operation and the way in which a team handles and transmits information, both internally and horizontally.

Spokespersons and Team Discipline

In football, one man calls the offensive team's signals to begin the play—the quarterback. In negotiations, the same principle applies—one person speaks for the team at the bargaining table. To continue the football analogy, just as the quarterback may not call his own plays, but merely executes the wishes of the coach, so a team's spokesperson may not really direct the team's decision-making.

To have clarity and consistency of position, each team speaks through one person. This is a generally accepted rule in both the public and private sectors, on both the employer and union sides. Typically, members of each team communicate at the table with the spokesperson by means of a written note or, if physical proximity allows, a whispered comment. To let the other side overhear and learn about any internal dissension will not only undermine a team's position, but also call into question the quality of leadership. For this reason, a "table caucus," a team's internal discussion conducted at the table, is not encouraged. Also one should never make a dissenting or disparaging comment about one's own team's position (or other team members) at the table. Certainly, undisciplined communication presents serious risks to any confidential strategic or tactical plans, not to mention privileged information or private data.

It should be emphasized that the team spokesperson is not necessarily the actual leader, i.e., the individual who dominates the team's caucuses and determines direction, goals and priorities. For example, when the Gotham Telephone Workers Union goes to the bargaining table, the team spokesperson is Stephanie Washington, an attorney with the international union. The local unit chairperson, Beverly d'Amato, is also the local president, but the real leader is Patricia DiCarlo, head of the grievance committee. Daniel Rawlings, chief spokesperson for the Gotham Telephone Company, is director of human resources, but Stanley Rose, vice president for corporate operations, is the real power on the team, because the company's chairperson has designated Rose as his personal representative for the negotiations, and Rose personally gives the chairperson daily negotiation status updates. Thus, the two real leaders, DiCarlo of the union and Rose of the company, are not the team spokespersons. Knowing who is the true team leader can be especially critical in such situations as shadow bargaining and mediation, when the other team leader and the mediator must be able to identify and deal with the individual with real power.

There are clues as to who the true team leader is if one observes carefully. For example, when the union is presented with the company's counteroffer, team spokesperson Washington asks the necessary questions so she and her team are clear as to exactly what is being offered. But it is DiCarlo, seated next to her, who whispers a comment to Washington, who then calls for a caucus. Similarly, when Marvin Cohen, the mediator, comes into the company caucus, he quickly notes that it is not Rawlings, the team spokesperson, who questions him, but Rose, the corporate vice president.

As noted earlier, whoever the real team leader is, he or she must act as a quasi-mediator for the good of the team, and one of the main tasks of a quasi-mediator is to maintain team discipline and cohesiveness. It is definitely not always an easy task, but a necessary one. A team without discipline is a team destined for failure.

For certain issues of great complexity or specificity, each side may designate some team member to engage in "subcommittee negotiations." In a large and complicated negotiation, such as the talks between the major steel companies, which bargain together, and the United Steelworkers Union, there may be subcommittees appointed to conduct concurrent negotiations in such areas as pensions, health insurance and contracting out of operations. Each party's subcommittee will usually engage in detailed and intense bargaining, but may not be empowered to make any binding commitments without the agreement of the full committee. By engaging in detailed study and discussion of a subject area, however, away from the heat of the main negotiations, often much valuable information may be exchanged, with the result that each team's position is better thought out and the parties are more likely to reach agreement.

Control of the Negotiation Process

In every negotiation, at any given time, one party is in control of the table, the agenda and the process—one party and only one party. Certainly, the control may shift back and forth numerous times, even within a short time span. Experienced negotiators will endeavor to maintain control as much as possible, and truly masterful negotiators maintain control by appearing to relinquish it gracefully.

What is this control? It is exercising management over the other party, the agenda, the pace of the discussion, and, ultimately, the outcome. Thus, the controlling party may even let the other side talk more, demonstrate, gesticulate and seem to monopolize the clock, but, in fact, never cede control.

Examples of control are giving the other party "permission" to speak, telling the other party when and how to caucus, and calling for a meal break. When both sides are speaking simultaneously, control is usually being exercised by the party who can restore order, or who can keep the tirade going until choosing to end it.

Not surprisingly, the party exercising control most often during negotiations will achieve a favorable settlement. What then gives one party this important element of control? The answer is a combination of negotiating skills, personal demeanor and behavior, and, underlying it all, masterful use of bargaining power, a topic previously discussed at some length.

Promoting Your Position

One technique experienced negotiators often utilize is to have the discussion of a particular issue be centered on their own proposal.

For example, shortly after being certified as bargaining agent, when the often emotional issue of union security is being bargained over for a first contract between a retail clerks local union and the owners of Calloway's department stores, the union negotiator, Kate Allison, puts her proposal on the table as a basis for discussion. ''As you can see,'' she says, "this is a union shop arrangement which is legal in this state. We feel that, since our union was overwhelmingly voted in by the employees, and because we represent everyone's interests, every employee should join and support our union."

The management negotiator, Joseph Scott, disagrees. Like many employer representatives, he is very reluctant to compel any employee to join and support a union. When he expresses his concerns, the union spokesperson responds that she can understand his position and she can agree that some employees might have philosophical or religious objections to joining her union. In that case she urges the company to consider her proposal for an agency shop. Under this arrangement, she explains, no one has to join any organization if they do not wish to; however, if they choose not to join the union, they must pay a fee for service to the union. By handing a paper with the agency-shop language across the table, the union is seeking to maintain control of the discussion. The union is simultaneously controlling the subject of negotiation, the language to be discussed and the philosophic dialogue. The union spokesperson says, "Since everyone in the bargaining unit will benefit from our negotiations, and we will represent anyone who has a grievance that may arise, it's only equitable that everyone pay their fair share. For example, every homeowner pays property tax, most of which goes to operate the public schools. Now, it doesn't matter if you have no school-age children, or if your children attend private school, you still have to pay your taxes. That's the way it is with paying for union representation—everyone should pay their fair share."

Note that the union is well-prepared, a basic requirement of successful bargaining. Further, by having a fall-back position ready, one she has previously cleared with her team, the union is able to move forward and maintain both control and the momentum of negotiations. To be sure, by taking this approach the union is not guaranteed of a successful outcome; however, by dealing with the other side's objections in a calm, well-prepared way, the union has helped defuse an emotional issue and has made it easier for the company to accept a form of union security.

To develop this illustration further, if the employer has also prepared and is ready to negotiate this subject, Joseph Scott might respond this way: "Yes, you're right that every homeowner has to pay property taxes, but realize that when they bought their home, they knew and understood they would have that obligation. When virtually all our employees hired on here, there was no union and they had no obligation to join or pay dues to a union. We are very concerned that our employees, all of them, not feel that we've abandoned them just because a union won a representation election. At the same time, we understand that a number of our employees do support your union and that's why we're here to reach

an equitable agreement with you. At this time we would like you to consider a maintenance of membership clause, a copy of which I have right
here for you to examine. As you will note, everyone is free to join your
union, but no one will be compelled to do so. We feel this arrangement
is fair to everybody because it provides for freedom of choice. You'll note
that once someone joins your union, they must maintain their membership for the duration of the agreement. We feel that gives you a real
measure of security while at the same time allowing for freedom of choice
among our employees.''

Now the company has regained control of the negotiations and has
benefited from the preparation done earlier. Further, note that if the company is seeking a longer-term agreement than the union has proposed,
the union may have a meaningful incentive to consider a longer contract.
The employer has thus been able to achieve a strategic advantage, as well.

The Union may choose to respond to the Company's proposal by accepting the maintenance of membership clause if the employer will accept the union's wage demand. This is the so-called ''horse trading'' side
of bargaining with which some readers may be familiar, but note that
each side is well-prepared for any dealing because of time well-spent
preparing and doing research in advance and then seeking to better position themselves by having the discussion at the table centered on their
own proposal in their own words.

It is always an advantage to have discussion focus on your team's
proposal, not the other side's. As experienced debaters will attest, he who
frames the issue of the debate often prevails.

Recorders and ''B-Books''

In the turbulent and often emotionally charged atmosphere of the
bargaining table, it is all too easy to get confused about what was said
by whom about a specific proposal, and what agreement, if any, was
reached. To avoid confusion and misunderstandings, each side will usually designate one of its members as a recorder. While it is common for
every team member to take some sort of notes during the bargaining sessions, the recorder has the specific responsibility of making and maintaining a complete and accurate record of what transpired. This is not
always easy, and it is a position of great responsibility. Long after the
negotiations are over, it is not uncommon for a dispute to arise over what
was agreed upon and its applicability to a current grievance. Should the
matter go to arbitration, the records and testimony of the recorder can
be critical.

Some teams give the recorder the responsibility of compiling and
maintaining the so-called ''b-book,'' which is a bargaining book of con-

tract language containing, in indexed form, the current contract language and each side's proposal to change that clause. Because there may often be so many clauses at issue in a dispute, the responsibility for the bargaining book may be spread among two or three team members, none of whom is the recorder.

Another use of bargaining books is found in impasse resolution. When the mediator, fact-finder or interest arbitrator enters the dispute, typically he or she knows virtually nothing about the unresolved issues. A jointly prepared and submitted clause book can give the outside neutral a rapid and yet comprehensive view of the disputed matters. On one page, for example, the neutral can quickly determine the current language and the position of each party. This clarity of presentation not only saves valuable time, it also serves to let the disputants themselves determine how close they may be to each other's position, and how close they may be to a successful resolution of the impasse.

Another technique to minimize the possible confusion is to "sign off" when an item is agreed upon. This entails both sides initialing and exchanging a document with the agreed-upon clause. Thus, at the end of the negotiations, each side has signed copies of all that has been agreed upon. If the parties have the resources, they may have each clause typed by a professional typist, then sign and exchange that document. Most parties lack the resources for a typist, and their "sign offs" are handwritten and often quite terse.

The parties will usually reach agreement in principle on an item and later have their representatives or attorneys jointly write the exact language of the agreement. Negotiating basic agreements on many items is difficult enough, and it is usually cumbersome to negotiate language at the table. In the event there is later a dispute when the language is being written, the recorder's notes are vital (as they are if the written language ends up in a dispute before an arbitrator) because they provide the best evidence of just what the parties agreed to. As discussed in the material on grievance arbitration, sometimes the parties' minds may not have met, or each side believes firmly that the other side agreed with a given interpretation. Oral recollection is good evidence of intent, certainly, but the written word is even better evidence.

For all of the above reasons, not only is the recording of notes important during bargaining, but it is imperative to maintain notes from prior negotiations, because quite often the same issue will surface again and again, negotiation after negotiation. Since union negotiating teams may alter composition due to elections and management teams change with promotions and retirements as well as administrations, good, legible records of previous years' bargaining sessions are vital for intelligent preparation for successful negotiations in the present—and the future.

The Persistence of Numbers

As negotiators begin to close the gap within the parameters already described, each side picks up cues from the other, and the same figures begin to be utilized on both sides, creating the outlines of the ultimate settlement.

For example, the Woodworkers Union has just proposed the following: 35¢ per hour across the board for a one year contract. The Acme Lumber Company comes back with a three-year offer providing 25¢ per hour across the board for each of the three years, or a total increase of 75¢. When the union responds, it proposes a two-year contract with a 40¢ increase the first year and a 35¢ increase the second year, for a total increase of 75¢ per hour, using the company's figure, albeit for a shorter time period. What is worth noticing is the repetition of the number, in this case 75¢ per hour total increase.

The reason for this persistence of the same number is the very human tendency, when seeking to cut a deal, to make the offer as attractive to the other side as possible. Notice here that the union was proposing a contract longer than its original one-year offer, and in so doing was appealing to management's usual preference for an agreement of greater duration. The reason for this is manifold, such as predictability of labor costs and stability of employee relations, as well as avoiding the resource- and energy-draining process of contract negotiations. Unions generally prefer a shorter duration of agreements, because they assume, usually correctly, that the more often they go to the table, the more they will get. Also, in times of inflation or economic insecurity, such as our society has been experiencing, greater flexibility is enjoyed with a shorter-term contract.

In the example above, the union was thus seeking to accommodate the company's goal of increased contract length while using the company's own 75¢ figure, again attempting to make the proposal not only more acceptable, but also less threatening.

In the public sector, often budgetary rules mandate agreements with one-year funding, but this has not completely prevented multiyear contracts. Often the parties will agree on nonmonetary, or "language," items for a two- or three-year duration, and each year will negotiate only on monetary items. This mode gives the parties increased stability while complying with the applicable laws, and enables the negotiations to have a clearer focus, usually requiring less time to reach agreement because the number of issues is greatly reduced.

Not surprisingly, some private sector relationships have also utilized this model because, while not statutorily limited in their funding, the parties will settle upon language items for two, three or even four years, enjoying the stability and predictability of a longer agreement and yet retaining economic flexibility by having wage and monetary reopened every year.

Packages, Parameters and Priorities

For illustrative purposes, most bargaining examples discussed so far have concentrated on one or two items, but it must be noted that each party approaches the table with a number of items and each individual item must be seen as related to all other items. Thus, an employer may establish a figure of $235,000 as what it can afford to pay as an increase in monetary benefits and wages. If $200,000 of that sum is absorbed by a wage increase, the employer will be very constrained to agree to a new optical-care plan, which costs $25,000 and a new benefit in the existing dental-insurance plan, which costs $20,000.

Put simply, the employer will likely be unwilling to exceed the limit of $235,000. Nonetheless, pressures such as those already described may persuade the employer to exceed this preset limit. Again, the employer may conclude that to agree to a package of $245,000—$10,000 more than originally expected—is worth the extra expense if it is vital to reaching an agreement. If, on top of this, the union seeks an additional paid holiday, the employer may well conclude that the further cost of $35,000 is too high to pay, and will resist, even if resistance entails a strike.

On the union side, the negotiators approach the table with their list of priorities. Experienced bargainers fully realize that they will not obtain everything on their list, but certain items are of greater importance than others, while other items may be more readily cast aside or traded for more important concessions. Concerning still other items, the membership may be satisfied with a relatively minor improvement.

For example, employees of the Zerring Manufacturing Company have long sought changes in their vacation and holiday schedules. Previously, employees have been unable to take vacations during the Christmas/New Year period, even though they may have had the time accumulated. This rule was originally established years ago by the company's founder, but now it appears unnecessary because few products are made or shipped during this holiday time, and employees complain they must report to work with little for them to do. The company, therefore, after closely studying the situation and discussing it with supervisors in production and shipping, determines that it can close down for this period with no undue harm to operations, which would allow supervisors to spend time with their families as well. The union agrees that, on other than Christmas and New Year's Day, the days the plant is closed will be mandatory vacation days. Note that this is a significant benefit achieved by the union at little or no cost to the employer, an example of positive change to one party with little loss to the other.

Unfortunately, such mutually satisfactory adjustments are not always possible, and often collective bargaining resembles a ''zero-sum game,'' wherein a gain to one side must be a loss to the other. It is for that reason that, as the parties get down to the actual process of bargaining, they must establish parameters and priorities. Generally, in the preparatory phases, when proposals and positions are being formulated, each side establishes its own opening position (or counteroffer) as well as its ''bottom line'' or fall-back position, representing the point beyond which it will not go.

For example, when the Truck Drivers Union formulates proposals, it plans to open with a demand for a 75¢-per-hour wage increase. Its bottom line is 35¢ per hour, meaning that the union is willing to strike rather than agree to less. The Truck Owners Association, a bargaining consortium of 16 trucking companies, plans as an opening position a counteroffer of 10¢ per hour, their bottom line being a 35¢-per-hour increase, meaning it will withstand a strike rather than agree to pay more than 35¢ per hour more.

In the above example, the subject of a wage increase is the highest priority for both sides, as is most often the case. Further, the parameters overlap and, therefore, barring communication barriers, the parties will reach a settlement on that issue. Because it is the key issue for both sides, they will likely come to a full agreement on all other matters as well. But what if the parameters do *not* overlap—if the highest the owners will go is 30¢, and the lowest the truck drivers will accept is 35¢?

Most likely there will be a strike, or the threat of one, and the dispute will be resolved by a contest of wills and economic power. If there is indeed a strike, what will occur is that, at some point, one side will determine that the continued cost of disagreeing is higher than the cost of agreeing, and a deal will be struck. Suppose the strike is entering its tenth day. By now, employees are feeling not only the impact of lost wages, but the uncertainty of the strike and consequent anxiety from inactivity. No one on either side knows with any certainty when the strike will end. Employers not only begin to lose revenue, plus having continuing overhead costs and customer unhappiness over the disruption of service, but also experience anxiety over whether all customers will return once service is resumed.

As discussed earlier, destabilizers will staunchly oppose efforts at compromise, and will argue, when victory is within sight, that it is time to stand up to the other side and ''hang tough.'' Conversely, stabilizers on each side will urge movement and encourage alteration of parameters that will more likely encompass a settlement figure. For example, John

Reddy, owner of Reddy Trucking, urges his fellow owners to move beyond their earlier agreed-upon 30¢ "bottom line" position; while union negotiating committee representative Carlos Martinez urges his team members to drop their fall back position below 35¢. Thus, when Truck Owners Association spokesperson Vincent Patrick meets with mediator Susan Olivas and union spokesperson Louis Lopez, there is already at least some support on each side for a compromise. When mediator Olivas suggests 32.5¢ as a settlement figure, both parties are willing to consider it. Each side must weigh the costs of continuing the strike with the costs of settlement at a figure beyond its parameters.

For the union, accepting a lower figure may entail significant economic and political costs. On the other hand, the inventory of loss facing each side continues to mount daily, and acceptance of the compromise figure brings with it the certainty of stability and a resumption of normal relations. Finally, when one side does accept the compromise settlement, it puts even greater pressure on the other side to accept and thus end the conflict. Additionally, the compromise offer, coming from the mediator, may mean each side can claim that it did not "give in" to the other side, and thus did not "lose" by accepting the mediator's offer.

Symbolic Concessions

Often, it may be possible for one side to make a concession which is truly not costly yet quite valuable to the other party. For example, many city and county personnel rules evolve over a lengthy period of time and may contain certain anachronistic provisions. In the days before the prevalence of air conditioning, it was not uncommon in some jurisdictions to have shortened summer workdays when the official temperature was recorded at over 95 degrees. Today, with the use of air conditioning in offices so widespread, such rules make little sense and have been eliminated through negotiations where there are public employee bargaining laws. Not surprisingly, unions have sought concessions from the employer in return for giving up the right to go home early on hot days.

Consider this situation involving the issue of length of the authorized lunch break during negotiations between the Gotham City Department of Public Health and the union representing the visiting nurses. All other Gotham City employees have a 30-minute unpaid break for lunch but, by custom and contract, the visiting nurses have 45 minutes.

City negotiator Todd Bledsoe is vitally concerned there be uniformity in lunch-break length, especially because other unions have argued that their members are as deserving as the visiting nurses of a longer period. Therefore, Bledsoe is clear that achieving a 15-minute reduction in the lunch break is a very high priority in negotiations with the nurses' union.

Sandra McIntyre, chief negotiator for the nurses, is aware of the city's position and in off-the-record talks with Bledsoe she has gotten a sense of the great importance of the lunch-break issue. In caucus with her bargaining team, she explores the ramifications of the issue. Pam Carroll, local president, tells McIntyre that the issue is really unimportant to her members who would willingly concede on this issue in return for gains elsewhere. Carroll explains that most of the visits that nurses make to patients' homes inevitably require more time than is allotted by management. Further, with hiring freezes and attrition, she feels her members are already stretched quite thin, having to really hurry to see all of their patients during their workdays. Therefore, there is no nurse who actually takes as long as 45 minutes for lunch, which is generally eaten on the run, if at all; now, the nurses are in a position to consider exchanging a "symbolic concession" in return for a "meaningful concession," structured over-time.

McIntyre thus proposes to the city that, in return for agreeing to reduce the length of the lunch break by 15 minutes, Gotham will agree to lift the freeze and immediately hire 50 additional nurses. After some back and forth negotiation, Bledsoe gets permission from the Mayor's office to agree to hire 36 additional nurses at the beginning of the first year of the new agreement and 14 additional nurses at the end of the first year of the agreement in return for the nurses' concession about their lunch break.

Note that in this illustration the union was able to make a symbolic concession in exchange for other promises they very much wanted. Nurses' negotiator McIntyre was successful in achieving her goal of increased staffing by emphasizing the unique nature of her members' work, and wisely couched her proposal in terms directly consistent with the mission of the public health agency. This approach enabled Gotham negotiator Bledsoe to keep the agreement unique to the visiting nurses' group. Had the nurses been seeking a direct salary increase tied to their lunch-period concession, Bledsoe might have had difficulty in coming to agreement for fear he might upset the pattern or parity of settlements, a topic previously discussed.

Closers and Clinchers

In the field of sales management, certain individuals are known as "closers" because of their ability to close a deal. Often, they will structure their sales presentation so that, when the prospect is seriously considering and weighing the proposal, the "closer" can provide a slight additional benefit or price concession that makes accepting the deal too advantageous to pass up. For example, when Jack Martin is considering purchasing a new car, at the critical moment sales manager Neil Simonds may say, "If you sign the purchase contract tonight, I'll throw in an AM-FM radio at no cost—but only if you buy tonight."

As discussed in the section on momentum, each negotiation has its own pace and rhythm. A negotiator, or mediator, will often want to close the deal, and, in so doing, offer a clincher to bring bargaining to a conclusion.

Consider negotiations between the Hammer Corporation, a diversified conglomerate, and the local union, which represents five engineers in a field laboratory in northern Wisconsin. For Carla Furillo, the Hammer Corporation's chief negotiator, travel from her Pittsburgh office to the location of negotiations in northern Wisconsin is very time consuming, involving more of her time than she can afford. The converse is true for Lana Bowers, an attorney and chief negotiator for the engineers, who has her office seven miles away in a neighboring Wisconsin town.

At this bargaining session, the fourth between the parties, Bowers can discern that her opposite number is tired of the travel, and, because this is a small bargaining unit, perhaps it is time to close the deal. Engaging in an authorized shadow bargaining session, Bowers tells Furillo that if she wants this to be the last bargaining session, the union wants to oblige her—but only if the corporation will make a really attractive offer on wages and professional development—the two principal unresolved items. The union's last position is a nine-percent wage hike and an increase in the number of professional development days (which are used for paid conference and seminar attendance) from four to eight per year. The corporation has offered a six-percent wage increase and one additional professional development day.

Furillo, who has reviewed her parameters, moves to a 7.5-percent wage increase and two additional professional development days, but only if Bowers will accept right now. Bowers counters by saying that while it is a very attractive offer, she could accept it only if it were sweetened— even just a little bit. Furillo responds by saying she is virtually at the extreme of her parameters, but if she can clinch the deal and get a contract she will make the following—and final—move. Since the proposed agreement is a two year contract, she will stay with her offer of 7.5 percent each year and two additional professional development days the first year, with an additional one professional development day in the second year of the contract. This is her final offer and is contingent upon immediate acceptance. Bowers has been empowered by the union negotiating team, and thus can, and does, accept the offer.

It is worth noting that here the time pressure was not related to a strike situation, but, rather, demands upon a negotiator's time. The corporation's chief negotiator has other responsibilities, and so decided her time was well worth the final concession. Perhaps the professional development day, while not an inexpensive benefit, is a concession that could more easily be given than, say, salary or vacation because it enhances the engineer's productivity. Certainly no competent negotiator is going to "give away the store," making costly concessions simply to save time or travel. If union negotiator Bowers had held out for a wage increase of nine percent, no doubt the deal would not have been so quickly consummated. And, finally, the small size of the bargaining unit involved, as well as its unique professional composition, affected the willingness of the corporation to settle.

Because the vast majority of Hammer's unionized employees are blue collar employees, the concession concerning professional development days will not likely be precedent setting for other bargaining units. Perhaps due to the characteristics of size and composition of the engineers' unit, the wage settlement will not lead to coercive comparisons by other groups. In any event, the corporation's negotiator must always be aware and sensitive to those possibilities. If the corporation's policy is to give all employee groups the same percentage of wage increase, then Furillo would not have been willing to go to a 7.5-percent settlement if corporate policy was for one percent. In sum, "clinchers" can "close" a deal, but the concession must be such that it is not seen as more costly than the value of reaching agreement.

In certain situations, individual negotiators may be called in by either side to deal with specific issues or to close the deal. For example, when the Flight Attendants Association negotiates with Federal Airways, the company may bring in a pension specialist to bargain over those specific items and give this expert latitude and decision-making power in that area.

The Flight Attendants Association might call in a "closer" from its central union two days before the current agreement expires. This individual is highly experienced in bargaining and is well versed in current conditions and recent settlements, having herself participated in the negotiating of some of the contracts. She thus knows what level of settlement can be expected and will be often relied upon by negotiating team members to evaluate the proposed agreements. In addition, many unions can pay strike benefits only if the international union's executive board is convinced that the strike is appropriate, and the board relies on its own experts to report on the negotiations. For example, if the bargaining specialist from headquarters determines that the local union's positions are unreasonable and irresponsible, he or she will not only urge the local to reexamine and alter its positions, but may also recommend to the international union that no strike funds be allocated.

Thus, at 11:45 P.M., a quarter of an hour before the expiration of the agreement and the beginning of a strike, when the flight attendants' negotiating team caucuses, Helen James, the local's president and chairperson of the team, asks George Kramer, the bargaining specialist, his opinion of the airline's last proposal. Kramer notes that the wage increase is right in line with two other comparably sized airlines, and, although improvements in the pension plan are modest at best, he concludes this contract is one the flight attendants can live with. He points out that the general financial state of the airline industry is not particularly robust, and, if the flight attendants strike, the airline might either lose customers to its major competitors, which it could ill afford, or seek replacement stewards and stewardesses among those laid off by other airlines. He concludes by urging acceptance of the agreement, and the committee follows his recommendations.

It is, of course, possible for the opposite situation to occur. The bargaining specialist may find the proposed agreement is not in the best interests of the employees or of the international union. Consider the following example: Federal Airways proposes that it be allowed to use some part-time flight attendants during its holiday business rush, a proposal the negotiating committee views with some suspicion but is willing to accept. However, Kramer, the bargaining specialist, tells the committee that the proposal can lead to a number of problems for the members, such as less overtime and possibly layoffs, which occurred at another airline. Thus, he convinces the team that it is in its best interests to oppose any use of part-time employees.

In conclusion, then, an outside expert may be a "closer," or may have just the opposite effect and successfully urge the team not to agree. In the example above, it the negotiating team followed Kramer's lead and opposed any use of part-time flight attendants, and this in turn sparked a strike, the international union would most likely lend its full support to the strikers with both strike-benefit payments and support personnel and publicity.

Points to Ponder

Consider one contract negotiation with which you are familiar—or, if not appropriate, use a bargaining simulation which you either participated in or observed. Did one side have better team discipline than the other? If so, how was it manifested and how do you think if affected the outcome? Did one side exercise greater control of the negotiation process? If so, which side was it and how did it manifest itself? Do you think it influenced the outcome? If so, how and why?

Table Dynamics

"There are no good guys,
There are no bad guys,
There's only you and me
And we just disagree."

—DAVE MASON

"It ain't what you're doing
when you're doing what you're doing,
It's what it looks like you're doing
when you're doing what you're doing."

—CHARLES WRIGHT &
THE WATTS 103rd STREET RHYTHM BAND
Express Yourself

IN THIS SECTION we examine the dynamics that affect the parties' relationship. Collective bargaining is an interactive relationship with each party's perceived actions having an effect on the other side, and simultaneously being affected by their perception and the other sides' actions. In labor–management relations—as in much of life—perceptions are all important.

Uncertainty: Creating Doubts

There are two aspects to getting the other party to alter its position.
The first is to create doubts about the wisdom of the other side's position, and the second is to create uncertainties about your own future actions: what will you do next? The other side isn't sure of what you'll do or the impact your actions will have on the outcome of the dispute.
The other party, no matter how strongly and staunchly they reiterate their position and its attendant rationale, has some doubts about the wisdom of its posture. For example, the management of Bradley Products

has repeatedly said that they must have a wage and benefits freeze to remain competitive in their very competitive industry. However, Helene Leonard, vice-president of Human Resources, seriously doubts if the union would ever accept a no-increase agreement. She knows how much the cost of living has increased over the past two years and foresees at least some inflation in the next two years. Perhaps, she wonders, the employees would accept just a cost of living increase to protect their purchasing power. A strike, even a brief one, would cost the company not only millions in lost sales but also valuable market share points, and, most importantly, create an aura of bad feelings all around.

Similarly, although Michael Higgins, the chief union negotiator, has constantly demanded a 10-percent wage increase, arguing that his members need to do more than simply match the pace of inflation, he is aware of the competitive industrial pressures on the employer as well as the costs to his membership of a strike. Would the company be forced into bankruptcy by a strike?

Both negotiators therefore are loudly and clearly advocating one position while harboring some doubts about the practical viability of their respective positions. It is the role of each side to create, foster and amplify these doubts.

The other side's position may be attacked factually, arguing that their numbers are wrong. For example, when the company contends that the per-employee productivity of the work force has not increased over the past two years, the union may counter that the same amount of work is being performed by fewer employees.

"Facts," statistics and all data are certainly subject to differing interpretations. Each side in negotiations is engaged in a constant effort to make the other party question its own most basic assumptions as to "fact," and advancing their own series of "facts."

The second aspect of this effort is to create uncertainties about the consequences of continued disagreement. In the most rudimentary illustration, the union argues that, if it calls a strike, all bargaining unit members will walk out and no work will get done. The company counters that, in the event of a strike, production will continue and it expects many bargaining unit members to cross the picket line and work with the supervisors.

The union says that no one will cross the picket line—but will they? How many bargaining unit members will cross? The union leaders wonder if the company will be able to recruit capable replacement employees— and will they cross the union's picket lines?

The company wants to conduct its operations normally and completely. Will bargaining unit members cross the picket line? How many? Will the number increase, decrease or remain constant over time? What about replacement workers? Can the company actually recruit, hire, train and get productivity from these new hires? If the company is planning on contracting out some operations during the strike, will the contractors live up to their agreements? What about the quality and cost of the work done? In these days of competitive markets, which is worse: producing no product or service or producing a lower quality product or service?

This uncertainty is compounded by the dynamic nature of human behavior. Each day people make new decisions—and this in turn affects other decisions. That's why during a dispute it's not uncommon to have the company's and union's reports of events differ so markedly. For example, the same day that the company announces that over one-third of the bargaining unit employees have crossed the line to work and more are expected tomorrow (this in addition to the over 300 replacement workers already at work, putting the employer at just about full efficiency), the union announces that less than 10 percent of bargaining unit members crossed the line, and less are expected tomorrow, this in addition to the employer's dismally unsuccessful efforts at getting only about 100 replacement workers who are marginally productive at best.

Obviously, they cannot both be right—and indeed neither may be totally correct, for the truth may lie somewhere in between the two advocates' versions. If the strike is failing, as the company contends, then those employees with an uncertain commitment to the union cause may be persuaded to cross the picket line, in effect, making the employer's statements a self-fulfilling prophecy. But if the union's pronouncements are correct, then wavering employees may be persuaded to stand fast in hopes of soon achieving a substantial increase in their financial position. It is for just this reason that unions may call for mass-picketing or large public rallies at which prominent politicians, civic leaders and celebrities may join with union advocates to promote the strike and convince wavering adherents.

In situations like this, it is not uncommon for the employer, in turn, to invite journalists for a plant visit and a chat with top company officials to demonstrate how efficiently operations are proceeding.

As the strike progresses, each side is constantly reassessing its relative position while attempting to increase their perceived strength in terms of bargaining power to advance their position. However, while this is occurring and each side is creating doubts and fostering uncertainty on the other side, each must deal with its own doubts and uncertainties. For example, no matter how rosy the employer's public reports may be, the reality may be that not as many of the strikers are crossing the picket line as hoped and newly hired replacement workers are proving slower to train than expected. Further, quality is slipping, total output is down and the supervisory staff is becoming exhausted as they seek to perform their own jobs plus added production tasks as well. Increasingly, top company officials are fearful of losing steady customers while fearing the harm to corporate acceptability in the community as a result of all the bad feelings generated by the bitter strike. Families in the area are being torn as some support the company while others feel the union is right.

At the union headquarters, the leaders maintain an outward calm and publicly comment that not only is their cause correct, but that victory is imminent. In private, however, serious doubts are being expressed. What if the strike breaks the company financially, driving it into bankruptcy? Then this will be a Pyrrhic victory, with no jobs, no financial security—and no union; or what if the company can actually function well without union workers? Perhaps the replacement workers, scabs in union parlance, who are willing to work cheaper than union members will become permanent and some or all jobs will be lost forever. What if the union actually loses the strike? It could happen.

The union's strike funds are becoming rapidly depleted while no dues income is being received. For example, having become involved in two large strikes, the national union may not be in the best financial health right now, and there is some question about the continuation of financial support from them. Many strikers are openly complaining about the insufficiency of strike benefit–payments which are only a small percent of normal take-home pay, and personal savings have already been depleted by a number of members. In addition, support by local political and civic leaders seems to be slipping a bit as the mayor and a prominent clergyman both publicly asked both sides to reconsider their respective positions in light of the economic and psychological damage being done to the community.

In this pressurized atmosphere, both sides are increasingly ready for a compromise settlement. It is the role of the mediator to help the parties reach a settlement and end the conflict.

The Untruths That Matter

As we discuss in the section of this book dealing with the different types of proposals, it is often very difficult for one party to determine the veracity of the other party's statements. For example, if management announces to the media that about 35 percent of bargaining unit members have crossed the picket lines today and reported to work, an increase of perhaps 10% over the day before, how accurate is that figure? If true, such a statistic would indicate that better than one out of three employees is abandoning the union's position, a not insignificant piece of information that might impel some additional wavering striking employees to likewise cross the picket line and resume work, perhaps creating a snowball effect which will destroy the union's power.

On the same day, however, the union announces to the media that only about seven percent of those striking have crossed the picket line, a few less than yesterday. This would indicate that the strike is strong and gathering strength daily. To those employees striking, this information may likely strengthen their resolve and deter any wavering workers from crossing the picket line and returning to work.

Which party is telling the truth? Whose figures should be believed?

This is why both labor and management are extremely concerned with reporting in the mass media, especially television, the simplest and most visual medium. Each side wishes to be perceived as supremely confident that they will prevail, no matter the reality.

Further, each party seeks to communicate with the affected employees, endeavoring to persuade them that the tide is turning in their favor.

Given this confusion and uncertainty, which is the one to believe? And if the significance of that which has already occurred is unclear, what will happen in the future?

Some naive observers have commented that their best interests lie in reaching a contract.

How then does a mediator work?

The mediator works to isolate the destabilizers—those who don't believe in resolution through the table process, and who harbor the least doubts.

How Mediators Really Succeed

What makes one mediator better than another? Why is it possible for mediator A to succeed in getting the parties to reach agreement when mediator B could not?

The quick answer is that the parties were not ready to reach agreement when B sought to mediate. Like most quick answers, there is some truth present, but not all of it.

The role of a mediator is to create a climate in which the parties can reach agreement. The parties would not be at an impasse if there was the *animus negotiandi*, the mutual commitment to resolve the dispute by negotiation and compromise. It is the task of the mediator to make both parties want to negotiate. The way the mediator accomplishes this is by creating or enlarging doubts that become so powerful they cause an attitudinal change.

This is not, to be sure, an easy task or one simply accomplished. In the first place, those on each party's negotiating team are the most deeply committed to that party and advancing or protecting its institutional interests.

On the union side, most, if not all of those serving on the bargaining committee are not being financially rewarded for their time and effort. Typically, these are men and women who so believe in the role of the union and the importance of achieving a satisfactory contract that they will meet in caucus and in joint conference for seemingly endless hours while receiving little or no compensation. Most union teams are headed by a business agent, or international representative who is usually a full time employee of the union, and paid a salary which assumes s/he will work all the hours necessary to get the job done.

Similarly, those on the employer negotiating team are generally full-time salaried employees who serve without extra compensation, often having to continue to meet their main job responsibilities such as sales managers, chief financial officers, production superintendents or directors of human resources. The long hours spent in preparation and research, joint conference and caucus are thus an additional demand upon their time and energy. These employer representatives serve in negotiations because of a commitment and concern for protecting and promoting the interests of the employer.

Those men and women representing the employer are obviously deeply committed, both professionally and personally, to the continued successful existence of the company or agency. For the institution to prosper in the future and to adequately meet the needs of their customers or clients, the employer must have the flexibility to operate efficiently. This means achieving the lowest cost and highest quality attainable in a new agreement. While the welfare of its employees is important, management must consider the concerns of other constituencies such as suppliers, vendors, customers and shareholders.

For those on the union negotiating team, the men and women most committed personally and professionally to best representing the interest of the employees, the new agreement must primarily protect and promote the economic security of their members while insuring equitable treatment of all.

The task of the mediator is, at first blush, somewhat daunting. Called into the dispute only when the parties are already at an impasse, when positions have hardened and bad feelings are everywhere, the mediator must somehow create an environment in which both parties feel that watching the parties maneuver in a strike environment is like witnessing a large chess board. It is true that, in a chess match, as in a strike, the winning strategy may not be readily apparent to the opponent. However, this analogy is highly simplistic because in chess each side only makes one clearly observable move at a time; in labor–management relations, the moves are often unclear, occur rapidly, may happen simultaneously and at the end the identity of the winner may not be readily apparent.

Selling a Settlement

It is axiomatic in marketing that the best salesperson never sells anything, but rather creates a context in which the customer wants to buy. A mediator attempts to do the very same thing: to sell a settlement by having the parties buy it; and the team leader, the quasi-mediator, must do the same thing among team members.

The best mediator is thus one who creates a context in which the parties become convinced their best interests are in reaching a settlement. Put another way, in order to get each side to come to agreement, a majority on each side must be convinced that the cost of agreeing is lower than the cost of continued disagreement. Because each side must come to this belief, usually the settlement will not favor one side completely. Typically, one side may emerge victorious in the sense of having the settlement contain more of what they sought than the other side's position. Unless the strike collapses completely and the union falls apart, or the employer totally capitulates and accepts the union demands in toto, the usual settlement involves some measure of compromise with neither company nor union achieving a complete, unqualified victory. There is usually at least some disappointment in the outcome by both sides, with the destabilizers being most acutely unhappy with the settlement.

Destabilizers, discontent with the settlement, may well create future problems on both sides of the relationship. On the union side, these destabilizers may seek a negative ratification vote and then they may seek top elective office, running on a platform that accuses the incumbents of being too friendly with management. On the employer side, managers dissatisfied with the outcome may attempt to sabotage implementation of the new contract and undermine those who support increased labor–management cooperation.

It is worth emphasizing that contract negotiations only comprise one component of the collective bargaining process.

Points to Ponder

Consider one contract negotiation with which you are familiar—or, if not appropriate, use a bargaining simulation in which you either participated or observed. Did one side emerge clearly victorious? Was the other side totally vanquished? If so, why do you think such a win–lose outcome occurred?

Or perhaps you might conclude the results were somewhat unclear. What did each side gain and lose? Do you feel one side won more than the other side? How did this occur—and why? Is it possible that both sides might justifiably claim each emerged victorious? Or that each side emerged a loser? Can there be lose–lose negotiations?

Table Tactics

"Play with fire."

—THE ROLLING STONES

*"Knowing when to leave can be
the hardest thing to do."*

—DIONNE WARWICK

IN THIS SECTION we present and analyze some of the more common tactical maneuvers used at the table. The list of techniques selected for this section are far from complete, but are often used in both public and private sectors.

Intentional Errors

In the often tense and trying atmosphere of negotiations, patience can wear thin and judgment can grow weak. It is therefore not impossible to make an error, a misstatement of position, a premature concession or a thoughtless remark one later regrets. The appropriate thing to do is own up to the error and seek to rectify it. For example, during negotiations for a new agreement between Gotham City and its Firefighters Union, city spokesperson Frank Kalinowski inadvertently agrees to an extra personal leave day as well as an additional holiday, when he had intended to give one or the other but not both. When the union leaves the room to take its caucus to consider the offer, Kathryn Kelley, the city's director of personnel, quickly points out the error to Kalinowski. He immediately goes to the firefighters' caucus room and informs them of his misstatement so that there can be no acceptance of his offer or any resultant change in the position of the union as a result of a misunderstanding.

One may wish, however, to use the technique of intentional error as a positive ploy. Such a purposeful error must be distinguished from the inadvertent one, both in occurrence and response. For example, such an intentional error may be committed by someone other than the team spokesperson, thus allowing official repudiation if necessary. For example, by prearrangement, the following occurs during a discussion of paid leave.

When Gotham spokesperson Kalinowski responds to the union proposal for both an increase in holiday and personal leave, he tells the firefighters they can have neither an additional holiday nor an extra personal leave day. Kathryn Kelley blurts out, "Why can't they have an additional personal leave day?" Kalinowski glares at Kelley and calls for an immediate caucus. This gives the union time to consider if a personal leave day is acceptable, an idea they know has at least some support on the other side of the table. Thus, when bargaining resumes, the firefighters can propose dropping their request for an additional holiday and stick with their proposal for the one additional personal leave day. Again, it must be stressed that this was an intentional error, designed to transmit certain information across the bargaining table to the other team. If this is not what was intended, immediate steps should have been taken to prevent a serious misunderstanding.

In a similar vein, when discussion begins about the amount of a wage increase, the city is at three percent and the firefighters are at five percent. City finance director Kevin Lynch passes a note to spokesperson Kalinowski, which reads, "Frank, remember we can't go over 3.5 percent." When the city team leaves the room for caucus, Lynch's note is intentionally left on the table for the firefighters to read and consider. Again, this is a message that the city wants the union to read and act upon. If it comes off successfully, the union will get a clear picture of the city's final position without the spokesperson having to put that figure on the table. However, if the firefighters have traditionally gotten the same settlement as the Gotham teachers, and if the city has just settled with the teachers at four percent, this note could cause great resentment. In short, the use of the intentional-error technique is not without its hazards and must be approached cautiously and executed flawlessly.

Mutt 'n' Jeff

This technique, sometimes called "good-guy/bad-guy," will not be unfamiliar to devotees of police interrogation methods. One person takes the role of the hardliner who is dissatisfied with everything and threatens dire consequences. The confederate takes the role of the peacemaker and argues that cooperation with him will be better than resistance to the hardliner. Analytically, the first person is playing the destabilizer, and the second, the stabilizer. Here is an example of this technique at work.

In negotiations between the Gotham Contractors Association and its unionized electricians, there is a dispute over the length of the agreement.

The union wants a one-year agreement because of inflation and economic uncertainty; the contractors' group wants a three-year agreement for stability and predictability in labor costs.

The spokesman for the contractors is Red O'Neill, who heads one of the larger companies. He is well known for his fiery temper and excitability. The contractor's vice chairman is Charlie Bates, who heads his own medium-sized firm and is known for his quiet demeanor and thoughtful comments. When the issue of contract length is being discussed at the table, the union makes its position clear: A one-year contract is all they will accept. O'Neill loses his temper and yells at Kirk Richards, the union spokesman, saying, "You guys are going to be locked out, I'm telling you! We need a longer contract, don't you clowns see that? Are you all so dumb?"

Bates puts a cautionary hand on O'Neill's arm and says softly, "Now, let's not talk lockout, Red. We all want a contract, and I'm certain the union will be reasonable about this. There's no need to call anyone dumb just because they don't agree with you." He turns his attention to Richards, the union team leader, and says, "Can't you fellows accept a longer agreement? How about, say, 30 months if three years is too long? What do you say?"

While the union may not accept a 30-month agreement, it may well move off its one-year position, which is the goal of the employers. By acting "reasonably" and urging the union to do likewise, Bates is taking some of the energy and heat out of the atmosphere and putting out a feeler, a suggestion, an idea that the union can consider. What Bates is saying contrasts with O'Neill's message and clearly demonstrates to the union that there is someone with a calm, dispassionate view of the proceedings on the other side. If the union counters by saying it might move from one year to, possibly, 18 months, the parties are developing momentum, the important subject previously discussed.

Wild-Man Steve

This is a technique with a great dramatic presentation and a strong effect, if successful. The spokesperson on one side, when presented with a position by the other side not to his or her liking, throws a temper tantrum, vilifies the other side and storms out of the room, slamming the door loudly. The confederate then rebukes the other side for causing the scene, arguing forcefully that if the position is not altered, negotiations are over for the foreseeable future. In effect, the "wild man" has become the center of control, and to placate his or her hurt feelings, a significant movement of position is demanded.

Here's an illustration of this technique: Steven Henson is spokesman for the Industrial Workers Union in its negotiations with Moffett Manufacturing Company. The union is avidly seeking a contractual provision that will make weekend overtime, now mandatory, voluntary. Henson has explained the union's position completely at each of the previous five negotiating sessions, and now the company's spokesperson, Mark Grant, has said that under no circumstances will the company change its position on this issue. Upon hearing this, Henson pounds the table and yells, "That's it! I've had it with you idiots!" He stands up and storms from the room and slams the door.

The company is thunderstruck. What do they do now? Union vice president Art Chambers says that the union cannot continue negotiations unless Henson returns, and the only way that will occur is if the company will agree to consider some type of voluntary weekend overtime provision, such as that no employee can be required to work more than six hours overtime per weekend, but can voluntarily work more. The company agrees to consider the proposal, and Chambers goes out and brings back Henson.

Will o' the Wisp

This negotiating technique involves taking a purposely vague approach toward a specific issue, which, in effect, throws the burden of specificity to the other side, thus giving the first party the advantage of being able to respond to the proposal.

For example, the union representing janitorial and custodial employees at the Anthony Manufacturing Company is led by Veronica Lyttel, who tells the company's chief negotiator, Nick Adams, that her union wants the company "to do something about the parking situation" at the plant. Adams responds, "Do you want us to install better lighting, or provide better maintenance or have a guard on duty?" To which Lyttel responds, "Yes! Yes! Yes!" Note that, while the company may well not promise all three items, the union now knows what the company sees as possible steps it might take. In effect, the specifics of the union's proposal have come from the company.

Similarly, when the Federal Oil Refining Corporation comes to the table to negotiate with the union that represents its production and maintenance employees, the company's chief spokesman, Ralph Berns, tells the union team leader, Sharon Olsen, that the company wants "something done about the problem of absenteeism before and after paid holidays." Olsen responds by asking if he wants employees to be required to work the day before and after the holiday to be eligible for holiday pay, and is he especially concerned about Christmas, New Year's Day and Thanksgiving?

Again, Berns now has a sense of the union's position on a couple of aspects of the issue and can work from there. Perhaps he may respond by saying he is concerned with all the holidays, or he may simply add two specifics to the list, July 4 and Memorial Day, giving Olsen a sense of where the company is leading.

An effective way of dealing with this approach is to recall the old Army maxim: Never volunteer. In the first example about "the parking situation," if Adams had responded by simply asking, "What, specifically, bothers you about it?" he would have avoided the trap, as would Olsen if she had asked what her opposite number wanted.

It must be noted that both Adams and Olsen took an action that could also be viewed in a positive light, because they gave the other side a clue as to where they might be willing to go on the issue. Removing some of the mystery probably assisted the other side in its assessment of what to do, and thus moved negotiations along by giving them some direction, or momentum.

Dotting "i's" and Crossing "t's"

The opposite approach is often practiced, wherein a negotiator seems as concerned with the specifics of an agreement as he or she is with the spirit of reaching agreement. While most negotiators first seek to gain agreement on a broad principle and mutually refine it to specifics, this technique involves exaggerated specificity and a punctilious attention to fine print. All possible scenarios to which the clause being negotiated could apply are laboriously explored and the possible outcomes dissected. This is why it is often said that lawyers, who are trained to be cautious in the use of words in a contract, are the most difficult and obstructionist negotiators.

Knowing When to Leave

It should be noted that walking out of negotiations is by no means synonymous with the use of either the strike or the lockout, though they are often used in concert. Thus, a union could continue negotiating while a strike is on, or the employer could lock out its employees and still be available for negotiations; or the union could break off negotiations but not strike, just as the employer could walk out of negotiations but not take any other action.

The more sophisticated and experienced negotiators are, the more flexibility and creativity they can bring to the negotiating table. This then would appear to be an appropriate point at which to leave our analysis.

Points to Ponder

Consider one contract negotiation with which you are familiar or, if not appropriate, use a bargaining simulation which you either participated in or observed. Did either team attempt to use any of the techniques described in this chapter? If so, what was the outcome? If none was used, why not? Were any techniques used that were not discussed? How did they work? If you worked with a mediator, what techniques did the mediator use to create doubts and uncertainties in the minds of both parties?

Promise Checking: Grievance Arbitration

"Here comes the judge."

—SHORTY LONG

IN THIS SECTION the "promise checking" phase of collective bargaining is examined, and an overview of the process and the participants is provided.

Contract Administration: Checking the Promises

While grievance arbitration is similar in conceptual approach to interest arbitration in that a neutral hears the positions of both parties and renders a binding decision, there is a fundamental difference between the two forms of arbitration. Grievance arbitration is concerned with the interpretation and/or application of already existing contract language that the parties themselves negotiated. That is the key to its widespread voluntary acceptance in both the public and private sectors.

As noted earlier, when the parties are unable to reach agreement during the contract-making process, resort may be made to interest arbitration, which serves to make promises for the parties. Once the parties have reached a contract and exchanged promises, the relationship changes. Now they are willing to give up overt weapons of conflict, such as the strike or lockout, in exchange for stability, continued production and wages.

Realizing the importance of a continuous uninterrupted functioning of the enterprise to both employer and employee, the parties have voluntarily surrendered their traditional weapons of strike and lockout in favor of grievance arbitration. This process is also called rights arbitration, because it determines the contractual rights of the parties under their agreement. As noted earlier, while the parties are reluctant to allow a neutral to write the contract for them, they willingly, often eagerly, encourage grievance arbitration. Indeed, it has been estimated that better than nine percent of collective bargaining agreements provide for some form of grievance resolution through the arbitration process.

This system is very pragmatic, because it provides for the resolution of a dispute while employees are working and getting paid, and while the employer is able to continue the production of goods or the delivery of a service. In England, for a quick contrast, the parties are free to take self-help steps, which, while they may be tactically astute, nonetheless allow a high inventory of loss to both sides on an ongoing basis. In the United States, the parties are willing to forgo the possible short-run tactical advantage in favor of the longer-term viability of the relationship.

Grievance Procedure

Typically, each agreement will define what is grievable and what is not, and then proceed to provide some mechanism to encourage grievance settlement in an orderly, or ''step,'' fashion.

Although there are considerable individual contractual variations, usually the first step of the grievance process is informal discussion between employees and the first, or lowest, level of supervision. If there is no resolution satisfactory to the parties, the next step provides for a written or formal grievance to be filed with the first-line supervisor, who then must respond within a stated time period, usually five days. It must be noted that the vast majority of grievances are resolved without resort to arbitration, and usually at one of these first two steps. This should not be surprising inasmuch as the parties most directly affected by the grievance are those best equipped to resolve it. Working together, day after day, the parties develop a relationship. While they may not love each other, they are bound together and must get along if the enterprise is to continue. Any organization, no matter how automated, cannot function without at least some employees. Employees, for a wide variety of reasons, are tied to that enterprise, for, if not, they will leave and others will take their places.

Unlike many relationships, labor and management *must* get along if they are both to prosper. Most employers, while not enamored with having their employees unionized, can accept and live with a union. Many union members may hold their employers in something less than high regard, but they can accept the reality that these people are in positions of authority and must be dealt with accordingly. Thus, there is interaction between the parties on a daily basis, with many opportunities for differences and disputes to arise. The grievance process is therefore a means of resolving the many and varied problems that occur.

If the first two steps of the grievance process do not resolve a particular dispute, the third step, consultation between higher officials of management and the union, will be invoked. Again, there are time limits provided, and they must be adhered to closely. A grievance is best resolved as quickly and expeditiously as possible, for it may be a thorn for both parties. The longer it remains unresolved, the more irritating it may become.

There may be a fourth and even a fifth step of the grievance procedure, wherein successively higher levels of authority on both sides are introduced to resolve the grievance. It is often said that, while those closest to the problem may be in the best position to know most about the grievance, they may be too personally and emotionally involved to be objective. As those with less personal connection with the grievance are brought in, their objectivity and often superior knowledge of the field of industrial relations may be of assistance in resolving the dispute.

The final step of most grievance procedures is binding arbitration. The parties typically provide a mechanism for the selection of a neutral to hear the case. The actual specific mechanisms may vary considerably, but there are similarities. Both parties have some say in the selection of the neutral, and it is rare that a neutral will be imposed upon the parties for a grievance arbitration.

Interestingly, it should be noted that the process of grievance negotiation does not end once the process of arbitration is invoked. Indeed, the parties will often successfully resolve the dispute the day before or even the morning of the hearing itself. Often, then, it appears that the imminence of an arbitrator's award serves as a spur to the parties to settle it themselves. This is as it should be, for the best resolution of any dispute flows directly from the disputants themselves; they best know their own needs. Any compromise settlement worked out by the parties means they shape and know the dimensions of the resolution; an arbitrator's binding award contains at least the possibility of some uncertainty, surprise and even total defeat.

Conceptually viewed, a grievance procedure offers the parties multiple opportunities to resolve the grievance at successively higher levels of each organization's hierarchy through negotiations (Chart 17).

Negotiating Grievances to Settlement

It is inherent in any conflictual relationship that there is the potential for surprise, for the unexpected. Often, shortly before a scheduled arbitration hearing, one side may discover evidence which seriously undercuts the theory and structure of their case. For example, the day before an arbitration hearing, management representative Karen Shea learns an unsettling piece of information. The reason for Ms. Allen's termination was the alleged failure to call in and report off, conduct for which she

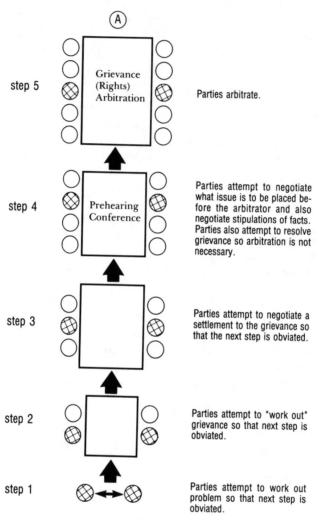

step 5   Grievance (Rights) Arbitration   Parties arbitrate.

step 4   Prehearing Conference   Parties attempt to negotiate what issue is to be placed before the arbitrator and also negotiate stipulations of facts. Parties also attempt to resolve grievance so arbitration is not necessary.

step 3   Parties attempt to negotiate a settlement to the grievance so that the next step is obviated.

step 2   Parties attempt to "work out" grievance so that next step is obviated.

step 1   Parties attempt to work out problem so that next step is obviated.

CHART 17

had previously been disciplined. Examining the ward's log book with the unit's head nurse, Cynthia Marks, Ms. Shea sees a notation that reads, "Jill Fisher called at 5:30 A.M.—her mother ill, won't be in today." She pauses and inquires about this entry. Head nurse Marks replies that, being new herself in her assignment, she doesn't know to whom this refers but she will check. A few minutes later she tells Ms. Shea that Jill Fisher is the grievant's step-daughter and in fact the former ward clerk who took the message knew that the call referred to Ms. Allen not being in that day.

In essence, at the eleventh hour, management representative Shea had just learned that she has no case. If she were to proceed to arbitration, she would definitely lose. But if she can negotiate a settlement she can cut her losses. Ms. Shea telephones the union representative, Margarita Arroyo, and arranges to meet with her in two hours.

At the meeting, Ms. Shea stresses the hospital's desire to work out a settlement fair to all concerned. Realizing the importance of trust in an ongoing relationship, the management representative candidly tells Ms. Arroyo what she just learned and that it appears the grievant was correct when she asserted during the earlier phases of the grievance process that she had called in and reported off. Nonetheless, Ms. Shea points out that Alice Allen had on a number of previous occasions failed to call in and further, that her attendance record is quite poor and merits some discipline.

Union representative Arroyo says that at this point the grievant has been out of work for three months and really wants her job back. Also, she is in quite desperate financial straits and has not been able to find another job. The union seeks full back pay and an immediate return to work.

Ms. Shea suggests the following settlement: Ms. Allen will return to work the next Monday, and will receive full back pay and benefits less a three-day suspension for failure to be regular in attendance. Further, the grievant will be on warning that she must report to work every day and must call in without fail if she will not be in to work as scheduled.

The union representative, who is fully familiar with Ms. Allen's poor record, is willing to agree but has one final demand: since the arbitrator will not be needed tomorrow, and a cancellation fee will be due, the hospital will bear the full cost of his fee.

Ms. Shea agrees and the matter is resolved. Consider the following points about this situation: first, it is not uncommon that relevant information is revealed at the eleventh hour. While it is true that preparation is the unquestionable key to success in arbitration, often one or both sides cannot devote the requisite time to research and prepare the case. In the real world, there are many demands upon one's time and limited resources. Second, there is nothing like the imminence of a hearing to concentrate one's attention on the relevant information regarding a case. And when a case is thoroughly researched, all sorts of information is revealed —information that may make your case stronger or weaker but information that directly and profoundly affects your case. Third, it is not uncommon to find participants in the process who have little or no prior background in the relationship. For example, a new supervisor, a new management representative and a newly-elected union grievance chairperson may be dealing with a grievance that arose before any of them entered the scene. And finally, and perhaps most importantly, historically, labor and management representatives have been resolving grievances by negotiation since the beginning of the trade union movement. Recently, however, there has been a great deal of attention focused on the process of grievance mediation, an extension of grievance negotiation, a topic considered later in this section.

Duty of Fair Representation

In every sector that grants a union exclusive representation status, a concomitant responsibility is also given to the union—that of fair representation. The significance of this doctrine in grievance administration is important. Basically, each union is charged with representing the interests of all those in the bargaining unit, regardless of membership status or race, religion, etc. Thus, a union must responsibly handle grievances brought by all those it represents, disregarding personal characteristics of the grievant. While this does not mean that the union must take every case to arbitration, it does mean that the union must seriously consider every grievance at each step of the grievance procedure. It cannot refuse to process or advance a grievance because the grievant is not a union member, or is black, female, etc. Many observers contend that this doctrine puts an undue burden on the union, both in terms of time and money, two precious resources, and leads many unions to process non-meritorious grievances out of fear that if they fail to do so, they will be sued for breaching their duty.

On the employer's side, many managers argue that they, too, are under similar pressures. Certainly, no employer would wish to be cited as having wrongfully discriminated among members of the workforce in terms of employment, conditions of work or imposition of discipline. On the other hand, it is often policy to support lower level managers. Thus, many employer officials often feel that they have been placed in a difficult position and are reluctant to settle a grievance which they believe is of unclear merit.

For all the above reasons, both labor and management representatives often wait until the "eleventh hour" before seriously beginning settlement negotiations; many grievance arbitrators have had the experience of settlements of scheduled cases the day before the hearing, or even at the hearing itself.

It may, therefore, be helpful to consider the following situations *after* the fourth or final prearbitration step of the grievance process as possible opportunities to settle a grievance:

(1) The parties' representatives may meet to discuss the process of selection of an arbitrator and request a list of arbitrators from the

American Arbitration Association, Federal Mediation and Conciliation Service or appropriate state agency, etc.

(2) The parties' representatives may meet to discuss the list of arbitrators provided and make a selection.

(3) Once the arbitrator has been selected, the parties' representatives may be in communication concerning scheduling of the hearing.

(4) As the date of the scheduled hearing approaches, the parties' representatives may discuss the preparation of joint exhibits and stipulations of issues and/or facts.

At each of these four times, the representatives examine their own cases and anticipate the other side's case. For example, it is not uncommon that, when the parties are discussing submission of joint exhibits and stipulations of fact, they may realize they are not so far apart and that compromise settlement of the grievance may be possible. Similarly, one side may see a fatal weakness in its case not noticed at a lower level and seek a settlement as an alternative to losing at a hearing before an arbitrator.

Advantages of Arbitration

The enormous acceptance of grievance arbitration is no doubt due to the advantages of the process. Compared to litigation in court, or administrative proceedings, rights arbitration is faster, less expensive and more informal. Unlike crowded court dockets and extensive waits to have a case heard, arbitration allows for the hearing to be conducted as quickly as the parties and the arbitrator can schedule it. Money is saved because no attorneys are needed, since the process usually is flexible and informal.

Unlike judges who hear a variety of matters and may not gain expertise in one particular field, labor arbitrators are well-versed in what is variously called "industrial jurisprudence" or "the law of the shop." Because both parties so empower the arbitrator, his or her decision is final and binding on both sides, and the arbitrator's award is enforceable in a court of law. This finality can be dramatically contrasted with the administrative and/or judicial appellate system, which can and often does take many years (and many dollars) to achieve finality.

Although it is possible to challenge an arbitrator's award in court, few parties do and far fewer still are successful in such a challenge. Typical grounds for a successful court challenge to an arbitrator's award would be those rare instances in which the arbitrator rendered an award exceeding his or her authority or had an undisclosed partisan interest in one side, such as an arbitrator whose law firm represented a union or employer. The net positive effect of the speedier hearing and the finality of the award is the creation of a better climate of human relations at the workplace, because the problem, the complaint and the grievance are irritants that may fester like an untreated wound, and, in time, infect and poison the atmosphere. Even if the ultimate resolution of the grievance, either during the grievance process or by arbitral award, is not fully to the liking of one of the parties, it *is* a *resolution*, and the parties are free to move on with their lives and work relationships.

Fundamentally, then, the basic advantage of arbitration is that the dispute resolution process belongs to the parties themselves, and they are jointly free to shape it and control it to meet their needs. From the selection of the arbitrator to the level of legality and formality desired, the process belongs to both labor and management. This is, of course, not true of judicial and/or administrative dispute resolution processes, wherein the selection of the judge, or hearing officer, is totally beyond the control of the disputants, as are procedural rules.

It must be emphasized that the arbitrator draws his or her authority from the parties and enjoys this power due only to this mandate. For example, once a final award is issued, the arbitrator is considered *functus officio*, or without any further power or authority over the case. Thus, after the issuance of the final award, should one party seek to have the arbitrator alter or clarify the award, the arbitrator may not do so unless jointly reempowered by both sides.

About Arbitrators: Selection and Cost

Since great power is given by the parties to the arbitrator, a closer examination of the arbitrator is clearly appropriate.

First, in our credential-happy society, wherein everyone from beauticians to electricians to realtors is licensed, arbitrators are not. There is no licensing exam, no education requirement, no certifying board, no paper one hangs on the wall saying "arbitrator." Put simply, you become an arbitrator when the parties—both of them—accept you as an arbitrator, and not before.

While there are no formal requirements to become an arbitrator, certain standards have evolved from common practice. The first is neutrality; that is, the arbitrator should not be an advocate one day and seek to be a neutral the next. A knowledge of industrial relations, the common law of labor relations, is certainly sought, as is the ability to write a comprehensible opinion. While most arbitrators have a legal background, not all are lawyers, and while many teach at colleges, law schools and universities, not all do. The profession of labor arbitration is changing as the original cadre, the War Labor Board neutrals, retire. One can only hope the new generation of arbitrators will maintain the high standards set by these distinguished individuals.

The parties look principally to two organizations to provide lists from which they will select an arbitrator. In a sense—but only in a minor sense—these organizations act as preliminary screeners of arbitrators through their admittance procedures. Both organizations require some background investigation and documentation before an arbitrator candidate is admitted, but, basically, it is always left to the parties themselves to select the arbitrator who will hear their case, a right the parties guard zealously.

The American Arbitration Association (AAA) is a not-for-profit organization dedicated to the voluntary resolution of a wide range of disputes—not only labor–management controversies, but commercial, construction, international, insurance and community disputes as well. The AAA as a nongovernmental entity can conduct employee representation elections, improper-practice hearings and other dispute resolution proceedings, such as fact-finding, even in jurisdictions or sectors with no law governing employee relations, provided the disputants so agree. The AAA has 35 regional offices across the United States and can administer cases anywhere in the country.

For a nominal fee, an AAA regional office will provide the disputants with a list of arbitrators, accompanied by a short biographical sketch of each arbitrator. The parties will often ask around about the names on the list if they are unfamiliar with them. Through a system of alternate striking or preference ranking, both sides select the arbitrator to hear their case. The fee each side pays to the AAA is for case administration, which means that important details, such as scheduling the hearing and requests for postponements, are handled by tribunal administrators, not the arbitrator herself or himself. This is not only a convenience for the arbitrator and the parties but, perhaps more important, it provides a buffer between the neutral and disputants that many feel serves to keep the process neutral.

The Federal Mediation and Conciliation Service (FMCS) is a federal agency that provides mediators free of charge to parties at impasse in contract negotiations. As part of its peacemaking and peacekeeping mission, the agency will also provide parties with lists of grievance arbitrators, allowing for a similar selection process. Like the AAA, the FMCS investigates the background of potential arbitrators in an effort to ensure that lists sent to the parties contain only the names of qualified neutrals. The FMCS does not charge a case administration fee, nor does it administer cases. Once the parties select an arbitrator, he or she contacts the parties directly and makes all necessary arrangements with no further involvement of the FMCS.

Some parties prefer the AAA and others prefer the FMCS, depending on cost considerations and their desire for more or less case administration assistance. Most successful arbitrators are on the lists of both organizations, and are thus available from whichever organization the parties wish to use. It is also not uncommon for the parties to agree to appoint directly an individual to serve as an arbitrator without using either organization.

Some state labor relations agencies or boards also have rosters of neutrals available to the parties. And, finally, some parties with a continuing volume of grievance arbitrations will create a permanent umpireship, wherein the same individual (or small group of neutrals) will hear all grievances. It is perhaps a misnomer to call these umpireships permanent, because the neutral serves at the pleasure of the parties and can be removed by either or both sides. Nonetheless, some umpires have served the same parties for many years and have become an integral part of the relationship.

In ad hoc arbitration, once the parties have received a list of names of arbitrators and examined the accompanying biographical sketches, they are ready to begin the actual selection of an arbitrator. How do parties make this important decision?

First, experienced advocates will often be familiar with one or more of the names on the list, perhaps from previous cases. Many law firms, employers and unions maintain, either formally or informally, some sort of roster or directory of arbitrators in which those who have had experience with the individual may record their impressions and/or file a copy of any decision and award issued. Those advocates who are unfamiliar with the work of a particular arbitrator will usually inquire among fellow advocates concerning the reputation of the arbitrator as to ability to run an orderly, productive hearing and issue a well-written, well-reasoned opinion and award. Many advocates utilize reporting services to gather information about a particular arbitrator and read any published awards issued. This provides a sense of the track record of the arbitrator.

Inherent in all of these approaches is the danger of considering an arbitrator's acceptability based solely on his or her "score card," the decisions issued for labor or management. This "score card" approach is probably not terribly effective in predicting the performance of a particular arbitrator because there is no way, short of reading all the opinions written by the arbitrator, of determining any bias or predilection. Put simply, no arbitrator would enjoy broad and continuing acceptability if he or she evidenced a pronounced bias toward one side or the other.

Arbitrators are paid for hearing time, travel time and study time. Per-diem rates vary with the arbitrator, but generalizations are still valid. In a typical case, the arbitrator will charge for one day to hear the case and two days to study, write and issue the award. Assuming a per-diem charge of $400, a typical case will cost the parties $1,200 in fees, plus travel, food and lodging expenses. The arbitrator's bill is usually split evenly by the two parties. Thus, in the illustration above, each party would pay about $625, assuming $50 in arbitrator expenses for travel, lodging and food.

The real expense of arbitration lies in each side's own case preparation costs. If outside legal counsel is used, if witnesses are called, if preparation time is taken (as it most certainly should be) before the hearing, the cost to each side alone may well be twice or three times the arbitrator's fee. Time spent preparing, investigating, documenting and presenting the case involves expense and lost work time. But case preparation, the key to successful arbitration practice, is well worth the expense, especially considering the risk of a negative decision. Put simply, if a matter were not of some importance, it would not have been brought to arbitration. Because the matter is at arbitration, it is important enough to warrant the expense and time for thorough preparation.

An additional benefit of comprehensive case preparation is that it enables a party to fully evaluate the merits of its case—and, as previously discussed, often encourages a prearbitration compromise settlement, or even an alteration in position, resulting in a withdrawal of the grievance by the union or a granting of the grievance by management.

Industrial Jurisprudence: Progressive Discipline

Over the years, a body of arbitral rulings has been created, referred to previously as "industrial jurisprudence." These rules, the equivalent of the common law of industrial relations, enjoy broad acceptance and are followed in both public and private sectors.

Broadly speaking, arbitration cases fall into two categories: discipline and contract interpretation. The first category represents by far the greatest volume of cases, covering as it does the gamut of disciplinary matters—from a letter of reprimand to the most severe of all industrial penalties, termination.

For example, a grievance typically arises over conflicting interpretations of the collective agreement, or how language should be applied to govern a factual situation. If the contract says that no employee shall be disciplined except for "just cause," was an employee properly given a three-day unpaid suspension for being tardy? The employee's prior tardiness record is important, as are records of any warnings, written reprimands, conferences, etc. Often there is no factual dispute—that is, the employee's attendance record is undisputed, and the controversy is simply over whether a three-day suspension under the circumstances is too severe. Other cases are simple factual disputes. Was the employee drunk? Who hit whom? etc.

One of the principles of industrial jurisprudence is that discipline must be corrective to the employee and not merely punitive. Under a system of progressive discipline, an employee is given numerous opportunities to correct his or her behavior, with counseling and penalties of increasing severity if the infractions continue. For example, if Bill Thomas is 15 minutes late to work and it is the first time he has been tardy, his supervisor may dock his pay and give him a gentle admonition not to be late again. The second time it happens, the admonition may be less gentle, and the third time a letter of reprimand may be issued that could become part of his permanent personnel file.

The supervisor would want to make certain that Thomas knew what his obligation was, and might suggest ways to ensure that the obligation would be met every day. The next lateness might result in a one-day suspension and progress through a three-day and one- or two-week suspension if the employee did not correct his behavior. Ultimately, the supervisor might conclude that the employee deserved termination because he had continued to report to work late. Often, as in this example, there may not be a factual dispute; both sides agree that the employee was late on 12 occasions over a seven-month period, but there may well be a dispute over the equity or severity of the penalty. In other disciplinary cases, there may be a critical dispute over tacts, such as who hit who first in a physical confrontation between a supervisor and an employee, or whether the employee was provoked into striking the supervisor.

Certain types of employee behavior may be considered so extreme that the usual steps of progressive discipline may not apply. Examples of this might be an employee stealing money or property from the employer, or an act of extreme insubordination. One of the basic tenets of industrial jurisprudence is that an employee must obey a lawful order of a supervisor so long as the employee's health or safety would not be placed in jeopardy by complying with that order. This rule is sometimes abbreviated as "don't leave, grieve," meaning the employee is not to refuse an order or leave work if she or he does not wish to comply, but should obey the order and *then* file a grievance. The worth of this system is that it gives the employee protection of his or her rights, and simultaneously allows the enterprise to continue its normal functioning.

Thus, under a contract providing mandatory overtime for least-senior employees, if a supervisor directs senior employee Fred Hamilton to stay and work overtime while telling Jack Camp, a junior employee, to go home, Hamilton should stay, work and then file a grievance. If

Hamilton refused to work and left, he would be committing an act of insubordination that in turn constitutes a violation of the contract. This would effectively serve as a waiver of his claim in a work assignment dispute.

Another principle of industrial jurisprudence is that ungrieved discipline is presumed valid and may not later be challenged. To return to our earlier example of Bill Thomas, the employee with the tardiness problem, consider that, when he received a one-week suspension, he served it and did not file a grievance. When he got a 30-day suspension, he grieved, and, at arbitration of the 30-day suspension, he sought also to attack the earlier one-week suspension as unjustified. Generally, most arbitrators would sustain the objection by the employer to an examination of the earlier discipline. As noted earlier, each contract contains time limits for filing a grievance and for appealing from one step to the next higher one. If there were no prohibition on reviving old grievances, each arbitration could potentially encompass all manner of prior disputes, and the proceeding would lose focus.

Even more fundamentally, as discussed earlier, because the parties are living together on a daily basis, it is vital that disputes not be allowed to fester like untreated wounds, which could turn into fatal infections. There must be clarity of the status of a dispute. If no grievance is filed in a timely fashion, then the matter must be considered closed and its resolution final. It is for this reason that many union stewards routinely grieve all discipline matters in order to preserve and protect employees' rights. Then, in the early steps of the grievance process, the union will withdraw its nonmeritorious claims and proceed with only meritorious grievances.

It should be noted that industrial jurisprudence has evolved with societal mores and behaviors. As one illustration, employees with alcohol or drug abuse problems are more commonly considered "sick," deserving and benefiting from treatment as opposed to earlier moralistic judgments that they were "bad" and deserved punishment. This means that, if an employee with a substance abuse problem misses work and/or is tardy too often, arbitrators today will be likely to look beyond the sum total of absences and latenesses and examine the reason for it.

If the employer has sought to understand and assist the employee in dealing with a problem, by, for example, encouraging attendance at counseling or therapy programs and the like, but the employee has not sought help, then the discipline will likely be upheld. However, if the employer has not demonstrated any sensitivity or understanding of the problem and has not supported the employee's sincere rehabilitation efforts, the discipline will likely not be sustained.

Industrial Jurisprudence: Contract Interpretation

The arbitrator decides contract interpretation cases guided by certain principles, many of which, like the parol evidence rule, are taken from contract law, and others which come from the body of industrial jurisprudence. An example of the latter is the maxim that one party may not successfully seek from the arbitrator's pen that which it failed to negotiate at the bargaining table.

Thus, if an employer proposed during contract negotiations that Sunday overtime, which had previously been voluntary, be compulsory, and the union rejected that proposal, the employer may not unilaterally impose mandatory Sunday overtime during the term of the contract. If the matter went to arbitration, most likely the arbitrator would sustain the union's grievance and conclude that the employer did not have the right to unilaterally alter a bilaterally negotiated agreement. Phrased another way, the arbitrator would not grant one party a right it had an opportunity to obtain in another more appropriate forum and did not.

The contract is obviously an important agreement to both sides and they usually treat it with great respect. The rules that govern the workplace emanate from the joint agreements of the parties. Thus, while discharge and discipline cases are far more common than contract interpretation matters, the latter are often of far-reaching importance and greater significance than the more dramatic disciplinary proceedings. The reason for this is that the contract belongs to all the parties, and a decision on its meaning affects all, while a typical discipline case, though of enormous significance to the grievant, often may mean nothing to other members of the bargaining unit. For this reason, union stewards will often encourage and even urge the filing of a grievance if they believe it may be of significance.

For example, in the contract between the Gotham Teachers' Association and the school board, each high school teacher is allocated one duty free planning period per day. This planning period may be taken away, the contract says, "only in emergency situations." When the board gives high school students the state-mandated so-called "accountability tests" (standardized skill-achievement exams), Dorothy Post is assigned to administer the test during her planning period. She feels that while she probably should not have to do this she will surrender the planning period.

Her union representative Carole Freed urges her to file a grievance because, as she explains, accountability tests are not a real emergency, such as a teacher suddenly becoming ill, but are rather scheduled, predictable events for which the board can obtain substitute teachers. Freed concludes by telling the teacher that if the board is permitted to take away a planning period from her for a nonemergency, then no teacher's planning period is safe. Thus convinced, Dorothy Post files a grievance because, even though the financial amount at stake may not be important to her, the matter is significant to her fellow teachers.

The reason this is so important lies in the concept of "past practice," which means that, under certain circumstances, the parties may by their conduct modify the written language of the agreement. In the illustration above, if the school board had been utilizing high school teachers' planning periods to give accountability tests for the past six years and there had been no grievance filed, a valid past practice may have been created that serves to alter the contractual provision concerning planning periods.

How does a behavior become past practice? In real property law, students are familiar with the concept of obtaining property rights by adverse possession. Thus, if for a number of years your neighbor has walked across a small patch of your land that abuts his property to get to the beach, he might get certain rights to your property. The same principle applies in contract administration. If one party engages in an act that is continuous, open, overt, unequivocal and clear, and that act is accepted, albeit tacitly, by the other side, a past practice may emerge that enjoys the same legal status as written contract language and gives the same rights.

To sum up, the authority of the arbitrator is limited by contractual provisions and precepts of industrial jurisprudence. The arbitrator is called in to determine what the parties' rights are under the agreement they negotiated. The arbitrator is not empowered to give one party what it failed to obtain by negotiation or past practice.

Contract language may not always be clear, and poorly written agreements are all too common because of pressures such as strike deadlines. At 3:45 P.M., after engaging in around-the-clock bargaining, exhausted parties may well be excused if their language was less than precise. Indeed, sometimes the parties may consciously choose unclear language and agree simply to wrap up a contract. Like Scarlett O'Hara, they "will think about it tomorrow."

Even if language is precise, unforeseen events may occur for which no contractual provision was negotiated. What then? Each side may well believe that existing language, past practice or equity demand that their position be sustained. If a settlement satisfactory to both sides cannot be negotiated—as it usually is—then recourse to arbitration will be pursued.

Conducting the Arbitration Hearing

Unlike judicial proceedings wherein a judge decides questions of law and a jury decides questions of fact, in labor arbitrations, the arbitrator judges both fact and law. Given this situation, the safeguards for the protection of the jury, i.e., the rules of evidence, are usually suspended, and the case is conducted in an informal manner.

It is appropriate to reiterate a key point: the process of arbitration belongs to the parties. Thus, if the parties agree that they want a formalized, legalistic hearing, the arbitrator will usually oblige, though most parties—and arbitrators—prefer an informal process. The rules of evidence are exclusionary in nature, and most arbitrators want to hear more, as opposed to less, about the case at hand. Most, but by no means all, arbitrators have sufficient legal training to conduct a formal hearing if the parties want it. Often, the parties may choose a formal approach for a number of reasons. For example, if there may be subsequent or collateral proceedings—as in the case of a grievance involving allegations of race or sex discrimination—the parties may wish to have a full record developed, including a verbatim transcript and strict adherence to the federal rules of civil procedure.

The rationale behind a nontechnical approach to arbitration goes deeper than a mere preference for informality. As the late Harry Shulman, perhaps the dean of labor arbitrators, once explained, the nature of labor arbitration is fundamentally different from normal litigation. He noted that, unlike litigants in a court, the parties in a collective bargaining agreement must continue to live with one another both during the dispute and after. He urged the parties to view grievance arbitration as a mutual problem that can affect the future relations of the parties and the smooth operation of the enterprise.

This means that the parties' approach must be radically different from that of litigants. Shulman wrote:

> A litigant does not care whether he wins his law suit because the tribunal understood the problem and made a wise judgment, or because the tribunal was actually confused or was influenced by wooden technicality, or irrelevant or emotional considerations. But the parties in a labor dispute submitted to arbitration, seeking an award with which they must both live harmoniously in the future, must seek not merely a victory but a wise and enlightened award based on relevant factors and full understanding of the problem. And they must, therefore, seek to have the arbitrator know as much as possible about their enterprise, their interest in it, and the problem involved.

In sum, then, grievance arbitration exists to resolve those problems arising during the course of the parties' ongoing relationship. It is a valuable tool of dispute resolution, and most parties use it wisely and well.

Arbitrability

This leads us directly to the area of arbitrability, or whether the matter is properly before the arbitrator for hearing or decision. There are two types of arbitrability: substantive and procedural. Procedural arbitrability asks whether the grievance has been processed properly by the parties. Often a union may miss an appeal deadline in the early stages of the grievance process. Assume a contract provides that the union has five working days to appeal from a Step-3 decision, and the union took six days. Most arbitrators would conclude that, while technically there was a procedural violation, to deny a hearing to the grievant on such narrow, technical grounds would be inconsistent with the goals of labor arbitration. For, if the arbitrator ruled the grievance procedurally defective and, therefore, inarbitrable, the grievant would never receive a hearing on the merits. The problem would remain unsolved and would be a continuing irritant to the parties. More likely than not, a new grievance would soon be filed claiming an identical or similar contractual violation. The process would begin again, not only with a duplication of effort and a waste of time and money, but with increasing bitterness between the parties.

Thus, most arbitrators approach procedural arbitrability questions rather flexibly and will be inclined to give full consideration to any reasonable explanation of tardiness. Common sense governs here, and a union that sat on its rights for two months without a plausible explanation will probably not receive the same consideration from an arbitrator. Flexibility and common sense—yes; implausibility and laxity—no. Additionally, in making his or her ruling, the arbitrator would consider such factors as the custom of the parties concerning adherence to deadlines. As an illustration, if both parties routinely deviated from the time limits in the grievance procedure and one side is now, for the first time, raising a procedural objection, the arbitrator could well be expected to view this claim with a rather jaundiced eye.

Substantive arbitrability is not viewed nearly as flexibly. A substantive claim in arbitrability means that one side is arguing that the grievance in question is not properly before the arbitrator because its substance is not covered by, or is excluded from, the collective bargaining agreement. An example of this would be the union seeking to have a supervisor (someone not in the bargaining unit) disciplined for some allegedly improper act. The employer would argue, successfully, that, under the language of the contract, an action management might or might not take concerning a supervisor is not subject to the grievance procedure and is simply not arbitrable.

Simply put, the arbitrator draws authority from the parties under an agreement, and if he or she lacks authority to hear a certain type of dispute under that agreement, then the grievance is substantively inarbitrable and the arbitrator may not pass on the merits of the case. It should be clear that substantive arbitrability is by no means a "technical ruling" in the sense that Professor Shulman found objectionable in arbitration. Indeed, such a ruling of substantive inarbitrability, if warranted, goes to the very heart of the parties' relationship, and is, therefore, vitally important to the content and future of the collective agreement.

Expedited Arbitration

When the parties have a large, ongoing volume of grievances requiring arbitration, and many of the cases are minor disciplinary matters, expedited arbitration may be utilized. Typically, the parties will jointly establish rules and procedures tailored to their own needs and proceed to preselect a small group of neutrals to hear the cases on a rotating basis.

For example, the Belmont Steel Company and the Industrial Union of Steel Workers agree to the following: all unresolved discipline grievances for which the penalty is a suspension of 30 days or less, and which present no contract interpretation issues of precedential value to either side, may be submitted to expedited arbitration. With the assistance of the local office of the American Arbitration Association, the parties select one arbitrator who will serve on their expedited arbitration and agree to bill at a uniform rate and not charge for study time. The arbitrators further agree that they will issue only awards, not opinions, within five business days after the hearing. The parties have decided that no transcript will be recorded at the hearing, and neither side will file post-hearing briefs or be represented by an attorney at the hearings which are to be conducted on an informal basis.

Such a system of expedited arbitration not only allows the parties to resolve a large number of cases quickly and economically, but enables them to clear up a potential source of friction between employees and their supervisors. When an expedited arbitration system is working in tandem with a smoothly functioning grievance process and a system for arbitrating major disciplinary and contractual matters, both parties can enjoy less tension at the workplace. As with disease, early detection and treatment can lead to better health at the workplace.

Constructive Adversarialism

Given the current perilous state of our economy and the enormously competitive global environment, increased cooperation between unions and employers seems to make such sense as to be self-evident. Surely, conflict at the workplace is bound to reduce efficiency just when higher productivity is most necessary. Obviously, the only way to proceed in the last decade of this turbulent century is whole-hearted labor–management cooperation—or is it?

First of all, to be successful, any joint labor–management effort requires a high level of mutual trust and respect. Too many of these cooperative programs are born out of desperation, threatened bankruptcy and closure of operations, under conditions of economic insecurity. Often at that late hour, the financial situation of the enterprise is so precarious that the hastily conceived and executed joint program is simply too little, too late, with the result that nothing short of a miracle could allow the avoidance of disaster. And in the real world miracles seldom occur.

Further, no amount of mutual cooperation can save an enterprise out of sync with the needs of the marketplace. Producing a poorly designed product, an overpriced one or an unreliable one puts the employer in such jeopardy that no amount of cooperative effort will be successful.

In these sorts of desperate situations where there is really no foundation of mutual trust between the parties, it is unlikely that there would be any joint labor–management program except for the impending financial disaster, and the cooperative activities will likely not be very successful coming from such negative motivation.

The key, therefore, to enjoying success in these endeavors is taking a pro-active approach, that is to build a relationship of mutual trust and respect over time so that, when and if it becomes necessary to take drastic steps such as a significant cutback in employment or a broad reduction of wages, the union members have the necessary information to enable them to make an informed judgment in assessing the employer's needs. Paradoxically, it is those same managers who have built a positive industrial relations climate of mutual trust and respect who rarely need the desperation measures discussed above.

Blurring of Roles

One of the principal pitfalls in engaging in cooperative programs is the possibility of the blurring of each party's role in the enterprise. Just how closely can the union work with the employer without becoming an arm of the company? In virtually every internal union election—at every level of the organization—the principal and often only issue is the question of whether the union incumbents have gotten too close with the management. Dissidents will invariably charge that their opponents, the current union leaders, have lost touch with the members and have begun to identify far too closely with the employer's interests. Union activists know too well the response to the following question: what do you call a union official who is extremely sensitive to the needs of management and sincerely works to insure its continued viability? A former union official.

Managers often zealously guard their prerogatives from union encroachment. To put a union representative on the board of directors is seen as a serious invasion of management rights, that area of decision-making from which unions are excluded. The fear employers have is that, once the union begins to influence the managerial decision process, the process will continue until the union runs the entire enterprise, and makes judgments based on improper criteria. For example, if a union were given veto power over what to produce, formerly a right exclusively controlled by management, the union might force the enterprise to continue to make products the marketplace rejects in order to maintain—at least for the short run—a high level of employment of dues-paying, voting union members.

It is by no means easy to reconcile these concerns of unions and managers over invasion of their domains. Nonetheless, if there is to be meaningful cooperation, each side must deal not only with their own concerns but those of the other side.

The Theory of Constructive Adversarialism

We espouse a theory called "constructive adversarialism" as a way to encourage mutual cooperation at the workplace without undermining the legitimate roles and rights of both the management and the union. How does this theory work?

In terms of workplace cooperation, the union should encourage wholehearted employee participation by its members while exercising flexibility on issues like job classifications and work assignments. However, the employee involvement process is a management process because the ultimate responsibility for its success—and the success of the enterprise itself—rests with the management. This means that within broad parameters management must have wide discretion to direct the enterprise in a flexible and efficient manner. The union's role is to protect its employees from the possible excesses of managerial decision-making. The precise definition of the parameters should be the subject of serious negotiations between the parties, preferably before the enterprise falls into fiscal peril.

Similarly, the union should have input into the managerial decision-making process through representation on committees at every level of the organization, from the workplace to the board room. Management cannot justify unilateral and total control of necessary information if they are asking their employees to trust them completely. In corporate decision-making, the union should have access to all relevant data but this does not mean the employees have veto power over crucial decisions.

Unions should be expected to cooperate with management but not to be co-opted by management. As in any business transaction, every good service has its price. To achieve the total cooperation of a union, management must be willing to accept the union as an integral part of the workplace environment. An employer cannot on the one hand seek to undermine or oust the union while at the same time seek union involvement and commitment for cooperative joint programs.

The union exists to represent, protect and advance the interests of employees. Clearly, the continued existence of the employer is a crucial part of a union's interest, for with no company there can be no jobs, no economic security, no bargaining unit. So the union must constantly balance aggressive advancement of employee interests with the realistic limits of the employer's financial ability, not often an easy task. This is constructive adversarialism, the union balancing conflicting interests, getting the most for its members without crippling the employer, winning and enforcing reasonable work rules which protect the worker from exploitation while not unfairly hobbling the efficient operation of the enterprise.

Management, on its part, then must be fair with the union, neither seeking to destroy the union nor meekly acquiescing to every union demand. No, finding the proper balance is not easy on either side of the table. But it is so necessary as to be more than worth the effort.

The Good Unions Can Do:

At a U.S. Department of Labor sponsored conference on labor–management cooperation, conferees suggested what unions might bring to the cooperative process:

1. Unions help weed out bad, flawed or deficient cooperative plans by providing a second opinion, a sounding board for ideas that may initially seem conceptually perfect but are not workable in the real world.

2. Unions keep companies from reverting to old ways in a crisis when there might be a tendency to revert to traditional unilateral decision-making and quick-fix-type solutions which, while quick, never do truly fix the problem.

3. Unions provide the institutional leadership for addressing and reforming glitches in the program without throwing out the whole process. Unions can maintain due process, equity, integrity and reciprocity in cooperative programs to insure that the program is not exploitative. Any program perceived to be exploitive will not last long.

4. A union is the only practical way to give workers a meaningful voice in the process consistent with principles of elective democracy. Just as citizens elect representatives, so too do workers elect union representatives to speak for them.

5. Unions are crucial for educating workers to make informed decisions and only unions have the institutional ability to both inform employees and provide the expertise to assist in decision-making.

6. Unions bring both legal status and economic power to the cooperative process which would not exist but for the exclusive bargaining agent. Both as a matter of legality and practicality, the employer is constrained in its unilateral power which provides a check, a counter-force on any ill-conceived management program.

To be sure, not all unions are going to approach the cooperative process with a total commitment to success. As in any relationship, one cannot simply create trust by fiat; it must be grown and nurtured on a daily basis throughout all levels of the organization. And while mutual trust between labor and management is not created quickly or easily, the rewards to both parties are well worth the effort; or put another way, the negative consequences of hostility between unions and employers are, like nuclear war, simply too deadly to contemplate, and like nuclear war, there are no victors—only losers and no survivors on either side.

The Fruits of Cooperation

Often, corporations may experience high profitability for a variety of reasons having more to do with good luck than planned strategy. Consider that oil companies have seen their finances respond to world geopolitical affairs both positively and negatively in recent years. It seems to matter little how efficiently their employees work given the powerful external market forces, and if there is no causal relationship between employees working harder and organizational success, there is no positive motivation to stimulate greater effort in times of high oil prices. Similarly, when the petroleum market declines, employees whose compensation is tied to net profits may become demoralized for, regardless of their individual or even collective efforts, the result will pay little or nothing.

A better approach to gain-sharing is a Scanlon plan which allows employees to receive a large portion of the savings in labor cost, an area over which they have great control. It is therefore possible to have a positive Scanlon plan payout to employees while the enterprise is not enjoying net profits and the shareholders are not being paid a dividend. However, on the other hand, it is also possible if the employees are not working efficiently for there to be large corporate profits but no Scanlon payout. Nonetheless, we believe that, because there is a strong causal relationship between working to reduce labor costs and receiving a Scanlon payout, such a plan makes the most sense in terms of worker motivation, in that it establishes a nexus between employee production, positive results and monetary reward.

Those few at the top of the corporate pyramid are often paid hundreds of times the average workers' salary. Not surprisingly, these top managers believe they earn their compensation packages by providing the sort of quality guidance and organizational leadership that results in success. For those who make the financial, marketing and other strategic and tactical managerial decisions, tying their compensation to organizational performance may well make sense. But for an employee who has no meaningful input into those crucial decisions, it seems that in many instances profit-sharing makes little sense. Perhaps the only exceptions would be situations such as retail or service organizations in which the employees *are* the corporation to its customers. However, even in these situations, it makes more sense to base financial rewards on either the individual's performance or a smaller operational unit such as one store or one service area.

Labor–Management Cooperation

Evaluation

How can a labor–management cooperative endeavor be judged? Certainly any activity that requires so much effort must be assessed carefully to evaluate its worth. Ten years ago, the American Arbitration Association, with a grant from the Federal Mediation and Conciliation Service, created the National Labor–Management Committee to discuss cooperative programs and worker participation programs as a means of improving productivity, organizational effectiveness and the quality of working life.

This group of practitioners reported that a labor–management committee would know it is proceeding on the right path when:

a) there is a shift in the labor–management relationship from hostility and secretiveness to advance notice, consultation and joint problem-solving;

b) there is a shift from a legalistic to a humanistic approach and diminishment of rules-mindedness while there is a simultaneous increase in substantive problem-solving;

c) there is an increase in scores in employee satisfaction surveys and an increase in quality of the production or service rendered; and

d) both sides receive benefits from these programs and believe it is worth continuing in the future.

In sum, these cooperative programs require a deep commitment from both sides in terms of time, energy and effort. And while there may be short-term benefits which are readily apparent to everyone, the greater and more important benefits may take longer to achieve but are deeper and more pervasive throughout the organization.

In sum, seeking the "quick fix" to serious problems at the workplace through joint labor–management cooperation is neither "quick" nor does it "fix" anything. It may be useful to recall that usually it takes many years for serious problems to foster and grow. It is unrealistic to expect that problems of great depth and complexity will be satisfactorily resolved after only a few brief joint meetings.

Grievance Mediation

In recent years, there has been a movement giving increased visibility to grievance mediation. In this process, an outside neutral is brought in to assist the parties in reaching a voluntary resolution of outstanding grievances. Often, the grievance mediator is faced with a large docket of unresolved grievances which may be symptomatic of a dysfunctional labor–management relationship. The grievance mediator may be able to provide the perspective of an outsider and assist the parties in forging a better relationship by helping resolve outstanding grievances.

For example, consider the situation at the Powell Products facility which distributes medical supplies. The warehouse workers and drivers are represented by a local of the Teamsters' Union which has filed about 75 grievances over allocation of overtime issues.

When Peggy Fong, a teacher of industrial relations courses at a nearby university, is brought in, she examines the situation and suggests to both parties that they consider the process of grievance mediation as a way to resolve the problems at the workplace and avoid the enormous drain of resources that the arbitration of so many cases would entail.

It must be emphasized that grievance mediation can be successful only with the sincere commitment and active cooperation of *both* labor and management representatives. The grievance mediator has no legal authority to bind the parties or compel either side to accept any settlement. If the parties have faith in both the process and the person selected, there is an increased likelihood of success. To be sure, when the parties have jointly selected an individual to mediate grievances and are interested in using the process, there is already a demonstrated predisposition for a positive outcome and the result is often exactly that.

Having read and digested all the pending grievances and the relevant sections of the parties' collective bargaining agreement, Dr. Fong is ready to begin the process. She meets jointly with company human resources vice-president Donna Kirk and the union's international representative Sally Shroeder. First, Dr. Fong makes clear the ground rules under which she is operating. Then she presents her analysis of the root causes of the allocation of overtime issues, explaining that the relevant clauses in the collective bargaining agreement seem quite vague and appear contradictory in part. Further, the record indicates that some supervisors approach the issue quite differently from other supervisors and this difference may well account for the bad feelings surrounding this issue. For example, she points out that, in the Receiving Department, overtime is offered strictly by seniority but in the Shipping Department overtime is allocated by the job assigned—a process known as "lines of progression," which combines both length of service and the work tasks performed. Although it is true that these two departments have operated for a long period of time under these differing rules, workers are increasingly upset and confused. Of course, employees talk among themselves about work and, depending upon each person's situation, s/he likes one system or the other. The Packing Department, for example, is constantly in turmoil as some employees and supervisors advocate one method for allocation of overtime, and their cohorts advance another. Dr. Fong suggests that this uncertainty must be resolved and all employees must be governed by the same rules or the situation will deteriorate further.

After some bluster on both sides, the two representatives warily agree that the present situation is untenable and far too many human resources are being wasted dealing with this conflict. Dr. Fong then asks both representatives to feel free to speak off the record about what they would conceptually want in an overtime allocation system. Not surprisingly, their interests are quite similar on the subject: both seek a predictable, simple, reliable system which is universally understood and operates the same for all concerned. Having gotten conceptual agreement, Dr. Fong is now ready to begin getting more specific agreements, first on what the parties need and want and then on the mechanics of achieving that goal.

After a number of intensive meetings, Donna Kirk, the company human resources vice-president, announces that, following discussions with production supervisors, the lines of progression system which combines both seniority and the work tasks performed is the one she prefers. Ms. Kirk explains that just using department-wide seniority may result in having employees working overtime at jobs they may not have fully mastered. Then, given the fact that there is a fatigue factor on top of lesser job skills, there can be problems with both safety and quality control, two important areas of concern.

Union representative Shroeder acknowledges the seriousness of the company's concerns and says that, as a general principle, she can agree with using the lines of progression system for allocating overtime but she has another, related concern. Each department maintains a weekly "overtime-desired" list which must be used by each supervisor in allocating overtime. The problem she hears from her members is that many supervisors require everyone who signs the weekly list to be eligible to work on any day during that week. Therefore, if an employee has an obligation such as a doctor's appointment after work on a Wednesday, s/he is effectively prevented from signing up and working overtime any day during that week. The union representative suggests that the company go to a daily overtime-desired list to deal with this problem.

The company representative counters that, while she understands the problems, the concept of a daily overtime-desired list seems administratively unworkable and would make planning for staffing a daily nightmare.

Dr. Fong suggests they consider a compromise on this issue: a weekly overtime-desired list but with space for an employee to preclude—in advance—the day or days s/he is unavailable during that week. This would enable supervisors to plan for their staffing needs while allowing employees to meet their after-work obligations.

Following candid and comprehensive discussions, both representatives reach agreement on how to manage the overtime-desired list and execute a written document containing the appropriate language.

Having fully resolved the issue of overtime allocation and having agreed to language effectuating their agreements, the parties, with the assistance of the grievance mediator, are now able to quickly settle all outstanding grievances filed on this subject, both clearing the backlog of unresolved grievances and making the labor–management relationship more positive and workable. In this instance, with the skill of the grievance mediator and the cooperation of the parties, the process has produced a good result for all parties.

Some final observations are in order. Clearly, grievance mediation is a useful process for not only resolving grievances but also creating a better workplace environment. However, this process can only succeed when both parties are truly committed to its success and are willing to work at resolving the problems.

Second, the grievance mediator must be knowledgeable about industrial relations concepts as well as gifted in dealing with conflict resolution. To be sure, the joint selection of the grievance mediator by both union and employer representatives presupposes that there is great confidence in the knowledge, skills and abilities of the grievance mediator. Nonetheless, the issues to be addressed are both substantive and emotional. It is far too simplistic to label these issues as merely "political," as if having consequences in either the employer or union organizational structure would render the dispute incapable of resolution. If the problems were so easily resolved, there would be no outstanding grievance backlog to be addressed. Yes, these are serious problems that are dealt with in grievance mediation and, with the assistance of a skilled practitioner, the process can be successful.

Third, while grievance mediation may well succeed, the parties are well-advised to create and maintain a workable grievance process which ends in final and binding neutral arbitration. As the authors observed about grievance negotiation and grievance med–arb, the availability of an adjudicatory resolution of any and all grievances through arbitration serves as a powerful hammer to impel advocates to fashion their own settlements, either by themselves or with the assistance of a trained neutral.

Finally, at the risk of belaboring the point, no one method of grievance resolution is "better" than any other. Each approach has its positive aspects and may be appropriate and successful in certain labor–management relationships at different times. The authors want to encourage the parties to explore, examine and consider each approach with open minds.

Grievance Med–Arb

In the previous case study, the parties resolved the grievance themselves directly through the negotiation process. It is worth emphasizing that a negotiated settlement, whether achieved through direct bargaining or with the assistance of a neutral, is usually preferable to an adjudicated one. When the parties can fashion the settlement, they can often better meet their mutual needs and provide a positive framework for dealing with future problems. An arbitration award, no matter how well-written or enlightened, can only resolve the immediate case and is not always designed to enhance the parties long-term relationship.

Often, when the parties cannot resolve a grievance through bilateral negotiation, they may seek the assistance of an outside, third-party neutral. Quite frequently, when an experienced arbitrator is brought in to hear and decide a grievance, the parties may encourage the arbitrator to mediate the dispute.

This is a matter that requires some delicacy and tact. Indeed, some arbitrators will not even consider mediation, believing their mission is to decide the matter and nothing else. Other arbitrators will not mediate but urge the advocates to discuss settlement while the hearing is in recess.

Many experienced ad hoc arbitrators, especially those with whom the parties are familiar and those who are permanent umpires, may seek the parties' permission to mediate the grievance. If either party refuses, the arbitrator will not proceed with the mediation but will rather conduct the hearing and subsequently issue an award. (When parties bring in an experienced neutral mediator or arbitrator specifically to mediate the case, many of these problem areas would be avoided.)

Why might an advocate be reluctant to have an arbitrator mediate the grievance? In the mediation process, the neutral often learns "facts" which, as an arbitrator, s/he would not have the opportunity to hear, matters such as opinions, beliefs and conjectures. Some advocates are concerned that, if the mediation process is unsuccessful and the neutral resumes his arbitral posture, his decision may be affected by material gleaned in his mediatory role.

For example, when arbitrator Lawrence Block is brought in to hear the discharge of machinist Donald Westlake, both parties are receptive to his attempting to mediate the dispute. In off-the-record *ex parte* discussions with management representative Arthur Lyons, he learns that the company believes Westlake hosts weekend parties in his home at which drugs are used and other machinists attend these parties. The company, like virtually all employers today, is unalterably opposed to the use of drugs anywhere, anytime. Arbitrator Block comments that Westlake was not fired for any drug-related behavior but was terminated because of an alleged safety violation on the job. Lyons, the management representative, acknowledges the stated reason for Westlake's discharge but says that the production superintendent is glad to have the opportunity to get rid of him, especially because of his weekend parties.

In his meeting with Brian Garfield, the union representative, arbitrator Block learns that the safety violation for which Westlake was fired was his attempting to clear a jam of pulp paper from a shredding mill while it was operating by means of attempting to push the pulp jam through a pipe with a metal rod. Garfield insists that, while it was foolish and unsafe, no one had previously been fired for doing this and that further, Westlake was a long-service employee with no prior discipline on his record. Finally, no one in plant history had been fired for a first-time safety offense except Westlake in the instant case.

If the parties are to succeed in mediation, Block realizes he must address the sub-textual issue of the weekend parties and drug use. In an off-the-record discussion, Block asks the union representative about these allegations. (Note that this subject would never have even surfaced during the arbitration hearing, and yet it is critical to a complete understanding of the true essence of this grievance.)

Garfield says that there was one party, seven months ago, at Westlake's house at which a neighbor—not a co-worker—brought over some marijuana which a few people smoked. But Garfield emphasized that this was a one-time occurrence that was evidently blown way out of proportion. Garfield assures Block that his grievant does not regularly use any drug and, if the company is concerned about this problem, they never commented on any decline in Westlake's work or attendance and have not asked him to submit to any drug test, as they have a right to do under the collective bargaining agreement if his behavior changes significantly. Indeed, after the safety violation incident for which he was terminated, the company could have required a drug test but did not.

The union representative says that his grievant committed an unsafe act and may deserve some discipline but that termination is an excessive penalty. While the union has asked in its formal position for Westlake's return back to work with full back pay and benefits, Garfield indicates he can be somewhat flexible in the remedy as long as the grievant gets his job back. He notes an earlier case he handled in which a discharge was converted through negotiations into a three-month suspension and a last-chance warning. That worker, Tim Stuart, has since done a good job at work, Garfield comments, and has learned his lesson.

When Block next meets with management representative Lyons, he has a number of questions to raise. Lyons admits that no one had been fired before for a first safety violation but he points out that Westlake is a trained machinist who is well-paid for his work. He, of all workers, should know the safe procedure for clearing out a plugged shredding mill. Lyons gives no reason why Westlake was not subjected to a drug test after the incident but suggests that most likely the maintenance manager, who knows the grievant well, did not think he was a drug user. The maintenance manager has told Lyons that Westlake is a good worker who probably was taking a shortcut to allow him to get to his next work assignment. Lyons is clear that the maintenance manager would welcome Westlake back on the job.

The arbitrator asks Lyons about prior disciplinary incidents for safety violations. Lyons responds that, in a previous case two years ago, Tim Stuart's discharge was converted into a three-month suspension with a ''last-chance'' agreement. But the production superintendent is upset about drug-use allegations and has been unwilling to settle with the union on similar terms in Westlake's case.

Block tells Lyons that, were he to decide this matter as an arbitrator, he would not uphold the discharge since the severity of the penalty seems disproportional, given the prior situations of other employees. The prior precedent of the Stuart case would be given great weight in his award. As for the drug-use allegations, they occurred off-premises during off-duty time and were not cited in Westlake's letter of discharge, and clearly they would be inadmissible in an arbitration hearing.

Lyons tells Block he needs to speak with the Production Superintendent, and Block asks Lyons what he will recommend. Lyons responds he thinks a settlement would be well-advised. "I wanted to settle this earlier but the Production Superintendent was adamantly opposed. Now that I can tell him what you've said, perhaps he will change his mind," Lyons remarks.

A half-hour later, the management representative tells Block that he has been empowered to negotiate a settlement that puts Westlake back to work with a disciplinary suspension and a last-chance agreement similar to the Stuart case.

The union is agreeable, the deal is quickly reduced to writing and both representatives as well as the grievant and the arbitrator sign it.

Some important observations are in order. First, grievance mediation can succeed only if both parties are willing to compromise. Second, the arbitrator can only mediate if both sides empower him to do so. Third, the arbitrator clearly indicated the direction that his arbitration decision would take if mediation were unsuccessful and this provides a powerful impetus for settlement.

As noted earlier, not all arbitrators will engage in grievance mediation and some who do will not indicate the direction of their arbitration award because they believe to do so fatally compromises the arbitral decision-making process.

Finally, it must be emphasized that both representatives knew the mediator was also empowered as an arbitrator with the right to issue a binding award. The authors call this power "the hammer" that drives grievance mediation and consider it the principal reason for its success.

Points to Ponder

In both the academic and training settings, there will often be mock arbitration cases presented from one fact pattern. If more than one arbitrator hears such a case he or she may offer a decision that differs markedly from other arbitrators' decisions. Why does this happen? What does this tell us about the arbitration process?

Concluding Comments

"And nothing's quite as sure as change."

—THE MAMAS AND THE PAPAS
Look Through My Window

"Let's be careful out there."

—SGT. PHIL ESTERHAUS
Hill Street Blues

IN THIS FINAL SECTION the future and uses of both this manual and the "table processes" are discussed.

About This Manual

This manual has endeavored to blend theory and practice, concept and reality. The notions presented and illustrations given have come out of not only the academic study of collective bargaining, but the participation in and observation of what actually occurs. Nonetheless, because of the dynamics and the ever-changing nature of the process, it is likely that periodic updates of this manual will be needed. Any revisions will come out of new insights and experiences, but their exact nature and dimensions cannot be predicted. This, then, is the peril and challenge of not only writing this manual, but of the field of collective bargaining itself.

Applicability of This Manual

Recent years have brought numerous adaptations of collective bargaining approaches, and especially of dispute resolution techniques. Environmental, community and family disputes are now being approached by a new breed of advocates and dispute resolvers who are adapting techniques from collective bargaining, such as bilateral, trilateral and hydralateral negotiations, as well as fact-finding, mediation and arbitration. Clogged court dockets and backlogged administrative agencies provide clear and convincing evidence that new methods are needed to resolve disputes. The future appears to present even more opportunities for new uses of these techniques in areas such as insurance and malpractice claims, employment discrimination and construction, housing and consumer warranties, to name but a few.

Certainly, statutory and administrative rule-making have created situations at least roughly analogous, if not directly comparable, to collective bargaining. Therefore, those concerned with dispute resolution in any field will likely find much here to relate and apply to situations they encounter.

The purpose of this manual is to raise the public consciousness of the "table processes" by defining, exploring, analyzing and differentiating among the various processes in the belief that the more that is generally known about them the more they will be used, resulting in less need for "street-and-field" processes.

Greater recourse to and experience with table processes will lead disputants to trust them more. Obviously, disputants will use tools they know and trust best. Disputants kill, burn, riot, engage in war, etc., because they believe that these are the only ways to achieve their goals. The success of peaceful labor relations dispute resolution in the United States over the years through the use of table processes offers hope that these tools may well enjoy wider applicability and even greater success in emerging and unstable relationships, not only in our society but throughout the world.

It follows, further, that more extensive experience with the table processes will begin a significant cycle: that of increasing awareness of a need for greater skill training in advocacy, which leads to more positive experiences with table processes, which in turn leads to increasing trust and greater use of the processes.

Dispute Resolution

Peaceful resolution of disputes in the field of employee relations is especially important in the 1990s as our industrial and commercial society undergoes deep and pervasive transformations. Peace and stability, flexibility to adapt responsibly to change, cooperation and not confrontation are all important goals, none of which is easily achieved. Simply put, peace is not the absence of conflict or dispute—an improbable situation—but, rather, peace rises out of the ability of all parties concerned to deal constructively with change and differing goals. This involves fashioning solutions acceptable to all, safeguarding promise checking so that relationships are maintained long after promises are exchanged, and protecting the interests of all parties to ensure a peaceful future. If this manual has, in some way, increased the skills and abilities of advocates and peacemakers, it has been an endeavor well worth the effort.

Appendix:

Time-Line Management in Negotiations

The following is designed to serve as a helpful checklist to guide you in managing the time-line in collective bargaining. It is far too easy to get caught up in the energy of the process and the tactical details of meeting and dealing with different proposals and in so doing to lose your overview of strategic planning and perspective in bargaining.

The three keys to success at the table are: time, feeling and focus. You must be willing to put in the time that good, comprehensive preparation requires and that the caucus and joint sessions demand. By feeling, we refer to the emotional commitment that is a fundamental part of the collective bargaining process. Our advice is always designed to help the negotiator keep emotions under control, but we don't deny the presence and importance of deep emotional feelings. This manual is written to help participants in the process achieve their goals through the process and we acknowledge the meaningful role of feelings.

Finally, the process is best approached with a clear focus on your ultimate long-term strategic goal. What do you wish to get out of the upcoming negotiations? What are your true priorities? What sort of relationships do you wish to have with your own constituencies and hierarchy? Where do you want to be with those on the other side of the table?

It should be evident at this point that the authors believe it is crucial for negotiators to maintain and develop positive relationships if the bargaining process is to prove constructive. We reiterate here that there is a unique and continuous relationship between a union and employer and all the employees. Unlike a typical commercial transaction, such as purchasing and selling real estate, the parties involved in collective bargaining are vitally connected to each other and their long-term interests are inextricably bound together after implementation; the keeping of the promises is critical. The interests of an employer and the union which represents the employees are both similar and different. It falls to negotiators to sort out these interests, to reach a mutually satisfactory agreement and to provide an appropriate enforcement mechanism. The job of those involved in collective bargaining is as difficult as it is important.

As you examine this checklist, you might consider whether you approach the process as a stabilizer, destabilizer or as a quasi-mediator, understanding that, while your perspective might change during the bargaining and is dependent upon the issues, there is an underlying characterological bent each of us brings to the table. [The authors would like to thank Alison Lobb, a Cornell ILR intern, who prepared this checklist for the American Arbitration Association.]

TIME-LINE MANAGEMENT IN NEGOTIATIONS

Prepared for the American Arbitration Association
by Alison Lobb.

I. THE BEGINNING GAME/PREPARATION PHASE

A. TASKS

1. Organize Preparation Phase
   a. Establish communication with Hierarchy; set communication channels to be used throughout negotiation process
   b. Determine Hierarchy's needs/goals
   c. Begin internal negotiations to influence goals and strategies
   d. Manage Hierarchy's expectations
   e. Determine time-line for Preparation Phase—ultimate bargaining deadline, personnel availability, resource availability
   f. Determine team's limits of authority
   g. Establish bureaucratic procedures

2. Choose/Develop Team
   a. Establish communications within team
   b. Team-building exercises
   c. Educate team members as to different styles of thinking
   d. Determine each member's strengths/roles—substantive experts, procedural experts, spokesperson(s), media expert, corridor lobbyists, leader/facilitator, recordkeeper/designated listener (including body language and sounds), keeper of ''B-Book'' editor/language expert, numbers expert
   e. Train team in the negotiation process
   f. Manage expectations of team members
   g. Balance stabilizers and destabilizers
   h. Assign Preparation Phase tasks to each member

3. Gather Information/Identify Data Needs
   a. For your side's position

   b. For the other side's position

   c. Collect information from contract administration
     —labor–management activity
     —grievance/arbitration activity

   d. Collect financial/operating data
     —cost data
     —performance data
     —wage, cost and performance data of organizations similarly
      situated by industry or region

   e. Identify external consultants and resources

   f. Identify options to negotiating/BATNA[1]

   g. Identify members of other team
     —identify possible cross–cultural communications problems
     —determine their relationship with their Hierarchy
     —determine their Hierarchy's/constituents' needs

4. Analyze Past Negotiations and the Implementation of Past
  Agreements

   a. Review past negotiations of both teams

   b. Assess past negotiations
     —did the team achieve what it strived for?
     —what procedures did it use?
     —evaluate strengths and weaknesses of past negotiations

   c. Develop an archive system for retention of data of past
     negotiations

   d. Assess the implementation of the last agreement
     —what issues came up in grievances or other disputes?
     —what items were difficult for us to comply with?
     —what items were difficult for the other side to comply with?

5. Identify Issues

   a. Determine negotiable and non-negotiable items

   b. Determine "throw-away" items

   c. Determine likely sticking points

6. Identify All Interested and Affected Parties

   a. Perform public relations activities to condition
     —the workforce
     —the public

   b. Build outside alliances

   c. Educate interested parties
     —in the negotiation process
     —as to the team's goals

—as to anticipated difficulties
—to lower expectations
—to avoid sabotage

7. Set Goals/Priorities
   a. Identify options for bargaining outcomes
   b. Set bottom-line
   c. Establish opening position
   d. Set strategy (i.e., the "roadmap" of the negotiations—what you want to have accomplished by when, signposts, desired timing of negotiations)
   e. Determine real and announced deadlines
   f. Contingency planning
   g. Anticipate and analyze other party's demands, both historical and new
   h. Prepare response to anticipated opening position of other team
   i. Reach consensus within team
   j. Receive a commitment to the bottom-line from the Hierarchy/constituency. Prepare proposals: opening and bottom-line positions, offensive/defensive proposals

8. Ensure the availability of administrative support
   a. clerical
   b. technical
   c. equipment
   d. security

9. Arrange First Meeting of Phase II
   a. Create opportunities for informal, pre-negotiations meeting with other team to
      —avoid surprises
      —establish the relationship
      —share information (if both sides so desire)
   b. Determine, with other team, time and place of first meeting, who will be there, if it is to be "open" or "closed," etc.

B. POTENTIAL PROBLEMS *(AND SOME SOLUTIONS)*

1. Hierarchy does not give enough authority to team, gives unclear or changing instructions
   Be flexible; create doubts in Hierarchy's mind

2. Mutually inconsistent goals
   Use consensus decision-making techniques

3. Team or Hierarchy lacks experience or continuity
   Training and education

4. Distractions caused by other work/responsibilities
   Manage time; delegate

5. Confusion caused by lack of procedure
   Get strategy in force early

6. Goals continuously change because of changing input from:
   —the public
   Public relations work
   —the union or management (the other team)
   Analysis of the history with the union or the management; review convention resolutions or the organization's strategy; review past labor–management meetings
   —the Hierarchy
   Improve communications with Hierarchy; good salesmanship
   —a changing economic climate
   Improve costing techniques

II. THE MIDDLE GAME/ACTIVE MEETING PHASE

A. TASKS

1. Negotiate Procedural Issues
   a. Introduce team members
   b. Make seating arrangements
   c. Set agenda for current meeting
   d. Set times and places for subsequent meetings
   e. Determine ground rules for negotiation
   f. Determine which team presents opening position first
   g. Establish how information is to be released to the media and to the public

2. Maintain Communication with Hierarchy
   a. Avoid surprises
   b. Lower expectations, cast doubt in their minds as to the viability of their own positions

    c. Maintain clear line of authority
    d. Assess progress of negotiations
    e. Constantly restate goals

3. Manage the Table Process
    a. Distribute a written summary of any previous meetings
    b. Build trust; avoid promises/compromises you can't deliver
    c. Prepare for possible mediation, litigation, arbitration, etc.
    d. Avoid surprising the other team
    e. Cast doubts in the other team as to the viability of their position
    f. Lower expectations
    g. Isolate stumbling blocks, bypass obstacles—go on to other items
    h. Don't let members "talk out of turn" or express disagreement at the table
    i. List concerns of both sides
    j. Rank priorities of both sides
    k. Avoid unduly pressuring other team
    l. Maintain physical and emotional edge (stamina, morale and confidence) by taking breaks, getting a "change of scene" and caucusing
    m. Keep communication with experts open (if they are not sitting on the team)
    n. Listen! Practice active listening!
    o. Constantly frame questions regarding other team's proposals
    p. Remain faithful to goals
    q. Keep negotiations on track
    r. Maintain tactical flexibility; remain open to new possibilities
    s. Make "If . . . Then . . ." supposals
    t. Identify allies on other team
    u. Identify opponents on other team and design specific responses to create doubt in their minds
    v. Identify the perceptions and assumptions underlying the other team's positions
    w. Timing: don't let negotiations move too quickly or get bogged down
    x. Take notes on both sides' evolving positions
    y. Clarify; constantly restate all agreements so far, constantly paraphrase other team's statements and positions
    z. Constantly check with data base; constantly analyze and cost out proposals
   aa. Take time to thoroughly explain positions

4. Accomplish
   a. Determine if and when closure might be reached
   b. Exchange proposals and responses
   c. Exchange information
   d. Educate the other team
   e. Air feelings (and allow other side to do the same) on items not to be negotiated (to facilitate a good, ongoing relationship)

5. The Caucus
   a. Maintain sight of goals by constantly restating them
   b. Cast doubt in stabilizers' and destabilizers' minds
   c. Lower expectations
   d. Educate the other team
   e. Analyze and react to other side's proposals
   f. Assess the other side's reactions to your proposals
   g. Control internal tensions
   h. Plan strategies
   i. Control the stabilizers and destabilizers

6. The Side-Bar Meeting—"Shadow Bargaining"
   a. Be honest, be yourself
   b. Don't surprise own team members—don't commit without first talking with them
   c. Be clear about empowerment

7. Prepare for Closing Phase
   a. Establish timing and tactics for approaching End Game
   b. Avoid pushing for closure prematurely
   c. Determine format of agreement

B. POTENTIAL PROBLEMS *(AND SOME SOLUTIONS)*

1. Being surprised by other team
   Caucus

2. "Un-psychability" of other team (unreadable)
   Have a "walk-in-the-woods" session (an informal, relaxed and private meeting); use a series of true/false or yes/no questions

3. Growth of number of issues
   The four "ings": clustering, dropping, giving, linking

4. Other side changes positions or lacks preparation
   Be patient; suggest a caucus

5. Other side inflexible
   Mediation

6. Poor communication with Hierarchy; Hierarchy changes goals, instructions; Hierarchy limits team's authority
   Reeducate, refocus

7. Lack of discipline within team; destabilizers
   Confront; replace; use peer pressure; create doubts

8. Failure to address adversary's needs
   Listen and ask questions; side-bar meeting between chief spokespersons

9. Team's strategy undercut by Hierarchy's posturing for public opinion concerns
   Use outside pressure (alliances with interest groups)

10. Information leaks
    Improve security

11. Lack of agreement on ground rules
    Side-bar meeting between chief spokespersons; group together items teams can agree on; compromise

12. High expectations on both sides
    Identify assumptions/perceptions, frame questions to seed doubt

13. Misperceptions
    Facts, data and cost analyses

14. Teams do not listen to each other
    Build trust, be consistent and fair; ask questions of the other team at the table and of own team in caucus

15. Difficulty maintaining unified purpose and approach, both within the team and with Hierarchy
    Ongoing communications

III. THE END GAME/CLOSING PHASE

A. TASKS

1. Maintain Control During Period of Accelerated "Horse-Trading"
   a. Identify and prioritize major unresolved issues, which are likely to be (in labor negotiations):

   —economic issues (wages and benefits)
   —work rules (union jurisdiction and overtime scheduling)
   —grievance procedure
   —workforce flexibility
   b. Update the bottom-line and BATNA[2]
   c. Assess likelihood of other team coming to an agreement above own team's bottom-line
   d. Carefully analyze possible ramifications of any changes on positions at this time
   e. Execute appropriate contingencies
   f. Maintain especially good (and quick) communication channels with Hierarchy
   g. Continue public relations work with employees and public
   h. Take careful, accurate notes
   i. Maintain a united front
   j. Predetermine a possible 11th hour dispute resolution mechanism
   k. Negotiate an implementation mechanism for the agreement
   l. Determine who will draft the agreement
   m. Determine how the agreement will be announced to the public and by whom
   n. Ensure administrative support availability

2. Monitor Union or Management (the Other Team) Activity
   a. With the press
   b. In current grievances or disputes
   c. On the job

3. Come to Verbal Agreement
   a. Assure agreement is within position
   b. Confirm that all parties understand proposed agreement

4. Sell the Agreement to All Concerned Parties
   a. Use other team's arguments to sell agreement to:
      —destabilizers
      —Hierarchy
      —constituents
      —outside interests
   b. Get as much as possible for the "losers"

5. Draft the Agreement
   a. Allow opportunity for comment, revision
   b. Check every draft with team in caucus

    c. Reconfirm with experts/data base
    d. Reconfirm with Hierarchy
    e. Reconfirm terms and language with the other team

6. Close
    a. Sign the agreement
    b. Observe any traditional ceremony/protocol
    c. Publicize the agreement
    d. Celebrate

B. POTENTIAL PROBLEMS *(AND SOME SOLUTIONS)*

1. Last-ditch efforts by destabilizers
    Educate destabilizers as to the cost of not closing

2. Attempts by other side to reopen issues already settled or to introduce new issues
    Establish ground rules to prevent introduction of new issues after designated cut-off

3. Stabilizers too anxious to close
    Remind them of wishes of constituents/Hierarchy

4. Agreement has gone beyond a position acceptable to constituents/Hierarchy
    Side-bar meeting

5. Change in external factors makes agreement untenable
    Bring in a mediator

6. One side gets ratification, other side does not
    Establish (through negotiations) a dispute settlement mechanism

7. Hierarchy enters the negotiations
    Get the two Hierarchies together (*if* they are educated/ experienced in the negotiation process)

8. Separate agreements are reached between factions of both teams
    Control own team

9. Hierarchy continues to insist on unrealistic goals
    Generate outside pressure on Hierarchy to accept agreement

10. Time constraints
    Identify managers authorized to make decisions at critical times

11. Breakdown of team spirit
    Periodic briefing of team members as to generalities and details

12. Negotiations over contract language continue after the table negotiations end
    Write language as articles are agreed to

13. Too many layers of authority in the negotiations
    Grant chief spokesperson more authority

---

[1] BATNA–Best alternative to a negotiated agreement. See *Getting to Yes* by Roger Fisher and Bill Ury.

[2] *Id.*

Postscript

The late Dr. Martin Luther King Jr., in a *Playboy* interview in January 1965, spoke of "militantly nonviolent" leaders. If we substitute quasi-mediator for "strong man," the quote applies to the actions of the quasi-mediator as a team leader:

> *"I mean to say that a strong man must be militant as well as moderate.*
> *He must be a realist as well as an idealist."*

Index